06/28

Salon. com.

The Best Democracy Money Can Buy

© Harry Borden

Greg Palast is an internationally recognized expert on the control of corporate power working with labor unions and consumer groups in the USA, South America and Europe. In America, among his more noted cases, he directed government investigations and prosecution of racketeering by nuclear plant builders and, for the Chugach Natives of Alaska, probed charges of fraud by oil companies in the grounding of the *Exxon Valdez*.

Five years ago, Palast turned his investigative skills to journalism. His 1998 undercover exposé of corruption at the heart of Tony Blair's cabinet, "Lobbygate," earned him the distinction of being the first journalist in memory berated personally on the floor of Parliament by a prime minister – as well as an award for Story of the Year. His column for Britain's *Observer* newspaper, "Inside Corporate America," and other writings, have won him the Financial Times David Thomas Prize (1997) and nomination as Business Journalist of the Year (1999).

In America, Palast broke the story of how Katherine Harris and Jeb Bush removed thousands of Black and Democratic voters from registration roles prior to the presidential election. The series of revelations appeared in *The Nation*, the *Washington Post*, *Harper's*, the *Guardian* – and in *Salon.com* which named the exposé Politics Story of the Year. Palast's investigative reports can also be seen on BBC Television – "*Newsnight's* own Sam Spade."

Publication of *Democracy and Regulation*, Palast's lectures at Cambridge University and the University of São Paulo, co-authored by Theo MacGregor and Jerrold Oppenheim, is forthcoming. He divides his time between London and New York.

Some comments on Greg Palast's writings:

"The journalist I admire most. His amazing work puts all the rest of us journalists to shame. I'm an avid reader of everything Palast writes – can never get enough of it." George Monbiot, *Guardian*

"Hearsay and misinformation." Official spokesman, International Monetary Fund (IMF)

"Great writing on the Evil Empire of the IMF." Jude Wanniski, former editorial page editor, *Wall Street Journal*

"The world's greatest investigative reporter you've never heard of." *Cleveland Free Times*

"To Americans who cannot read his stories printed in Britain's *Observer*, he is America's journalist hero of the Internet." Alan Colmes, Fox Television

"Intrepid investigative reporter who first broke the news that tens of thousands of likely Democratic voters were disenfranchised in Florida before the 2000 election." *US Journalism Hall of Fame*

"The Most Evil Man in the World." *Private Eye*

"Amazing reporting. I can't wait for the next installments." David Ruppe, *ABC News*

"The Liar! Sleaze Reporter!" *Mirror*

"[Palast's reports] have not one shred of evidence!" Prime Minister Tony Blair

"Tony Blair's nightmare." *Harper's & Queen*

"George Bush's nightmare." Laura Flanders, Working for Change Radio

"The information is a hand grenade." John Pilger, *New Statesman*

"Rubbish ... rubbish." Official spokesman, World Trade Organization (WTO)

"Courageous writing (on the WTO) – when no one else will do it." Maude Barlowe, Council of Canadians

"The type of investigative reporter you don't see anymore – a cross between Sam Spade and Sherlock Holmes." Jim Hightower

"All power to Palast's pen!" Will Hutton, author, *The State We're In*

"Should be read all over America." Andrew Tobias, author, *The Invisible Bankers*

"Greg Palast is investigative journalism at its best. No one has exposed more truth about the Bush Cartel and lived to tell the story." *Baltimore Chronicle*

"Your Bullshit axe to grind with Bush is just another example of how far a punk ass loser will go to slander our president." (Signed) "A Real American."

The Best Democracy Money Can Buy

An Investigative Reporter Exposes the Truth
about Globalization, Corporate Cons
and High Finance Fraudsters

Greg Palast

Pluto Press

LONDON • STERLING, VIRGINIA

First published 2002 by Pluto Press
345 Archway Road, London N6 5AA
and 22883 Quicksilver Drive, Sterling, VA 20166–2012, USA

www.plutobooks.com

British Library Cataloguing in Publication Data
A catalogue record for this book is available from the British Library

ISBN 0 7453 1846 0 hardback

Library of Congress Cataloging in Publication Data
Palast, Greg.
   The best democracy money can buy : an investigative reporter exposes
   the truth about globalization, corporate cons, and high finance
   fraudsters / Greg Palast.
      p. cm.
   ISBN 0–7453–1846–0
   1. Political corruption. 2. Corporations—Corrupt practices. I.
   Title.
   JF1081 .P35 2002
   364.1'323—dc21

                                                            2001008116

Reprints: 10   9   8   7   6   5   4   3

Printed in the United States of America

We cannot trust some people who are non-conformists.

Ray Kroc, chairman, McDonald's Corp, deceased

The thing about the Golden Straitjacket is, the tighter you wear it, the more gold it produces.

Thomas Friedman on globalization

I don't have to be nice to the spirit of the Anti-Christ.

Dr ("Reverend") Pat Robertson

Contents

Forewords
Joe Conason and Will Hutton

When I first knew Greg Palast years ago in New York, he was an extraordinarily determined and talented investigator, toiling away for a consortium of labor unions. Among the frustrations of his job was the necessity of explaining complex financial issues to doltish journalists. At some point since then, very much to the public benefit, he decided to pick up the pen himself and take on the world.

This fascinating book is really a world tour with Palast as guide. Those who join him will learn the previously unrevealed secrets of globalization, a term which really is a new "brand name" for very old forms of international investment and exploitation.

Joining the techniques and values of investigative journalism with his background in economics, Palast scrutinizes the global marketplace in ways that enlighten readers and frighten corporate chieftains. It is a salutary occupation that brings a touch of moral hygiene to institutions that badly need cleaning. Palast's bracing hosedown is a rare experience for the denizens of the corporate sector, who are accustomed to "business reporting" focused on stock prices and balance sheets.

It is ironic that we in the USA must turn to Britain for this American's unfettered reporting about our businesses and institutions – including some of the most important stories about last year's disputed presidential election. Readers who think they can no longer be shocked by that assault on democracy are ... well, they're in for a shock.

Palast is a tough and salty character, but one wishes he weren't quite so unique. A few more reporters chasing these stories with his passion and perspicacity might be able to change the world.

Joe Conason, New York
Salon.com and *New York Observer*

Those in authority will not agree, but we need more Greg Palasts. Palast is instinctively on the side of the underdog, and knows that those with power and money are generally being economical with the truth. A journalist to his quick, he also takes the view that news is something that someone somewhere does not want in the public domain. Greg is determined to get it there.

I first met him during the *Observer*'s famous scrape with authority over the Cash-for-Access Lobbygate scandal when I was editor. Greg had gone undercover to expose corporate lobbyists' influence on Tony Blair's New

Labour government, and his revelations were devastating (see Chapter 7). This was investigative journalism at its best – brave, painstaking and more than justified by the results.

His collection in this book is tribute to his techniques. As his reputation has grown so has the flow of the anonymous documents reaching his desk, again a tribute to the way he is seen by those inside and outside authority. You are not sent documents unless the sender believes in your capacity to understand and use them to maximum effect. Greg can be relied upon for both.

But Greg is not just an effective journalist dedicated to cocking a nihilistic snook at the powers that be. He has the best of America's commitment to genuine democracy and the ability of well-informed citizens to make rational judgements and hold the powerful to account – if only they have the information. Greg does pretty well by himself, but if we had a dozen Palasts the world would be a very different place.

Will Hutton, London
Author of *The State We're In*

For
LINDA LEVY,
whose work is here plagiarized without mercy.

For video links to these stories, documentation and updates,
go to www.GregPalast.com

Who Gives a Shit? An Introduction

You read the papers and you watch television, so you know the kind of spider-brained, commercially poisoned piece-of-crap reporting you get in America. If you're reading this in Britain, you stand a chance of getting some real information, but *your* news is so censored and twisted in a knot that ... well, that's another story (read Chapter 8, "Kissing the Whip").

You could call this book: What You Didn't Read in the *New York Times*. For example,

> Five months before the November 2000 election, Governor Jeb Bush of Florida moved to purge 57,700 people from the voter rolls, supposedly criminals not allowed to vote. Most were innocent of crimes, but the majority were guilty of being Black.

I wrote that exposé for page 1 of the nation's top newspaper. But it was the wrong nation, Britain. It ran in the *Guardian* and its Sunday sister paper, the *Observer*. You could see it on television too, on BBC TV's *Newsnight*, which airs my investigative reports.

(Want to know what was in that diseased sausage called a presidential election? Read Chapter 1, "Jim Crow in Cyberspace", which contains reports never printed in the US and new investigative material not yet reported on either continent.)

There's a lot more not printed in the US, barely seen in Britain. There's the story about Monsanto's genetically modified, milk-making hormone. It turns out, the company's test cows dripped pus into the milk buckets. Yummy. Monsanto fixed that problem the easy way – by burying test data. US officials helped out, slipping the company confidential regulatory documents. (See, "The Ignoble Prize in Chemistry", in Chapter 5.)

And you didn't read about accusations from inside the FBI and CIA that, prior to September 11, 2001, Bush's national security chiefs killed investigations into Saudi Arabian billionaires' funding of terror networks.

You didn't read about how the "Reverend" Dr Pat Robertson secretly, illicitly used his Christian Crusade *jihad* assets to boost his berserker get-rich-quick business schemes.

Nor did you read about Anibal Verón, an Argentine bus driver. Last year, Verón hadn't received his pay for nine months, protested in the road and was shot dead. Demonstrators charged that the IMF had a plan to force Argentina to cut wages. Anti-globalization conspiracy theory? I'll show you the document. You'll find Verón's story in Chapter 2, "Sell the Lexus, Burn the Olive Tree: Globalization and its Discontents".

If you read the pro-globalization gurus such as Thomas Friedman or Anthony Giddens, you get the line that the New World Order is all about the communications revolution and cell phones that will call your broker and do your laundry at the same time. Wow. And if you're against it, you're against the future. The kids in the streets are just a bunch of unsophisticated jack-offs. That's what you get in the media and, in the US especially, there's no dissent from this slap-happy view of globalization.

I'm not going to argue with Friedman and Giddens and the guys in favor of The Future. What I will do is show you documents: Country Assistance Strategies, an Article 133 diplomatic letter, the GATS committee memos. Most are marked "confidential", "not for public disclosure" – and walked out of filing cabinets inside the IMF, World Bank, World Trade Organization and related agencies you've probably never heard of.

There's nothing in those documents about mobile phones for the Incas. Rather, there's a lot about raising water prices and what one insider described as "The IMF riot", the social explosion the World Bank expects and figures into its plans.

Not all of my work is so grim. In July 1998, I was in London and caught the front page of the *Mirror*, one of Britain's biggest-selling papers. The whole front page was a picture of this nasty-looking bald guy – me – under a four-inch-tall headline: THE LIAR. And I thought, *"Damn, it doesn't get any better than this."*

I didn't have time to enjoy it: my deputy editor and Prime Minister Tony Blair *and* my wife were all planning my punishments, for varied if related reasons. (See Chapter 8.) The *Mirror* did not like a story I had written with Antony Barnett for the *Observer*. To get the story, I'd gone undercover and exposed a stinky little deal-making operation running through Blair's cabinet.

That story "Cash for Access – Lobbygate" grew out of this idea: *Why not apply the techniques of investigations I've conducted in government racketeering cases to news reporting?* This would be a quantum leap in dig-out-the-facts methodologies rarely used even by "investigative" journalists. That's what makes these writings a bit different – lots of facts, many from documents thought by their writers to be hidden away in desk drawers, from mis-sent faxes and from tape recordings made when big mouths didn't know who they were talking to.

If Britain's government was selling its nation, corporate America was buying. That's my main beat: "Inside Corporate America", the title of my column in the *Observer*. Those columns – updated, all fresh material – are in Chapter 5. There you will get, for example, the skinny on Wal-Mart ("What Price a Store-gasm?") and the tale of the strange little deal cut by a big-time environmental group and the number one lobbyist representing polluters ("How the Filth Trade Turned Green").

So why have you not seen these stories, or few? Take that story of the theft of the US election. In America, editors looked at their shoes and whistled – and hoped it would go away. Though not everyone ignored it: I got lots of letters like this one: "*Stay out of our politics, you English pig!*" I hate to quibble, but I'm not British.

I'm from Los Angeles. Actually, the scum-end of LA, in the San Fernando Valley, raised in a pastel house between the power plant and the city garbage dump. It was not as glamorous as abject poverty, but not far above it. Half the kids in my school were Mexican-American and, brown or white, we were pretty much tagged as America's losers. You graduated, worked minimum wage at Bob's Big-Boy Burger on Van Nuys Boulevard, got your girlfriend pregnant and, if Vietnam didn't kill you, overtime at the Chevy plant would.

America was a carnivore and we were just food. Anyway, I got out and so did my sister – how we did is neither interesting nor remarkable.

Am I bitter? Why shouldn't I be when I look at the privileged little pricks that call the shots on this planet, whose daddies could make the phone calls, write the checks, make it smooth? Daddy Bush, Daddy Koch, Daddy Bin Laden – I've got a list.

As a scholarship kid at the University of Chicago, I witnessed the birth of the New World Globalization Order. It was the mid-1970s and I'd worked my way into Milton Friedman's postgraduate seminar and into a strange clique, which later became known as the "Chicago Boys". That was the little cabal of South America's budding dictators and "neoliberal" economists who would turn Chile into an experiment in torture and free markets.

Even then I was undercover, working for Frank Rosen, head of the United Electrical Workers Union, and Eddie Sadlowski, the dissident steel workers' leader, for a greater purpose I could only dimly understand.

I avoided journalism. Starting in 1975, from a desk in the basement of the electrical workers' union hall, I began grinding through account books of US corporations. Using their own abstruse financial codes, I challenged gas company heating charges. I negotiated contracts for steel and iron workers. I was broke and I was in heaven. My dad had been a furniture salesman. He hated furniture. If it were up to him, we would have eaten sitting on the floor. Mom worked in the school cafeteria (you know, hairnet and creamed corned) until she became a hypnotist for McDonald's (really – see Chapter 3). From them, I gained a deep and abiding fear of working for a living.

Bang: One minute I was this dead-broke anti-corporate scourge with his head buried in bureaucratic file cabinets – and the next I was "America's number one expert on government regulation bar none" (I read that in the papers), with an office bigger than God's hairpiece on the 50th floor of the World Trade Center in New York City, giving lectures in São Paolo.

Still, I kept my nose in the dusty files. I found things like this: Executives of a megalith power company, Long Island Lighting of New York, swore under oath that their nuclear plant would cost $1.8 billion. Internal confidential memos said the plant would cost $3.2 billion. I convinced the government to charge them with civil racketeering, and a jury said they should pay $4.8

billion. Then, the governor of New York, a slick operator named Mario Cuomo, called the chief federal judge in New York – and poof! – the jury's verdict was thrown out. That's when I learned about love, and that there is no love greater than the love of politicians for the captains of finance.

So am I bitter? See above.

Then I quit. It was during my investigation of the *Exxon Valdez* crack-up (see Chapter 4). I was working for the Chugach natives of Alaska. Our team quickly discovered the oil spill was no accident: before the tanker's grounding, Exxon shut off the ship's radar to save money and a British Petroleum affiliate had faked the safety equipment reports.

That's when I realized, from a kyak in the Prince William Sound, *who can hear you scream?* The press had f'd-up the *Exxon Valdez* story something awful. That was five years ago. I decided from then on I'd write these stories myself, an idea immediately encouraged by the *Guardian's* Alex Brummer, the *Observer's* Will Hutton and Ben Laurance (all since moved to more lucrative venues), then producer Meirion Jones at BBC's *Newsnight*.

While American journalists spent those years smothered in Monica Lewinsky's panties, I had the luxury of diving into the filing cabinets of the Reverend Pat Robertson, the World Trade Organization and George Bush's favorite billionaires.[1]

So where are you, America? Don't you want to know how your president was elected? How the IMF spends your money?

I got a hint of the answers from Mike Isikoff, a reporter with the *Washington Post/Newsweek* group. A couple of years ago, he passed me some truly disturbing information on President Clinton, not the usual intern-under-the-desk stuff. I said, "Mike, why don't *you* print this?" And he said, *"Because no one gives a shit."*

But if you're one of the few who do, here's your book.

---

1 Not all my work is undercover gumshoe stuff. For those hungry for the grand theory behind all this journalism, Pluto Press is issuing a companion policy book, *Regulation and Democracy*, in cooperation with the United Nations International Labor Organization, which grew out of my lectures at Cambridge University and the University of São Paolo. Theo MacGregor and Jerrold Oppenheim are co-authors.

Figure 1. In July 1998, I was in London and caught the front page of the *Mirror*, one of Britain's biggest-selling papers. On the front page was this nasty-looking bald guy – me. Britain's Prime Minister Tony Blair was unhappy with the *Observer*'s undercover investigation into US corporate purchase of favors from his cabinet members. And when the Prime Minister is unhappy his press puppies attack. On my side of the Atlantic, a White House insider also reviewed my writings, "We hate that guy."

1

Jim Crow in Cyberspace:
The Unreported Story of How They Fixed
the Vote in Florida

In the days following the presidential election, there were so many stories of African-Americans erased from voter rolls you might think they were targeted by some kind of racial computer program. They were.

Silence of the Lambs:
American Journalism Hears No Evil,
Sees No Evil, Reports No Evil

Here's how the president was elected:

In the months leading up to the November balloting, Florida Governor Jeb Bush and his Secretary of State Katherine Harris ordered local elections supervisors to purge 57,700 voters from registries on grounds they were felons not entitled to vote in Florida. As it turns out, these voters weren't felons, at most a handful. However, the voters on this "scrub list" were, notably, African-American (about 54 per cent) and most of the others wrongly barred from voting were white and Hispanic Democrats.

Weeks after the election, first reports of this extraordinary news ran, as they should, on page 1 of the country's leading paper. The country: Britain. In the US, it ran on page 0 – the story was not covered on the news pages. The theft of the presidential race in Florida was also given big television network coverage. But again, it was on the wrong continent: on BBC television, in London.

Was this some off-the-wall story that the British press misreported? The chief lawyer for the US Civil Rights Commission called it the first hard evidence of a systematic attempt to disenfranchise Black voters; and the Commission held dramatic hearings on the evidence.

So why was this story investigated, reported and broadcast in *Europe*, for God's sake?

I'd like to know the answer. That way I could understand why a Southern California ho'daddy with his wife and kiddies has to commute to London to tell this and other stories about my country. How did 100,000 US journalists sent to cover the election *fail* to get the vote theft story and print it (preferably *before* the election)?

Investigative reports share three things: they are risky, they upset the wisdom of the established order and they are *very expensive* to produce. Do profit-conscious enterprises, whether media companies or widget firms, *seek* extra costs, extra risk and the opportunity to be attacked? Not in any business text I've ever read. I can't help but note that my paper, the *Guardian* and its Sunday sister, the *Observer*, are the world's only leading newspapers owned by a not-for-profit corporation, as is BBC television.

But if profit-lust is the ultimate problem blocking significant investigative reportage, the more immediate cause of comatose coverage of the election and other issues is what is laughably called America's "journalistic culture". If the Rupert Murdochs of the globe are shepherds of the New World Order, they owe their success to breeding a flock of docile sheep – the editors and reporters snoozy and content with munching on, digesting, then reprinting a diet of press releases and canned stories provided by officials and corporation public relations operations.

Take this story of the list of Florida's *faux* felons that cost Al Gore the presidential election. Shortly after the UK story hit the world wide web, I was contacted by a CBS TV network news producer ready to run their own version of the story. The CBS hotshot was happy to pump me for information: names, phone numbers, all the items one needs for a quickie TV story.

I also freely offered up to CBS this information: the office of the Governor of Florida, Jeb Bush, brother of the Republican presidential candidate, had illegally ordered the removal of the names of felons from voter rolls – real felons, but with the right to vote under Florida law. As a result, *another 40,000 legal voters* (in addition to the 57,700 on the purge list), almost all Democrats, could not vote.

One problem: I had not quite completed my own investigation on this matter. Therefore, *CBS would have to do some actual work*, reviewing documents and law, obtaining statements. The next day I received a call from the producer who said, "I'm sorry, but your story didn't hold up." Well, how did the multi-billion dollar CBS network determine this? Answer: "We called Jeb Bush's office." Oh. And that was it.

I wasn't surprised by this type of "investigation". It is, in fact, standard operating procedure for the little lambs of American journalism. One good, slick explanation from a politician or corporate chieftain and it's *case closed*, investigation over. The story ran on television anyway: I reported it on the BBC's *Newsnight*.

Let's understand the pressures on the CBS TV producer that led her to kill the story on the basis of a denial by the target of the allegations. The story required a massive and quick review of documents, hundreds of phone calls and interviews, hardly a winner in the slam-bam-thank-you-ma'am US school of journalism. Most difficult, the revelations in the story required a reporter to stand up and say that the big name politicians, their lawyers and their PR people were *freaking liars*.

It would be much easier, a heck of a lot cheaper and no risk at all to wait for the US Civil Rights Commission to do the work, then cover the Commission's canned report and press conference. No one ever lost their job writing canned statements from a press release. Wait! You've watched *Murphy Brown* or *The Front Page* so you think reporters hanker every day to uncover the big scandal. Bullshit. Remember, *All the President's Men* was so unusual they had to make a movie out of it.

Meanwhile, back in sunny England ...
My paper received about 2,000 bless-you-Britain-for-telling-us-the-truth-about-our-elections letters from US Internet readers circulating the *samizdat* presidential elections coverage. And I received a few like this:

> *You pansey brits seem to think that the average American is as undereducated and stupid as the average british subject. Well comrad, I'm here to tell you ...*

which ended with some physically unfeasible suggestions of what to do with the Queen.

Meanwhile, back in the US ...
Salon.com, the Internet magazine, ran my story on the theft of the elections. It wasn't exactly "print", but at least it was American. And now columnists like Bob Herbert of the *New York Times* picked it up, and some radio talk shows ... but still not one news editor called, not even from my "sister" paper, the *Washington Post*, with whom the *Guardian* shares material.

From a news view, and the flood of site hits, this was *Salon*'s biggest politics story ever – and they named Part I their political story of the year. But where was Part II? On their web-site and on radio programs the magazine was announcing Part II would appear in two days ... and in two days ... and in two days ... and *nothing appeared*. Part II was the story blown off by the CBS Nightly News about an additional 40,000-plus voters whom Jeb Bush barred from voting. The fact that 90 per cent of these 40,000 voters were Democrats should have made it news ... because this maneuver alone more than accounted for Bush's victory.

I was going crazy: Gore had not yet conceded ... the timing of Part II was crucial. Where the hell was it? Finally, an editor told me, "The story doesn't check out. You see, we checked with Jeb Bush's office and they said ..."

Agh! It was *deja vu* all over again.

Another staffer added, as a kind of explanation, "The *Washington Post* would never run this story."

Well, he had me there. They hadn't, they didn't. Not yet. At least *Salon* helped me sneak the first report past the border patrols. So God bless America.

While waiting for America to awaken, I took my BBC film crew to Florida, having unearthed the "smoking gun" documents proving that Florida's Republican officials had knowingly knocked thousands of innocent Black voters off the Florida voter roles before the election. I had a page marked "confidential" from the contract between the state of Florida and the private company that had purged the voter lists. The document contained cold evidence that Florida knew they were taking the vote away from thousands of innocent voters, most of them Black.

It was February. I took my camera crew into an agreed interview with Jeb Bush's director of the Florida Department of Elections. When I pulled out the confidential sheet, Bush's man ripped off the microphone and did a 50-yard dash, locking himself in his office, all in front of our cameras. It was killer television and wowed the British viewers. We even ran a confession from the company. Newsworthy? Apparently not for the US.

My program, *Newsnight*, has a film-trading agreement with *ABC Nightline*, a kind of "sister" show. Over 20,000 net-heads in the US saw the BBC webcast, a record; and they banged ABC TV with demands to broadcast the BBC film, or at least report on it. Instead, *Nightline* sent down its own crew to Florida for a couple of days. They broadcast a report that ballots are complex and Blacks are not well educated about voting procedures. The gravamen of the story was, *Blacks are too frigging dumb to figure out how to vote.* No mention that in white Leon County, machines automatically kicked back faulty ballots for voter correction; whereas in Gadsden County, very Black, the same machines were programmed to eat mismarked ballots. That was in our story, too.

Why didn't ABC run the voter purge story? Don't look for some big Republican conspiracy. Remember the three elements of investigative reporting: risk, time, money. Our BBC/*Guardian* stories required all of those, in short supply in US news operations.

Finally, in February, my Part II on the theft of the elections found asylum in that distant journalistic planet not always visible to the naked eye, *Nation Magazine*. Bless them.

In May, the US Civil Rights Commission prepared to report on the election in Florida. They relied heavily on the material uncovered by BBC for the core of their Commission's finding of systematic voter disenfranchisement in Florida. Our documents were their main evidence used in witness cross-examinations.

And then, *mirabile dictu*, the *Washington Post* ran the story of the voter purge on page 1, including the part that "couldn't stand up" for *CBS* and *Salon* ... and even gave me space for a by-lined comment. Applause for the *Post*'s courage!

Would I be ungrateful if I suggested otherwise? The *Post* ran the story in *June*; though they had it at hand seven months earlier when the ballots were still being counted. They waited until they knew the findings of the US Civil Rights Commission Report, so they could fire from behind that big safe rock of Official Imprimatur. In other words, the *Post* had the courage to charge out and shoot the wounded.

Black-out in Florida

These are the stories you weren't supposed to see: the reports that ran in Britain's Observer *and* Guardian, *bits of script from the BBC television investigation and, to help set out the facts, the US stories from* Salon, Nation *and the* Washington Post *– and new material, never before printed nor broadcast on either continent. Documents keep bubbling up from the cesspool of the Florida state offices. I've saved it for you here, having run out of the patience needed to knock heads with "respectable" US papers and networks.*

In June last year, an editor at one of the biggest newspapers in the US told me, "The Committee has decided not to continue printing stories about the presidential vote. We think it's over. We don't want to look partisan."

I thought, what "Committee"? And I picked up that I wasn't supposed to ask.

The first story of the voter purge ran on November 26, 2000, in my column, "Inside Corporate America" in the *Observer*, under the heading, "Black-out in Florida".

A Columbia University journalism student had posted a note on the *Mother Jones* Internet bulletin board flagging a story in the *Palm Beach Post* from months before the election that 8,000 voters had been removed from the voter rolls – by mistake. A researcher passed it to me. Given the *Sturm und Drang* in Florida, you'd think that an American journalist would pick up the story. Don't hold your breath. Undoubtedly, any curious reporter might have been waylaid by the *Post*'s assurances that the "mistake" had been *corrected*.

But what if the Florida press puppies had been wrong? What if they had stood on their hind legs and swallowed a biscuit of bullshit from state officials? It was worth a call.

From London, for the *Observer*, I contacted a statistician at the office of the County Elections Supervisor in Tampa. Such an expert technician would have no reason to lie to me. The question at the top of my list: *"How many of the voters on the scrub list are* Black?"

And the statistician said, "You know, I've been waiting for someone to ask me that."

This is what I wrote.

Vice-President Al Gore would have strolled to victory in Florida if the state hadn't kicked up to 66,000 citizens off the voters' registers five months ago as former felons. In fact, only a fraction were ex-cons. Most were simply guilty of being African-American. A top-placed election official told me that the government had conducted a quiet review and found – surprise! – that the listing included far more African-Americans than would statistically have been expected, even accounting for the grievous gap between the conviction rates of Blacks and Whites in the US.

One list of 8,000 supposed felons was supplied by Texas. But these criminals from the Lone Star State had committed nothing more serious than misdemeanors such as drunk driving (like their governor, George W. Bush).

The source of this poisonous blacklist: Database Technologies, acting under the direction of Governor Jeb Bush's frothingly partisan secretary of state, Katherine Harris. My thanks to investigator Solomon Hughes for informing me that DBT, a division of ChoicePoint, is under fire for misuse of personal data in state computers in Pennsylvania. ChoicePoint's board is loaded with Republican sugar daddies, including Ken Langone, finance chief for Rudy Giuliani's aborted Senate run against Hillary Clinton.

Florida's Ethnic Cleansing of the Voter Rolls

At the end of November 2000, the vote count in Florida was still on; Gore was still in the race. Word was, Gore's camp was split, with warriors fighting the gray-heads of the Establishment pushing the Democrat to lie down and play dead, advice he'd ultimately follow.

But at that time the race was wide open. Joe Conason, maybe the toughest investigative reporter in the US, insisted to his editors at *Salon* that they bring my story back to America. That would not be easy or cheap. The Texas list error – 8,000 names – was corrected, said the state. That left the tougher question: what about the 57,700 *other* people named on that list?

The remaining names on the list were, in the majority, Black – not unusual in a nation where half of all felony convictions are against African-Americans. But as half the names were Black and if this included even a tiny fraction of *innocents*, well, there was the election for Bush.

The question was, then, was the "corrected" list in fact corrected? Finding the answer would not be cheap for *Salon*. It meant big bucks, redirecting their entire political staff to the story and making hotshot reporters knuckle down to the drudgery of calling and visiting county elections offices all over Florida.

Just before we hit the electronic streets with it, someone called a key player in the White House and Gore's inner circle about the story *Salon* would soon break. The Big Insider said, "That's fantastic! Who's the reporter?" The tipster said, "This American, he's a reporter in Britain, Greg Palast."

Mr White House Insider replied, "Shit! We *hate* that guy."

But that's another story. In the meantime, the *Salon* team – especially contributors Alicia Montgomery, Daryl Lindsey and Antony York (thank you all) – came back with a mother-load of evidence that, by the most conservative analysis, Florida had purged enough innocent Black voters to snatch the presidency from Al Gore. I said, "Well God bless America," and, on December 7, 2000, wrote this.

If Vice-President Al Gore is wondering where his Florida votes went, rather than sift through a pile of chad, he might want to look at a "scrub list" of 57,700 names targeted to be knocked off the Florida voter registry by a division of the office of Florida Secretary of State Katherine Harris. A close examination suggests thousands of voters may have lost their right to vote based on a flaw-ridden list of purported "felons" provided by a private firm with tight Republican ties.

Early in the year, the company ChoicePoint gave Florida officials a list with the names of 8,000 ex-felons to "scrub" from their list of voters.

But it turns out none on the list was guilty of felonies, only misdemeanors. The company acknowledged the error, and blamed it on the original source of the list – the state of Texas.

Florida officials moved to put those falsely accused by Texas back on voter rolls before the election. Nevertheless, the large number of errors uncovered in individual counties suggests that thousands of eligible voters have been turned away at the polls.

• Florida is the only state that pays a private company that promises to provide lists for "cleansing" voter rolls. The state signed in 1998 a $4 million contract with DBT Online, since merged into ChoicePoint, of Atlanta. The creation of the scrub list, called the central voter file, was mandated by a 1998 state voter fraud law, which followed a tumultuous year that saw Miami's mayor removed after voter fraud in the election, with dead people discovered to have cast ballots. The voter fraud law required all 67 counties to purge voter registries of duplicate registrations, deceased voters and felons, many of whom, but not all, are barred from voting in Florida. In the process, however, the list invariably targets a minority population in Florida, where 31 per cent of all Black men cannot vote because of a ban on felons.

If this unfairly singled out minorities, it unfairly handicapped Gore: in Florida, 93 per cent of African-Americans voted for the vice-president.

In the ten counties contacted by *Salon*, use of the central voter file seemed to vary wildly. Some found the list too unreliable and didn't use it at all. But most counties appear to have used the file as a resource to purge names from their voter rolls, with some counties making little – or no – effort at all to alert the "purged" voters. Counties that did their best to vet the file discovered a high level of errors, with as many as 15 per cent of names incorrectly identified as felons.

News coverage has focused on some maverick Florida counties that decided not to use the central voter file, essentially breaking the law and possibly letting some ineligible felons vote.

Three weeks after the election, the *Miami Herald* reported that after research-ing voter records in twelve Florida counties – but primarily in Palm Beach and Duval counties, which didn't use the file – it found that more than 445 felons had apparently cast ballots in the presidential election.

But Palm Beach and Duval weren't the only counties to dump the list after questioning its accuracy. Madison County's elections supervisor, Linda Howell, had a peculiarly personal reason for distrusting the central voter file. She had received a letter saying that since she had committed a felony, she would not be allowed to vote.

Howell, who said she has never committed a felony, said the letter she received in March 2000 shook her faith in the process. "It really is a mess," she said.

"I was very upset," Howell said. "I know I'm not a felon." Though the one mistake did get corrected and law enforcement officials were quite apologetic, Howell decided not to use the state list because its "information is so flawed". She's unsure of the number of warning letters that were sent out to county residents when she first received the list in 1999, but she recalls that there were many problems. "One day we would send a letter to have someone taken off the rolls, and the next day, we would send one to put them back on again," Howell said. "It makes you look like you must be a dummy."

Dixie and Washington counties also refused to use the scrub list. Starlet Cannon, Dixie's deputy assistant supervisor of elections, said, "I'm scared to work with it because of lot of the information they have on there is not accurate."

Carol Griffin, supervisor of elections for Washington, said, "It hasn't been accurate in the past, so we had no reason to suspect it was accurate this year."

But if some counties refused to use the list altogether, others seemed to embrace it all too enthusiastically. Etta Rosado, spokeswoman for the Volusia County Department of Elections, said the county essentially accepted the file at face value, did nothing to confirm the accuracy of it and doesn't inform citizens ahead of time that they have been dropped from the voter rolls.

"When we get the con felon list, we automatically start going through our rolls on the computer. If there's a name that says John Smith was convicted of a felony, then we enter a notation on our computer that says convicted felon – we mark an 'f' for felon – and the date that we received it," Rosado said. "They're still on our computer, but they're on purge status," meaning they have been marked ineligible to vote.

"I don't think that it's up to us to tell them they're a convicted felon," Rosado said. "If he's on our rolls, we make a notation on there. If they show up at a polling place, we'll say, 'Wait a minute, you're a convicted felon, you can't vote.' Nine out of ten times when we repeat that to the person, they say 'Thank you' and walk away. They don't put up arguments."

Rosado doesn't know how many people in Volusia were dropped from the list as a result of being identified as felons.

Hillsborough County's elections supervisor, Pam Iorio, tried to make sure that the bugs in the system didn't keep anyone from voting. All 3,258 county residents who were identified as possible felons on the central voter file sent by the state were sent a certified letter informing them that their voting rights were in jeopardy. Of that number, 551 appealed their status, and 245 of those appeals were successful.

Some had been convicted of a misdemeanor and not a felony, others were felons who had had their rights restored and others were simply cases of mistaken identity.

An additional 279 were not close matches with names on the county's own voter rolls and were not notified. Of the 3,258 names on the original list, therefore, the county concluded that more than 15 per cent were in error. If that ratio held statewide, *no fewer than 7,000* voters were incorrectly targeted for removal from voting rosters.

Iorio says local officials did not get adequate preparation for purging felons from their rolls. "We're not used to dealing with issues of criminal justice or ascertaining who has a felony conviction," she said. Though the central voter file was supposed to facilitate the process, it was often more troublesome than the monthly circuit court lists that she had previously used to clear her rolls of duplicate registrations, the deceased and convicted felons. "The database from the state level is not always accurate," Iorio said. As a consequence, her county did its best to notify citizens who were on the list about their felony status. "We sent those individuals a certified letter, we put an ad in a local newspaper and we held a public hearing. For those who didn't respond to that, we sent out another letter by regular mail," Iorio said. "That process lasted several months."

"We did run some number stats and the number of Blacks [on the list] was higher than expected for our population," says Chuck Smith, a statistician for the county. Iorio acknowledged that African-Americans made up 54 per cent of the people on the original felons list, though they constitute only 11.6 per cent of Hillsborough's voting population.

Smith added that the DBT computer program automatically transformed various forms of a single name. In one case, a voter named "Christine" was identified as a felon based on the conviction of a "Christopher" with the same last name. Smith says ChoicePoint would not respond to queries about its proprietary methods. Nor would the company provide additional verification data to back its fingering certain individuals in the registry purge. One supposed felon on the ChoicePoint list is a local judge.

While there was much about the lists that bothered Iorio, she felt she didn't have a choice but to use them. And she's right. Section 98.0975 of the Florida Constitution states: "Upon receiving the list from the division, the supervisor must attempt to verify the information provided. If the supervisor does not determine that the information provided by the division is incorrect, the supervisor must remove from the registration books by the next subsequent election the name of any person who is deceased, convicted of a felony or adjudicated mentally incapacitated with respect to voting."

But the counties have interpreted that law in different ways. Leon County used the central voter file sent in January 2000 to clean up its voter rolls, but set aside the one it received in July. According to Thomas James, the information systems officer in the county election office, the list came too late for the information to be processed.

According to Leon election supervisor Ion Sancho, "there have been some problems" with the file. Using the information received in January, Sancho sent 200 letters to county voters, by regular mail, telling them they had been identified by the state as having committed a felony and would not be allowed to vote. They were given 30 days to respond if there was an error. "They had the burden of proof," he says.

He says 20 people proved that they did not belong on the list, and a handful of angry phone calls followed on election day. "Some people threatened to sue us," he said, "but we haven't had any lawyers calling yet."

In Orange County, officials also sent letters to those identified as felons by the state, but they appear to have taken little care in their handling of the list. "I have no idea," said June Condrun, Orange's deputy supervisor of elections, when asked how many letters were sent out to voters. After a bit more thought, Condrun responded that "several hundred" of the letters were sent, but said she doesn't know how many people complained. Those who did call, she said, were given the phone number of the Florida Department of Law Enforcement so that they could appeal directly to it.

Many Orange County voters never got the chance to appeal in any form. Condrun noted that about one-third of the letters, which the county sent out by regular mail, were returned to the office marked undeliverable. She attributed the high rate of incorrect addresses to the age of the information sent by DBT, some of which was close to 20 years old, she said.

Miami-Dade County officials may have had similar trouble. Milton Collins, assistant supervisor of elections, said he isn't comfortable estimating how many accused felons were identified by the central voter file in his county. He said he knows that about 6,000 were notified, by regular mail, about an early list in 1999. Exactly how many were purged from the list? "I honestly couldn't tell you," he said. According to Collins, the most recent list he received from the state was one sent in January 2000, and the county applied a "two-pass system". If the information on the state list seemed accurate enough when comparing names with those on county voter lists, people were classified as felons and were then sent warning letters. Those who seemed to have only a partial match with the state data were granted "temporary inactive status". Both groups of people were given 90 days to respond or have their names struck from the rolls.

But Collins said the county has no figures for how many voters were able to successfully appeal their designation as felons.

ChoicePoint spokesman Martin Fagan concedes his company's error in passing on the bogus list from Texas. ("I guess that's a little bit embarrassing in light of the election," he says.) He defends the company's overall performance, however, dismissing the errors in 8,000 names as "a minor glitch – less than one-tenth of 1 per cent of the electorate" (though the total equals 15 times Governor George W. Bush's claimed lead over Gore). But he added that ChoicePoint is responsible only for turning over its raw list, which is then up to Florida officials to test and correct.

Last year, DBT Online, with which ChoicePoint would soon merge, received the unprecedented contract from the state of Florida to "cleanse" registration lists of ineligible voters – using information gathering and matching criteria it has refused to disclose, even to local election officials in Florida.

Atlanta's ChoicePoint, a highflying dot-com specializing in sales of personal information gleaned from its database of four billion public and not-so-public records, has come under fire for misuse of private data from government computers.

In January 2000, the state of Pennsylvania terminated a contract with ChoicePoint after discovering the firm had sold citizens' personal profiles to unauthorized individuals.

Fagan says many errors could have been eliminated by matching the Social Security numbers of ex-felons on DBT lists to the Social Security numbers on voter registries. However, Florida's counties have Social Security numbers on only a fraction of their voter records. So with those two problems – Social Security numbers missing in both the DBT's records and the counties' records – that fail-safe check simply did not exist.

In its defense, the company proudly points to an award it received from Voter Integrity Inc. for "innovative excellence [in] cleansing" Florida voter rolls. The conservative, non-profit advocacy organization has campaigned in parallel with the Republican Party against the 1993 motor voter law which resulted in a nationwide increase in voter registration of seven million, much of it among minority voters. DBT Online partnered with Voter Integrity Inc. three days later, setting up a program to let small counties "scrub" their voting lists, too.

Florida is the only state in the nation to contract the first stage of removal of voting rights to a private company. And ChoicePoint has big plans. "Given the outcome of our work in Florida," says Fagan, "and with a new president in place, we think our services will expand across the country."

Especially if that president is named "Bush". ChoicePoint's board, executive suite and consultant rosters are packed with Republican stars, including former New York Police Commissioner Howard Safir and former ultra-Right congressman Vin Weber, ChoicePoint's Washington lobbyist.

A Blacklist Burning for Bush

By this time we were confident that at least 7,000 innocent voters had been removed from voter rolls, half of them Black, and that swung the election. But my investigation was far from over – and I found yet another 1,704 eligible voters targeted for the purge, almost all Democrats. (Bush won the official Florida count by only 537 votes.) It was December 10, 2000 – Gore was still hanging in there – I wrote this in the Observer *for British readers.*

Hey, Al, take a look at this. Every time I cut open another alligator, I find the bones of more Gore voters. This week, I was hacking my way through the Florida swampland known as the Office of Secretary of State Katherine Harris and found a couple thousand more names of voters electronically "disappeared" from the vote rolls. About half of those named are African-Americans. They had the right to vote, but they never made it to the balloting booths.

On November 26, we reported that the Florida Secretary of State's office had, before the election, ordered the elimination of 8,000 Florida voters on the grounds that they had committed felonies in Texas. None had.

For Florida Governor Jeb Bush and his brother, the Texas blacklist was a mistake made in Heaven. Most of those targeted to have their names "scrubbed" from the voter roles were African-Americans, Hispanics and poor white folk, likely voters for Vice-President Gore. We don't know how many voters lost their citizenship rights before the error was discovered by a few skeptical county officials before ChoicePoint, which has gamely 'fessed-up to the Texas-sized error, produced a new list of 57,700 felons. In May, Harris sent on the new, improved scrub sheets to the county election boards.

Maybe it's my bad attitude, but I thought it worthwhile to check out the new list. Sleuthing around county offices with a team of researchers from Internet newspaper *Salon*, we discovered that the "correct" list wasn't so correct.

Our ten-county review suggests a minimum 15 per cent misidentification rate. That makes another 7,000 innocent people accused of crimes and stripped of their citizenship rights in the run-up to the presidential race, a majority of them Black.

Now our team, diving deeper into the swamps, has discovered yet a third group whose voting rights were stripped. The state's private contractor, ChoicePoint, generated a list of 1,704 names of people who, earlier in their lives, were convicted of felonies in Illinois and Ohio. Like most American states, these two restore citizenship rights to people who have served their time in prison and then remained on the good side of the law.

Florida strips those convicted in its own courts of voting rights for life. But Harris's office concedes, and county officials concur, that the state of Florida has no right to impose this penalty on people who have moved in from these other states. (Only 13 states, most in the Old Confederacy, bar reformed criminals from voting.)

Going deeper into the Harris lists, we find hundreds more convicts from the 35 other states that restored their rights at the end of sentences served. If they have the right to vote, why were these citizens barred from the polls? Harris didn't return my calls. But Alan Dershowitz did. The Harvard law professor, a renowned authority on legal process, said: "What's emerging is a pattern of reducing the total number of voters in Florida, which they know will reduce the Democratic vote."

How could Florida's Republican rulers know how these people would vote? I put the question to David Bositis, America's top expert on voting demographics. Once he stopped laughing, he said the way Florida used the lists from a private firm was "a patently obvious technique to discriminate against Black voters". In a darker mood, Bositis, of Washington's Center for Political and Economic Studies, said the sad truth of American justice is that 46 per cent of those convicted of felony are African-American. In Florida, a record number of Black folk, over 80 per cent of those registered to vote, packed the polling booths on November 7. Behind the curtains, nine out of ten Black people voted for Gore.

Mark Mauer of the Sentencing Project, Washington, pointed out that the "White" half of the purge list would be peopled overwhelmingly by the poor, also solid Democratic voters.

Add it up. The dead-wrong Texas list, the uncorrected "corrected" list, plus the out-of-state ex-con list. By golly, it's enough to swing a presidential election. I bet the busy Harris, simultaneously in charge of both Florida's voter rolls and George Bush's presidential campaign, never thought of that.

And at the bottom of the story I added ChoicePoint's reaction.
It was Thursday, December 7, 2 am. On the other end of the line, heavy breathing, then a torrent of words too fast for me to catch it all. "Vile ... lying ... inaccurate ... pack of nonsense ... riddled with errors ..." click! This was not a ChoicePoint whistleblower telling me about the company's notorious list. It was ChoicePoint's own media communications representative, Marty Fagan, communicating with me about my "sleazy disgusting journalism" in reporting on it.

I was curious about this company that appears to have chosen the next president for America's voters.

They have quite a pedigree for this solemn task. The company's Florida subsidiary, Database Technologies (now DBT Online), was founded by one Hank Asher. When US law enforcement agencies alleged that he might have been associated with Bahamian drug dealers – although no charges were brought – the company lost its data management contract with the FBI. Hank and his friends left and so, in Florida's eyes, the past is forgiven.

Thursday, 3 am (I should say both calls were at my request). A new, gentler voice gave me ChoicePoint's upbeat spin. "You say we got over 15 per cent wrong – we like to look at that as up to 85 per cent right!" That's 7,000 votes-plus – the bulk Democrats, not to mention the thousands on the faulty Texas list. Gore may lose the White House by 500 votes.

I contacted San Francisco-based expert Mark Swedlund. "It's just fundamental industry practice that you don't roll out the list statewide until you have tested it and tested it again," he said. "Dershowitz is right: they had to know that this jeopardized thousands of people's registrations. And they would also know the [racial] profile of those voters."

"They" is Florida State, not ChoicePoint. Let's not get confused about where the blame lies. Harris's crew lit this database fuse, then acted surprised when it blew up. Swedlund says ChoicePoint had a professional responsibility to tell

FLORIDA'S 'FELON' SCRUB LIST

This is one screen page from the computer 'scrub' list of thousands tagged for removal from voter registration rolls.

The key is race On the full list, more than half are Black, mostly innocent citizens with common names (*Jackson, Butler, Roberts, Ramos, Smith)* matching a birthday and race with one of several million listed felons. JC Smith (#346) shares initials, race and birthday with a felon Smith. Despite the possibility there is more than one Smith in Florida, the state paid for, but refused to use several methods for verification. As a result, the list is at best 15% wrong (company claim) or 90.2% wrong (from statistical sampling). Either way, the errors were enough to swing the election from Gore to Bush.

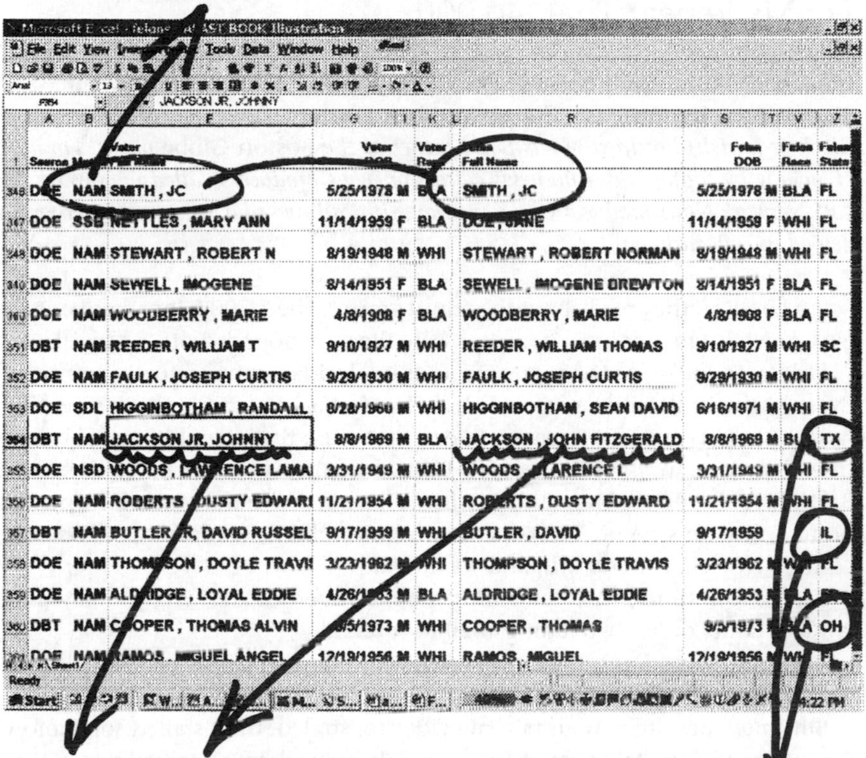

	Source		Voter Full Name	Voter DOB		Voter Race	Felon Full Name	Felon DOB		Felon Race	Felon State
346	DOE	NAM	SMITH , JC	5/25/1978	M	BLA	SMITH , JC	5/25/1978	M	BLA	FL
347	DOE	SSB	NETTLES , MARY ANN	11/14/1959	F	BLA	DOE , JANE	11/14/1959	F	WHI	FL
348	DOE	NAM	STEWART , ROBERT N	8/19/1948	M	WHI	STEWART , ROBERT NORMAN	8/19/1948	M	WHI	FL
349	DOE	NAM	SEWELL , IMOGENE	8/14/1951	F	BLA	SEWELL , IMOGENE BREWTON	8/14/1951	F	BLA	FL
350	DOE	NAM	WOODBERRY , MARIE	4/8/1908	F	BLA	WOODBERRY , MARIE	4/8/1908	F	BLA	FL
351	DBT	NAM	REEDER , WILLIAM T	9/10/1927	M	WHI	REEDER , WILLIAM THOMAS	9/10/1927	M	WHI	SC
352	DOE	NAM	FAULK , JOSEPH CURTIS	9/29/1930	M	WHI	FAULK , JOSEPH CURTIS	9/29/1930	M	WHI	FL
353	DOE	SDL	HIGGINBOTHAM , RANDALL	8/28/1960	M	WHI	HIGGINBOTHAM , SEAN DAVID	6/16/1971	M	WHI	FL
354	DBT	NAM	JACKSON JR, JOHNNY	8/8/1969	M	BLA	JACKSON , JOHN FITZGERALD	8/8/1969	M	BL[illegible]	TX
355	DOE	NSD	WOODS , LA[illegible]ENCE LAMA	3/31/1949	M	WHI	WOODS , [illegible]LARENCE L	3/31/1949	M	[illegible]HI	FL
356	DOE	NAM	ROBERTS , [illegible]USTY EDWAR	11/21/1954	M	WHI	RO[illegible]RTS , DUSTY EDWARD	11/21/1954	M	[illegible]HI	FL
357	DBT	NAM	BUTLER [illegible]R, DAVID RUSSEL	9/17/1959	M	WHI	BUTLER , DAVID	9/17/1959			IL
358	DOE	NAM	THOM[illegible]SON , DOYLE TRAVI	3/23/1962	[illegible]	[illegible]HI	THOMPSON , DOYLE TRAVIS	3/23/1962	[illegible]	[illegible]	FL
359	DOE	NAM	AL[illegible]RIDGE , LOYAL EDDIE	4/26/1[illegible]53	M	BLA	ALDRIDGE , LOYAL EDDIE	4/26/1953	[illegible]	[illegible]LA	[illegible]
360	DBT	NAM	C[illegible]OPER , THOMAS ALVIN	[illegible]/5/1973	M	WHI	COOPER , THOMAS	9/5/1973	[illegible]	[illegible]A	OH
361	DOE	NAM	RAMOS , MIGUEL ANGEL	12/19/1956	M	WHI	RAMOS , MIGUEL	12/19/1956	M	WH[illegible]	FL

Over the contractor's objection, the state purged voters whose names are close, but not exact matches, to felons. Johnny Jackson Jr (#354) lost his vote because John Fitzgerald Jackson committed a crime in Texas.

On the unlikely chance that Jackson of Florida is the same Jackson who served time in Texas, Florida now admits it had no right to take away his vote. In this small sample, Jackson of Texas, Butler of Illinois (#357) and Cooper of Ohio (#360) had the right to vote no matter their record. This error alone cost Gore six times as many votes as Bush's official victory margin.

Figure 2. Florida "felon" scrub list. This is one screen-page from the computer "scrub" list of thousands tagged for removal from voter registration rolls.

the state to test the list; ChoicePoint says the state should not have used its "raw" data.

Until Florida privatized its Big Brother powers, laws kept the process out in the open. This year, when one county asked to see ChoicePoint's formulas and back-up for blacklisting voters, they refused – these were commercial secrets. So we'll never know how America's president was chosen.

Florida's Disappeared Voters: Yet Another 40,000 Located. Let Me Repeat That: 40,000

Now it gets weird. Salon was showered with praise – by the New York Times, LA Times, Washington Post, Cleveland Plain Dealer *columnists (almost to a one Black or Jewish) horrified by, as Bob Kuttner of the* Boston Globe *put it, Florida's "lynching by laptop". But no news editors or news producers called me (except the CBS Network News producer who ran away with tail tucked as soon as Governor Jeb denied the allegations).*

So, in London, they read about the "third group", the 1,700 felons from outside Florida who had a right to vote, but were illegally bounced off the registries.

I began to look into the rights of felons in Florida – those actually convicted. Every paper in America reported that Florida bars ex-criminals from voting. And as soon as every newspaper agrees, that's the first signal it probably isn't true. Someone *wants* the papers to believe this. So I reached a clerk in First Brother Jeb's office who said, "Call me tomorrow before official opening hours." And this heroic clerk spent two hours the next morning telling me, "The courts tell us to do *this*, and we do *that*."

I asked four times, "Are you telling me the governor knowingly violated the law and court orders, excluding eligible voters?"

And four times I got, "The courts tell us to do *this* [allow certain felons to vote] and we do *that* [block them]."

But *Salon*, despite a mountain of evidence, stalled, then stalled some more. Resentment of the takeover of the political coverage by an 'alien' was getting on the team's nerves. I can't blame them. And it didn't help that *Salon* was facing bankruptcy, staff were frazzled and it was nearly Christmas. And *Salon*'s fact-checkers got a message that stops US news outlets like a cross freezes a vampire: a flat-out denial and soft-shoe explanation from a state official. Jeb Bush's people said they were innocent, they had the *right* to block these voters.

The remains of the year were lost while I got hold of legal opinions from top lawyers saying Bush's office was wrong; and later the Civil Rights Commission would also say Bush was wrong. But the political clock was ticking and George W. was oozing toward the Oval Office. And there was another problem that delayed the story. I had written about the case of a Black pastor in Alachua

County illegally barred from voting. Doubts were raised about the story by reporters who saw my drafts. They could not understand why a middle-aged Black man, an ex-con to boot, did not raise a ruckus in a county office in the rural South to demand his rights. After all, voters in Palm Beach had no problems complaining publicly.

E.J. Dionne of the *Washington Post* told me, "*You have to get this story out, Greg, right away!*" Notably, instead of directing me to the *Post*'s newsroom, he told me to call *Nation*, a kind of refugee center for storm-tossed news reports.

After double-checking and quintuple-checking the facts, *Nation* printed a summary of my research, "Scrub Helps Shrub", and the story of the "third group" of wrongly purged ex-felon voters (the list now hit 2,800), and a *fourth* group of voters wrongly barred from registering in the first place – *yet another 40,000 of them, almost all Democratic voters*.

It was now February 5, 2001 – so President Bush could read this report in *Nation* from the White House ...

In Latin America they might have called them *votantes desaparecidos*, "disappeared voters". On November 7, 2000, tens of thousands of eligible Florida voters were wrongly prevented from casting their ballots – some purged from the voter registries and others blocked from registering in the first instance. Nearly all were Democrats, nearly half of them African-American. The systematic program that disfranchised these legal voters, directed by the offices of Florida's Governor Jeb Bush and Secretary of State Katherine Harris, was so quiet, subtle and intricate that if not for George W. Bush's 500-vote eyelash margin of victory, certified by Harris, the chance of the purge's discovery would have been vanishingly small.

The group prevented from voting – felons – has few defenders in either party. It has been well reported that Florida denies its nearly half a million former convicts the right to vote. However, the media have completely missed the fact that Florida's own courts have repeatedly told the governor he may not take away the civil rights of Florida citizens who have committed crimes in other states, served their time and had their rights restored by those states.

People from other states who have arrived in Florida with a felony conviction in their past number "clearly over 50,000 and likely over 100,000," says criminal demographics expert Jeffrey Manza of Northwestern University. Manza estimates that 80 per cent arrive with voting rights intact, which they do not forfeit by relocating to the Sunshine State. In other words, there are no fewer than 40,000 reformed felons eligible to vote in Florida.

Nevertheless, agencies controlled by Harris and Bush ordered county officials to reject attempts by these eligible voters to register, while, publicly, the Governor's Office states that it adheres to court rulings not to obstruct these ex-offenders in the exercise of their civil rights. Further, with the aid of a Republican-tied database firm, Harris's office used sophisticated computer programs to hunt those felons eligible to vote and ordered them thrown off the voter registries.

David Bositis, senior research associate at the Joint Center for Political and Economic Studies in Washington, DC, suggests that the block-and-purge program "must have had a partisan motivation. Why else spend $4 million if they expected no difference in the ultimate vote count?" Bositis notes that, based on nationwide conviction rates, African-Americans would account for 46 per cent of the ex-felon group wrongly disfranchised. Florida's Black voters gave Al Gore nine out of ten of their votes.

White and Hispanic felons, mostly poor, vote almost as solidly Democratic as African-Americans. A recently released University of Minnesota study estimates that, for example, 93 per cent of felons of all races favored Bill Clinton in 1996. Whatever Florida's motive for keeping these qualified voters out of the polling booths on November 7, the fact is that they represented several times George W. Bush's margin of victory in the state. Key officials in Bush's and Harris's agencies declined our requests for comment.

	your socialist slanted news/reporting
Date:	1/7/01 2:20:41 PM GMT Standard Time

From: wild.bill@mtaonline.net (wildbill)
To: Gregory.Palast@guardian.co.uk

hey greg,
Let me begin by saying that your "article"on the Florida "black list" is so transparently a socialist/democrat attempt to help your socialist cousins in the states that it laughable.You pansey brits seem to think that the average American is as undereducated and stupid as the average british subject.Well comrad,I'm here to tell you that that is not the case.While your average british male was chasing his classmates around the dorms trying to get a little buggery time in,The Average American male was in class paying attention to the subject matter at hand.One of the first things I learned was to spot a liar,and in your case it was'nt hard.Yor story is so full of outright lies and half truths that a 6th grader here in the states could find you out.You claim to be places and to have spoken to people that would be extreemly hard if not impossible to a member of the legitimate press and a genuine miracle for a representative of a third world(yes greg,britain is considered here in the states to be a third world country,and one populated by fourth rate acedemics)socialist rag.We yanks have kicked your worthless limey butts twice so far,is that what has your panties in a twist?Does'nt matter anyway,I just wanted to drop you a line to tell you to say hi to prince chuck for me,you know who I'm talking about don't you?He's the one member of the boil family that is squatting in Buckingham palace,the one that from head on looks like a volkswagon with both doors open.Oh,and I almost forgot,tell that bitch the Queen the next time you bugger her that she needs to lose some weight &Stay out of our politics you english pigs.<>

Figure 3. More fan mail. How unfair to call me "English."

The National Association for the Advancement of Colored People, tipped off to the racially suspect voter purge by early reports of this investigation, added the tainted felon hunt to its lawsuit, filed on January 10, 2001, against Harris, her elections unit chief Clay Roberts and their private database contractor. The suit accuses them of violating the Voting Rights Act of 1965 and the Constitution's equal protection amendment. The NAACP demands an immediate injunction to halt the felon purge.

The disfranchisement operation began in 1998 under Katherine Harris's predecessor as Secretary of State, Sandra Mortham. Mortham was a Republican star, designated by Jeb Bush as his lieutenant governor running mate for his second run for governor.

Six months prior to the gubernatorial contest, the Florida legislature passed a "reform" law to eliminate registration of ineligible voters: those who had moved, those who had died and felons without voting rights. The legislation was promoted as a good government response to the fraud-tainted Miami mayoral race of 1997.

But from the beginning, the law and its implementation emitted a partisan fragrance. Passed by the Republican legislature's majority, the new code included an extraordinary provision to turn over the initial creation of "scrub" lists to a private firm. No other state, either before or since, has privatized this key step in the elimination of citizens' civil rights.

In November 1998 the Republican-controlled Office of the Secretary of State handed the task to the single bidder, Database Technologies, now the DBT Online unit of ChoicePoint Inc. of Atlanta, into which it merged last year.

The elections unit within the Office of the Secretary of State immediately launched a felon manhunt with a zeal and carelessness that worried local election professionals. The *Nation* has obtained an internal Florida State Association of Supervisors of Elections memo, dated August 1998, which warns Mortham's office that it had wrongly removed eligible voters in a botched rush "to capriciously take names off the rolls". However, to avoid a public row, the supervisors agreed to keep their misgivings within the confines of the bureaucracies in the belief that "entering a public fight with [state officials] would be counterproductive".

That November, Jeb Bush had an unexpectedly easy walk to the governor's mansion, an election victory attributed, ironically, to his endorsement by Black Democratic politicians feuding with their party.

Over the next two years, with Republicans in charge of both the governorship and the Secretary of State's Office, now under Harris, the felon purge accelerated. In May 2000, using a list provided by DBT, Harris's office ordered counties to purge 8,000 Florida voters who had committed felonies in Texas. In fact, none of the group was charged with anything more than misdemeanors, a mistake caught but never fully reversed. ChoicePoint DBT and Harris then sent out "corrected" lists, including the names of 437 voters who had indeed committed felonies in Texas. But this list too was in error, since a

Texas law enacted in 1997 permits felons to vote after doing their time. In this case there was no attempt at all to correct the error.

The wrongful purge of the Texas convicts was no one-of-a-kind mishap. The Secretary of State's Office acknowledges that it also ordered the removal of 714 names of Illinois felons and 990 from Ohio – states that permit the vote even to those on probation or parole. According to Florida's own laws, not a single person arriving in the state from Ohio or Illinois should have been removed. Altogether, DBT tagged for the scrub nearly 3,000 felons who came from at least eight states that automatically restore voting rights and who therefore arrived in Florida with full citizenship.

A ChoicePoint DBT spokesman said, and the Florida Department of Elections confirms, that Harris's office approved the selection of states from which to obtain records for the felon scrub. As to why the department included states that restore voting rights, Janet Modrow, Florida's liaison to ChoicePoint DBT, bounced the question to Harris's legal staff. That office has not returned repeated calls.

Pastor Thomas Johnson of Gainesville is minister to House of Hope, a faith-based charity that guides ex-convicts from jail into working life, a program that has won high praise from the pastor's friend, Governor Jeb Bush. Ten years ago, Johnson sold crack cocaine in the streets of New York, got caught, served his time, then discovered God and Florida – where, early last year, he attempted to register to vote. But local election officials refused to accept his registration after he admitted to the decade-old felony conviction from New York. "It knocked me for a loop. It was horrendous," said Johnson of his rejection.

Beverly Hill, the election supervisor of Alachua County, where Johnson attempted to register, said that she used to allow ex-felons like Johnson to vote. Under Governor Bush, that changed. "Recently, the [Governor's Office of Executive] Clemency people told us something different," she said. "They told us that they essentially can't vote."

Both Alachua's refusal to allow Johnson to vote and the governor's directive underlying that refusal are notable for their timing – coming after two court rulings that ordered the secretary of state and governor to recognize the civil rights of felons arriving from other states. In the first of these decisions, *Schlenther* v. *Florida Department of State*, issued in June 1998, Florida's Court of Appeal ruled unanimously that Florida could not require a man convicted in Connecticut 25 years earlier "to ask [Florida] to restore his civil rights. They were never lost here." Connecticut, like most states, automatically restores felons' civil rights at the end of their sentence, and therefore "he arrived as any other citizen, with full rights of citizenship".

The *Schlenther* decision was much of the talk at a summer 1998 meeting of county election officials in Orlando. So it was all the more surprising to Chuck Smith, systems administrator with Hillsborough County, that Harris's elections division chiefs exhorted local officials at the Orlando meeting to purge all out-of-state felons identified by DBT. Hillsborough was so concerned about this order, which appeared to fly in the face of the court edict, that the county's elections office demanded that the state put that position in writing – a request duly granted.

The *Nation* has obtained the text of the response to Hillsborough. The letter, from the Governor's Office of Executive Clemency, dated September 18, 2000, arrived only seven weeks before the presidential election. It orders the county to tell ex-felons trying to register that even if they entered Florida with civil rights restored by another state's law, they will still be "required to make application for restoration of civil rights in the state of Florida," that is, ask Governor Bush for clemency – the very requirement banned by the courts. The state's directive was all the more surprising in light of a second ruling, issued in December 1999 by another Florida court, in which a Florida district court judge expressed his ill-disguised exasperation with the governor's administration for ignoring the prior edict in *Schlenther*.

Voting rights attorneys who reviewed the cases for the *Nation* explained that the courts relied on both Florida statute and the "full faith and credit" clause of the US Constitution, which requires every state to accept the legal rulings of other states. "The court has been pretty clear on what the governor can't do," says Bruce Geai, assistant general counsel for the NAACP. And what Governor Bush can't do is demand that a citizen arriving in Florida ask him for clemency to restore a right to vote that the citizen already has.

Strangely enough, the Governor's Office does not disagree. While Harris, Bush and a half-dozen of their political appointees have not returned our calls, Tawanna Hayes, who processes the requests for clemency in the Governor's Office, states unequivocally that "we do not have the right to suspend or restore rights where those rights have been restored in another state". Hayes even keeps a copy of the two court decisions near her desk and quotes from them at length. So, why have the governor and secretary of state ordered these people purged from the rolls or barred from registering? Hayes directed us to Greg Munson, Governor Bush's assistant general counsel and clemency aide. Munson has not responded to our detailed request for an explanation.

A letter dated August 10, 2000, from Harris's office to Bush's office, obtained under Florida's Freedom of Information Act, indicates that the chief of the Florida State Association of Supervisors of Elections also questioned Harris's office about the purge of ex-cons whose rights had been restored automatically by other states. The supervisors' group received the same response as Hillsborough: strike them from the voter rolls and, if they complain, make them ask Bush for clemency.

While almost all county supervisors buckled, Carol Griffen did not. Griffen, Washington County's elections chief, concluded that running legal voters through Jeb Bush's clemency maze would violate a 1993 federal law, the National Voter Registration Act, which was designed to remove impediments to the exercise of civil rights. The law, known as "motor voter", is credited with helping to register seven million new voters. Griffen quotes from the Florida section of the new, NVRA-certified registration form, which says: "I affirm I am not a convicted felon, or if I am, my rights relating to voting have been restored." "That's the law," says the adamant Griffen, "and I have no right stopping anyone registering who truthfully signs that statement. Once you check that box there's no discussion." Griffen's county refused to implement the scrub, and the state appears reluctant to challenge its action.

But when Pastor Johnson attempted to register in Alachua County, clerks refused and instead handed him a 15-page clemency request form. The outraged minister found the offer a demeaning Catch-22. "How can I ask the governor for a right I already have?" he says, echoing, albeit unknowingly, the words of the Florida courts.

Had Johnson relented and chosen to seek clemency, he would have faced a procedure that is, admits the Clemency Office's Hayes, "sometimes worse than breaking a leg". For New Yorkers like Johnson, she says, "I'm telling you it's a bear." She says officials in New York, which restores civil rights automatically, are perplexed by requests from Florida for nonexistent papers declaring the individual's rights restored. Without the phantom clemency orders, the applicant must hunt up old court records and begin a complex process lasting from four months to two years, sometimes involving quasi-judicial hearings, the outcome of which depends on Jeb Bush's disposition.

Little wonder that out of tens of thousands of out-of-state felons, only a hardy couple of hundred attempted to run this bureaucratic obstacle course before the election. (Bush can be compassionate: he granted clemency to Charles Colson for his crimes as a Watergate conspirator, giving Florida resident Colson the right to vote in the presidential election.)

Was Florida's corrupted felon-voter hunt the work of cozy collusion between Jeb Bush and Harris, the president-elect's brother and state campaign chief, respectively? It is unlikely we will ever discover the motives driving the voter purge, but we can see the consequences. Three decades ago, Governor George Wallace stood in a schoolhouse door and thundered, "Segregation now! Segregation tomorrow! Segregation forever!" but failed to block entry to African-Americans. Governor Jeb Bush's resistance to court rulings, conducted at whisper level with high-tech assistance, has been far more effective at blocking voters of color from the polling station door. Deliberate or accidental, the error-ridden computer purge and illegal clemency obstacle course function, like the poll tax and literacy test of the Jim Crow era, to take the vote away from citizens who are Black, poor and, not coincidentally, almost all Democrats. No guesswork there: Florida is one of the few states to include both party and race on registration files.

Pastor Johnson, an African-American wrongfully stripped of his vote, refuses to think ill of the governor or his motives. He prefers to see a dark comedy of bureaucratic errors: "The buffoonery of this state has cost us a president." If this is buffoonery, then Harris and the Bushes are wise fools indeed.

What Really Happened In Florida?
BBC Television's *Newsnight* Investigates

What did the Nation *story tell us? About 80 per cent of registered voters actually vote in presidential elections, and about 90 per cent of this illegally excluded group, out-of-state ex-felons, vote Democratic. Therefore, about 36,000 would have voted for Gore, 4,000 for Bush. You do the arithmetic: that was the election right there.*

And that would be the last new investigative report on the matter in the US press and TV news. America had, as Katherine Harris requested, "moved on".

... But I hadn't.

A few things still bothered me. As always, it was the money. I looked into state files and discovered that ChoicePoint's DBT was not the first contractor on the job. The Florida Department of Elections terminated a contract with a small operator who won the work with a bid of $5,700. Florida then gave the job to DBT for a fee of $2,317,800 – no bidding. When I contacted database industry experts about the fee paid by Florida, 27 cents per record, their eyes popped out – *"Wow!" "Jeez!" "Scandalous!"* – easily *ten times* the industry norm.

Something else bothered me: it was the weird glee, the beaming self-congratulations, from the ChoicePoint public relations man over my reporting that 15 per cent of the names on his purge list were wrong (even though the error turned around an election). To ChoicePoint, my story was good news: in effect, they said, I reported their list was "85 per cent" correct. But was it?

The list was 85 per cent "accurate", said ChoicePoint's PR man, because they used Social Security numbers. That was convincing – until I checked the felon scrub lists themselves and *almost none* of them listed a voter's Social Security number. Floridians, until recently, did not have to provide their Social Security number when registering.

Four days after I ran my first report in England, on November 30, 2000, the Bloomberg business news wire interviewed Marty Fagan of ChoicePoint, one of the PR men who'd spoken to me. Based on the big "success" of its computer purge in Florida, ChoicePoint planned to roll out its voter-purge operation across to every state in the Union. This could become a billion-dollar business.

Fagan crowed to Bloomberg about the accuracy of ChoicePoint's lists. The company, he said, used 1,200 public databases to cross-check "a very accurate picture of an individual," including a history of addresses and financial assets. That was impressive. And indeed, every database expert told me, if you want 85 per cent accuracy or better, you will need at least those three things: Social Security numbers, address history and a check against other databases. But, over the weeks and months I discovered:

- ChoicePoint used virtually *no* Social Security numbers for the Florida felon purge;

- of its 1,200 databases with which to "check the accuracy of the data", ChoicePoint used exactly *none* for cross-checking;
- as to the necessary verification of address history of the 66,000 named "potential felons", ChoicePoint performed this check in exactly *zero* cases.

There was, then, not a chance in hell that the list was "85 per cent correct". And we knew this: one county, Leon (Tallahassee), had done the hard work of checking each name, one by one, to verify independently that the 694 named felons in Tallahassee were, in fact, ineligible voters. They could verify only 34 names – a 95 per cent error rate. That is killer information. In another life, decades ago, I taught "Collection and Use of Economic and Statistical Data" as an adjunct professor at Indiana University. Here's a quicky statistics lesson. The statewide list of felons is "homogeneous" as to its accuracy. Leon County provides us with a sample large enough to give us a "confidence interval" of 4.87 at a confidence "level" of 99 per cent. Are you following me, class? In other words, we can be 99 per cent certain that *at least 90.2 per cent of the names on the Florida list are not felons – 52,000 wrongly tagged for removal.*

OK, you want to argue and say not everyone tagged was actually removed. There might be some problems in the sample group. Maybe it's not 52,000 wrong names, but 42,000 or 32,000. Excuse me, but Gore "lost" by 537 votes. But I digress.

Now I was confident the list was junk – it had to be, because ChoicePoint did not use the most basic tools of verification. But why didn't they? Is ChoicePoint incompetent, didn't know how to verify a list? That's unlikely – this is the company hired by the FBI for manhunts, and the FBI doesn't pay for 90 per cent wrong.

And why would ChoicePoint lie about it? How did it happen? Did someone want it wrong? Could someone, say, want to swing an election with this poisoned list? And more documentary evidence piled up: including one sheet marked "DBT CONFIDENTIAL AND TRADE SECRET".

"When the going gets weird," Hunter Thompson tells journalists, "the weird turn pro." In London, I showed this "CONFIDENTIAL" sheet to the ultimate pro, Meirion Jones, producer with BBC Television's *Newsnight*. He said, "How soon can you get on a plane to Florida?"

Our BBC *Newsnight* broadcast began with a country and western twang off the rental car radio:

"After hundreds of lies ... fake alibis ..."

Newsnight's camera followed me up to the 18th floor of the Florida's Capitol Building in Tallahassee to my meeting with Clayton Roberts, the squat, bull-necked Director of Florida's Division of Elections.

Roberts, who works directly under Secretary of State Katherine Harris, had agreed to let us film our chat. We exchanged pleasantries as we both sat in his reception sofa outside his office. His eyes began to shift, then turned into panic as he read the heading of the paper on the sofa next to me: "CONFIDENTIAL". He certainly knew what I had when I picked up the paper and asked him if the state had checked whether DBT (the ChoicePoint company) had verified the accuracy of a single name on the purge list before they paid the company millions.

Roberts responded by saying, "No I didn't ask DBT," sputtered a few half-started sentences, ripped off his lapel microphone, jumped up and charged over the wires and slammed the office door on me and the camera crew giving

---

EXHIBIT A

(DBT CONFIDENTIAL AND TRADE SECRET INFORMATION)

Pricing Structure:

1. Phases I-IV (1998-1999)* $2,197,800
   (includes manual verification using
   telephone calls and statistical sampling)   120,000

                                                      Total $2,317,800

   * Based on the processing of 8,140,000 CVF Records @ S.27/record

2. -Year Two (Optional Renewal) (1999-2000) $1,024,000
   (includes manual verification using
   telephone calls and statistical sampling)

3. Year Three (Optional Renewal) (2000-2001) $1,024,000
   (includes manual verification using
   telephone calls and statistical sampling)

Figure 4. This is a photocopy of a page from the contract that won the election for George W. Bush – between the State of Florida and DBT Online (later owned by ChoicePoint Corp. of Atlanta) to identify "felon" voters to remove from registration rolls.

$2,317,800 for the first year's work. On this no-bid deal, DBT replaced a company charging only $5,700. The rate of "$.27/record" is, say experts, at least ten times industry norms.

What could account for the big difference in payment? The crucial words are, "telephone calls." Had DBT done the expensive work of making thousands of "manual verification" calls, voters, overwhelmingly Democrats, would never have been barred from the polls. But someone in the Florida Secretary of State's elections department told DBT they could skip that work and still get their millions.

Florida Governor Jeb Bush and his Secretary of State, Katherine Harris, jointly testified under oath to the US Civil Rights Commission that "verification" of this list was not left to their office and their contractor, DBT, but to county officials. They testified before BBC television unearthed this document.

chase. We were swiftly escorted out of the building by very polite and very large state troopers.

Before he went into hiding and called the Smokies, Roberts whipped around and pointed an angry finger at the lens, "Please turn off that camera!"

Which we did – BBC rules. But he didn't add, "and turn off the microphone", so our lawyers ruled we could include his parting shot, "You know if y'all want to hang this on me that's fine." I will. Though not him alone. By "this" he meant the evidence in the document, which I was trying to read out to him on the run.[2]

What was so terrorizing to the Republican honcho? The "CONFIDENTIAL" page, obviously not meant to see the light of day, said that DBT would be paid $2.3 million for their lists *and "manual verification using telephone calls and statistical sampling"*. No wonder Roberts did a runner. He and Harris had testified under oath to the US Civil Rights Commission that verification of the voter purge list was left completely up to the county elections supervisors, not to the state or the contractor, ChoicePoint DBT.

In fact, it was the requirement to *verify* the accuracy of the purge list that justified ChoicePoint's selection for the job as well as their astonishingly high fee. *Good evening, Mr Smith. Are you the same Mr John Smith that served hard time in New York in 1991?* That becomes expensive repeated thousands of times, but necessary when civil rights are at stake. Yet DBT seems to have found a way to cut the cost of this procedure: by not doing it. At least, there is no record of DBT having made extensive verification calls. And even if the manual verification process was implemented, why didn't it catch the fact that every single record on the Texas felon list was wrong?

(Later, I confronted DBT at their Florida headquarters about the verification calls, but our camera crew was barred entry. After returning to London, we received a call from one of their executives explaining that "manual verification by telephone" did not "require us to actually make telephone calls" to anyone on the list. Oh, I see.)

From the evidence, BBC broadcast that the *faux* felon purge and related voting games cost Al Gore 22,000 votes in Florida. One could quibble with the sum, but, tweak it as you will, it was 40 times the margin of victory for Bush certified by Katherine Harris. Now the British public knew who won the election.

Jim Crow in Cyberspace: New Unreported Evidence

But I had more questions, leading to the big one: was it planned – the purge of innocents and other voting games?

2 You can watch the film of Roberts's bunny-hop by visiting:
http://news.bbc.co.uk/olmedia/cta/progs/newsnight/palast.ram

A company charging $5,700 is booted out for one, with big Republican ties, charging $2.3 million, with no competitive bidding. A "little birdie" told George Bruder, ChoicePoint DBT's senior vice-president, to enter that astonishing bid, he said later. What else did the little birdie tell him?

The evidence piled up.

The missing statistician

First, there's the matter of the missing statistician. Florida's contract states:

> During the verification phase, DBT shall use academically-based and widely utilized statistical formulas to determine the exact number of records necessary to represent a valid cross-section [sample] of the processed files. DBT shall consult a professional statistician ... Upon the return of the processed data, DBT shall supply the formulas and mathematical calculations and identify the professional statistician used during the verification process.

The 8,000-name Texas list had a 100 per cent error rate – which seemed a wee bit high to me. What kind of "academically-based formula" was used to verify the accuracy of these data? Who was the statistician? Inscrutably silent on whether he or she exists or existed, ChoicePoint DBT referred me back to Clay Roberts. His Department of Elections cannot name this Man of Mystery either, although the contract requires DBT to provide evidence of the statistician's hiring and analysis. The name, the info, were not in state files.

No independent technician, no expert to see it go rotten, no one to blow the whistle.

Millions and millions of records – ignored

And what happened to the 1,200 databases, the millions and millions of records that DBT used in its Carl Saganesque sales pitch to the state? In fact, the state paid for this vital cross-check – or at least DBT's bid said that for their big-bucks bid, they offered artificial intelligence for "cross-referencing, linked databases ... simultaneously searching hundred of data sources, conducting millions of data comparisons, compiling related data for matching and integration". In all, they had *four billion* records to check against. Under "Offer and Bid" it read:

> *DBT will process total combined records from:*
> *8,250,000 Criminal Conviction Records*
> *62,000,000 National Change of Address ...*

And so on. The phone calls, the massive data-crunching, it all justified the big pay-off to DBT and scared away competitors who could not match DBT's database firepower, a bid promising, "273,318,667 total records to be processed".

But once the contract was nailed, another little birdie in the state told DBT not to bother with all that expensive computing work. In the state files, on the DBT bid, I found a hand-written notation, "*don't need*", next to the listing of verification databases (the 62 million address histories, etc.), though this work was included in the price.

These cross-checks were the justification for hiring DBT without competitive bidding, and for its high price. For example, Republican officials told the federal government that DBT's special expertise was needed to obtain and analyze out-of-state felon lists. Yet Janet Modrow, the state's liaison with DBT, confessed to me that DBT merely downloaded the lists from the dozen states that make the data available publicly, such as Texas. Any high school kid with a Mac and a credit card could have grabbed the names off the Internet. And that was OK with the state, even though eight of the eleven states should not even have been used. Had the state told DBT to complete its cross-check as paid for, the 57,700 list would have been cut to a fraction of the original number, allowing thousands more Black citizens to vote.[3]

So we have this: the state of Florida pays a contractor what appears to be several times more than a standard fee for services and then does not object when the costly part of the work is simply not done – or done so poorly that it is worse than not done at all.[4]

One can only conclude that Harris's office paid an awful lot of money for either (a) failed, incomplete, incompetent, costly, disastrous work that stripped innocent citizens of their rights or (b) services performed exactly as planned.

3 When I asked DBT to provide evidence that they had made the required calls to verify felons list or performed any other of the cross-checks, the company sent me, instead of evidence, a *Miami Herald* article stating, "the responsibility of verifying the accuracy was" left to the "67 county supervisors of elections". That was repeated by Harris and Jeb Bush to the US Civil Rights Commission under oath: verification was in the hands of the counties.

While I would not normally question a public official testifying under penalty of perjury, nor any fact printed by such an august journal as the *Miami Herald*, I thought it best to direct DBT to the contract itself. It says in black and white: "DBT will then verify the accuracy of the data contained in the output files", the scrub lists given to the state. The means of verification – "manual, telephone, and statistical methods" – are detailed.

4 DBT's seeming negligence in passing on the bogus Texas list cost Florida and its counties a pretty penny to attempt to reverse the error. Yet Mudrow, in Harris's office, says the state has either demanded reimbursement nor sought any penalty as permitted under the contract. In fact, the state awarded DBT another contract renewal, bringing total fees to over $4 million. Why didn't the watchdog bark? (Following my first reports, when the stats hit the fan, ChoicePoint DBT agreed to a one-year extension of their contract without charge.)

"Wanted there to be more names than we can verify ..."

Was DBT paid to get it wrong? Every single failure – to verify by phone, to sample and test, to cross-check against other databases – worked in one direction: to increase the number of falsely accused voters, half of them Black. ChoicePoint, such an expert outfit, did such a horrendous job, without complaint from their client, you'd think their client, the state, *ordered* them to get it wrong.

They did. Just before we went on air in February 2000, ChoicePoint's vice-president, James Lee, called us at the BBC's studios with the first hint that the state of Florida *told* the company to give them the names of innocents. The state, he said, "wanted there to be more names than were actually verified as being a convicted felon."

We broadcast the story with their statement – and ChoicePoint went ballistic, demanding in writing to network chiefs in London that we retract it all. On the Internet, a self-proclaimed expert on a pro-Bush web-site wrote that we had faked the Roberts tape, "unethical as you can get," because we clearly must have hidden away "the two-hour interview that preceded" Roberts's running away – fantasy footage that would have made Roberts look honest.

The BBC wouldn't back down an inch, detailing evidence we had yet to broadcast. Jones of *Newsnight* roared back at the Internet wingnuts.[5]

Following the broadcast, I received a call from Congresswoman Cynthia McKinney, who represents Atlanta, home of ChoicePoint's headquarters. She demanded their executives appear before a special hearing in Atlanta. The company would not answer questions from me, but if they came from her they might hesitate about shucking and jiving a member of the US Congress. On April 17, ChoicePoint's James Lee opened his testimony before the McKinney panel with notice that, despite its prior boast, ChoicePoint was getting out of the voter purge business. Then the company, in highly technical, guarded language, effectively confessed to the whole game, fingering the state.

For example, Lee said that the state had given DBT the truly insane directive to add to the purge list people who matched 90 per cent of a last name – if Anderson committed a crime, Andersen lost his vote. DBT objected, knowing this would sweep in a huge number of innocents. The state ordered DBT to shift to an 80 per cent match. It was programmed-in inaccuracy. Names were reversed – felon Thomas Clarence could knock out the vote of Clarence Thomas. Middle initials were skipped, "Jr" and "Sr" suffixes dropped, nicknames and aliases were added to puff up the list. And DBT sent in – quite quietly – its objections in e-mails it now produced. Were these true objections to this slaughter of civil rights – or just "CYA" (Cover Your Ass) memos? No

5 The BBC had unexpected proof that we didn't play editing games with the Roberts interview. While I taped Roberts, a documentary film crew taped me taping Roberts (a truly postmodernist scene). The cameramen with *Counting on Democracy*, by Emmy Award-winning producer Danny Schechter, filmed the interview from handshake to door slam.

matter. "DBT told state officials," testified Lee, "that the rules for creating the [purge] list would mean a significant number of people who were not deceased, not registered in more than one county or *not a felon* would be included on the list. Likewise, DBT made suggestions to reduce the numbers of eligible voters included on the list."

But the state said, *Forget about it.*

ChoicePoint's "confession" made my work easier, though I already had many of these state e-mails, like one (of June 14, 2000) about the "tweaked" data on middle names and "short names" – e.g. allowing Edward and Edwin to match.

Experts told me the state could have chosen criteria that could have brought down the number of "false positives" to less than a fragment of 1 per cent (as is done for medical records). One, Mark Hull, said it made him ill to learn what the company had agreed to do. He had been senior programmer for CDB Infotek, a ChoicePoint company.

Hunting the Black voter

They were *hunting* for innocents and, it seems, the blacker the better. To swing an election, there would be no point in knocking off thousands of legitimate voters if they were caught randomly – that would not affect the election's outcome. The key was color. And here's where the computer game got intensely sophisticated. How could it be that some 54 per cent of the list were Black? Yes, half of America's felons are Black, but how could it be that the *innocent* people on the list were mostly Black?

In November, ChoicePoint's PR men jumped up and down insisting in calls to me that "race was not part of the search criteria" – which the company repeated in press releases after they were sued by the NAACP for participating in a racist conspiracy against citizens' civil rights. DBT complained to editors, to the investigators. Race was not a search criterion, period! Then, I obtained a letter dated June 9, 2000 from ChoicePoint DBT's Vice-President Bruder written to all county elections supervisors:

> The information used for the matching process included first, middle, and last name; date of birth; *race*; and gender; but not Social Security Number.

But they had *not* lied to me. Read closely. They used race as a *match* criterion, not a *search* criterion. The company used this confusion between "match" and "search" criteria to try to pull the BBC off the track. They tried to slide the race question by the US Civil Rights Commission. But, at the Commission's request, on the morning of February 16, the day after our broadcast, I had faxed the Commission the June 9 letter and other key documents. Later that day, the Commission questioned Bruder.

COMMISSION: Was race or party affiliation a matching criterion in compiling that list?

BRUDER: [under oath] No ...

COMMISSION: [June 9 letter read into record.] Did you write this letter? It has your signature on it.

BRUDER: Can I see it, please?

COMMISSION: So, you misinformed the Florida Supervisors of Elections that race would be used as a matching criterion?

BRUDER: Yes.

Wise answer, Mr Bruder. Misleading elections officials is not a crime; perjury would be. He pleaded confusion. So if race was not a match criterion, how did Black people get matched to felons?

I was mightily confused until I looked again at the scrub sheets: ChoicePoint DBT simply *identified* race for every real felon, and the Secretary of State provided the race of the voters. It was left to the county supervisors to finish the Jim Crow operation: reasonably, they would accept racial matches as "proof" that the right person was named. Therefore, a Black felon named Will Whiting – this is an actual case – wiped out the registration of an innocent Will Whiting (Black) but not the rights of an innocent Will Whiting (White).

This methodology also explained another discovery. While Blacks made up about half the list of 57,700 targeted for the purge, of those ultimately expunged from the voter rolls, it appears *over 80 per cent are African-American*.

Evidence vanishes

And then, evidence began to disappear.

The counsel for the Civil Rights Commission told me he was most concerned about the purge of the 2,834 felons who did have a right to vote (he'd read my *Nation* article) – a wilful violation of two court orders. Proof of the illegal procedure was a September 18, 2000 letter to county supervisors. The letter was read to me by a county clerk, not sent.

So I called Janet Keels in Governor Jeb Bush's Office of Executive Clemency; I wanted a hard copy of the letter. A crew filming *An American Coup* captured the call on camera ...

My name is Gregory Palast and I'm calling from London.

My name is Troy Walker.

Troy, maybe you can help me. There is a letter from Janet Keels' [Governor's] Office of Executive Clemency, dated September 18, 2000. This is to Hillsborough Board of Elections dealing with registration of voters who moved to the state, committed a felony but have received executive clemency. I'm sure you have a copy of it ...

We do have a letter referencing something close to that.

OK, what date is that letter?

This letter is dated February 23, 2001.

What? He then read me a letter from Keels saying the *exact opposite* of the September 18 memo.

> September 18 (before the elections): convicts from other states moving to Florida "would be required to make application for restoration of civil rights in the State of Florida".
> February 23 (*after* the election): out-of-state convicts "need *not* apply for restoration of civil rights in Florida".[6]

The post-election letter was drafted one week after the Civil Rights Commission began to question Florida about the illegal maneuver – and now Troy was telling me there was *no record* of the first letter in Keels's files, or in the office's files, or in the state computers. From other sources, I obtained the incriminating September 18 memo, on Governor Bush's letterhead with Keels's signature.

The pre-clearance deception

The US Voting Rights Act assumes something very unkind about Florida, that the Old South state will twist the process to stop African-Americans from voting. Florida cannot be trusted to change voting procedures on its own. So, with the handful of other states named in the 1965 Act, Florida must "pre-clear" voting operations changes with the US Justice Department. The state must certify any new voter registration process will have no "disparate impact" on Black voters.

How in the world did Florida zing this racially bent felon purge scheme past the Feds? In 1998, the Justice Department smelled something rotten and asked a few questions, including, Why did Florida need to hire an outside contractor? On July 21, 1998, a lowly state legislative aide drafted a soothing memorandum of law to the Justice Department, dismissing the purge operation as mere administrative reform. The aide – Clayton Roberts – worked with a State Senator – Katherine Harris. In 1998 they sowed; in 2000 they reaped.[7]

Voting machine apartheid

The office of Leon County Supervisor of Elections Ion Sancho is right across the road from the State Capitol in Tallahassee. While researching files in his office

6 The tenacious Dave Ruppe of ABC.com news discovered this document switch-a-roo independently, though the network did not broadcast the story.
7 A huge amount of follow-up research on the presidential race (and other stories in this book) was conducted by a large team of researchers, most unpaid volunteers, some the top names in their technical fields, some inspired amateurs. The intensely complex research unravelling Florida's deceptive moves to obtain pre-clearance was conducted by Paul Lukasiak.

on the felon purge, the camera crew with *Counting on Democracy* asked to take a picture of me "voting" – putting my paper ballot into the practice voting machine set up in the Elections Office, to get what we call "B-roll" atmospheric footage. I deliberately made a mistake – voting both Nader and Buchanan. I put my pretend ballot into the machine and – *grrrr-zunt!* – it shot back into my hands. In other words, you could not make a voting mistake on this machine, called an "Accuvote". Mighty cool. So I asked a clerk: does every county using paper ballots have this machine? Yes and no. The adjoining county, Gadsden, also had machine-read paper ballots, *but did not activate the reject mechanism.* It's incredibly easy to make a wrong mark on a paper ballot. Make one wrong mark on your ballot in Gadsden, the machine accepts it – then the ballot is not counted.

So I asked what I call The Florida Question: "By any chance, do you know the racial profile of counties where machines accept bad ballots?"

Then I got The Florida Answer: "We've been waiting for someone to ask us that." The clerk then pulled out a huge multi-color sheet, listing, for every Florida county, the number of ballots not counted. In a presidential race decided by 537 votes, Florida simply *did not count* 179,855 ballots. And whether your vote counted depended a lot on your color. In Leon (Tallahassee), a White county, only one in 500 ballots was spoiled. In neighbouring Gadsden, with a high population of Black voters, one in eight ballots were rejected, never counted. In the Black counties, for example, some voters had checked off *and written in* the name "Al Gore" – yet their vote did not count for Gore.

Here's the breakdown of ballots not counted in Florida's blackest and whitest counties:

Black counties
25+ per cent African-American residents

		Ballots not counted
Gadsden	52 per cent	12 per cent
Madison	42 per cent	7 per cent
Hamilton	39 per cent	9 per cent
Jackson	26 per cent	7 per cent

White counties
Fewer than 5 per cent African-American residents

Citrus	2 per cent	½ per cent
Pasco	2 per cent	3 per cent
Santa Rosa	4 per cent	1 per cent
Sarasota	4 per cent	2 per cent

Detect a pattern? And as the Tallahassee officials demonstrated to me, whether a ballot was counted or not had almost nothing to do with the voters' education or sophistication – but an awful lot to do with the type of machine and *how the buttons are set.*

Was the governor or Katherine Harris aware of this racially-loaded technical problem? Their offices were literally a stone's throw away from the test machine. The technicians told me, "That's why we set up this machine, so they could see it – *before* the election."

Cover-up and counterspin

While virtually none of the new investigative material reached America's shores, the counterspin machine was in full throttle. The *Wall Street Journal*, usually unbiased, ignored the racial demographics of the mountains of spoiled ballots and proclaimed that there was no racial difference in the geographic division of sophisticated voting machines.

My felon purge reports got Florida's press poodles up in arms. Months after the election, *Palm Beach Post*, ChoicePoint DBT's home-town paper, announced dramatically, "thousands of felons voted in the presidential election last year ... It's likely they benefited Democratic candidate Al Gore." Wow! Thousands!

The *Post*'s FELONS VOTED! shock-horror story run one week before the US Civil Rights Commission aimed to blast the state/DBT purge list as garbage. What did the *Post*'s sleuths use to hunt for felons? The DBT list. They then looked for voters who matched, by name, birthday, race and gender, "felons" among the six million Florida voters. It was DBT Lite. They failed to do even the lame cross-checks done by the state and counties.

The *Post* did not find "5,643 felons voted", or anything close to it. Rather, they simply had a list of common names (e.g. John Jackson) and birthdays, maybe some misdemeanor violators or felons with clemency. (Think of this: if every birthday were a city, America would have 365 cities with 750,000 people in it. How many in that city's phone book would have the name "Joe White"?)

This was just not bad journalism, it smacked of a disinformation campaign. There's good reason to suspect the motive and method of the *Post*'s story. This is the paper, remember, that began to sniff the fake purge before the election, but then swallowed what a secret pre-election memo from the state to DBT's Bruder called the "Department of Elections News Coverage Game Plan". In that memo, discovered after the election by our researchers, the Department of Elections gloat how they got the *Palm Beach Post* to "correct" their story and planted happy-talk stories in the *Sun-Sentinel* and other papers.[8]

The ultimate measure

And there's the ultimate test of the veracity of DBT and *Post* lists: the Attorney General of Florida, Bob Butterworth, told me he absolutely would prosecute

8 E-mail dated June 26, 2000, from Janet Carabelli, Department of Elections, to Dee Smith, Bruder, others; obtained through Florida Open Records Act.

anyone who illegally voted or registered. A felon voting has committed a new felony – that means jail time. The idea that 57,700 Floridians – or even 5,643 – would chance years in pokey to vote was on its face incredible. If DBT and the *Post* found criminals, why haven't they been arrested? Butterworth is now checking a *handful,* and as of this writing, has not busted one single "felon voter".

The Theft of the Presidential Election – 2004

From the Washington Post

Twisted press coverage murdered the story of ethnic cleansing of the voter rolls. But that wasn't good enough for the *New York Times, Washington Post,* CNN and the other keepers of the New Information Order. With other major new outlets joined together as "The Consortium", they spent a wagon-load of cash to hire the National Opinion Research Center (NORC), of the University of Chicago, to conduct what was wrongly called a "recount" of the ballots. For months they held back the results. Finally, more than a year after the election, they released their findings. "Bush would have won anyway," headlines reassured us. So shut up, move on, get over it: the Lion of Kabul won fair and square.

Or did he? First, understand that NORC did not "recount" the ballots. Rather, its teams described each of the 180,000 ballots that Katherine Harris barred counties from including in the official total. This was the *first* count of these ballots. Second, NORC "coders" were not allowed to state the intent of the voter, merely provide physical descriptions of each ballot. They could note, in code, "Paper ballot, Gore circled," but could not count that ballot as a vote for Gore. The newspaper and television executives and editors, not the NORC experts, called the "winner" in this one.

Most Americans would have thought the news groups spent millions to found out whom Floridians wanted to vote for. That tends to be what we mean by "democracy". But the news bosses were in no mood for a democracy that threatened the legitimacy of authority, especially with a war on in Afghanistan and an economy in the toilet. So, despite the fact that NORC coders clearly found that the majority of Florida voters thought they had voted for Gore, the papers called the NORC findings for Bush. Like, huh? NORC has put its data on the web, so the Gore majority is there for all to see (for those who bother to look). The media chiefs' trick was to say that, going by various Florida rules, which knock out ballots with stray markings, Bush would have won. Well, we knew that. That's how Katherine Harris called it for Bush – on technicalities, not votes. Through this editorial three-card monte, the Republic was saved. I watched the NORC operation at first hand in Miami in February 2001. There was an Alice in Wonderland weirdness in the process – "First we announce the winner, then we count the ballots." It was not difficult to discern whom the

Figure 5. Clayton Roberts runs for cover. Who told DBT they would get paid even if they did not do the promised "manual verification by telephone" required by the "confidential" page of their contract? Whoever made that decision cost the state treasury millions – and cost thousands, mostly Democrats, their right to vote. I decided to ask the Director of the Florida Department of Elections about it. In February 2001, Republican Clayton Roberts agreed to talk with me in his Tallahassee office. Yet, when I began to show the elections chief the page of his contract with DBT marked "confidential," Roberts did a quick dash from our cameras and hid in his office. Roberts's run was caught on video by the crew from my program, BBC's *Newsnight*, and by filmmaker Danny Schechter, producer of *Counting on Democracy*, from which these shots are taken. (© 2001 Globalvision)

voters wanted. "It screamed at you," said one counter. If someone circled "Gore" exactly whom do you think they wanted as president? Yet, such ballots were not included in the official count simply because of a wrongly placed or stray mark – often made by the voting machine itself, as it turns out. The Consortium members did not comment on this exclusion of tens of thousands of clearly marked ballots, which the NORC data reveal – or on the effect of this exclusion: the inauguration of the wrong person.

Still, the big theft of voting rights was not the failure to count the ballots (though that nailed the election shut), but the blocking of voters through the felon purge. It would be unfair of me to say the big-dog US papers refused to run my story. It took six months, but the *Washington Post* finally, cautiously, re-reported the *Salon* and *Nation* stories on the theft of the last election – and gave me a platform to warn about the theft of the *next* election. In "The Wrong Way to Fix the Vote" I commented:

Lord, save us from "reform".

If you liked the way Florida handled the presidential vote in November, you'll just love the election reform laws that have passed since then in ten states, and have been proposed in 16 others. These laws mandate a practice that was at the heart of the Florida débâcle: computer-aided purging of centralized voter files. The laudable aim is to rid registries of the names of the dead, as well as of felons and others legally barred from voting. But the likely result will be the elimination of a lot of legitimate voters and an increased potential for political mischief.

You would think other states would run from Florida's methods. But in their current legislative sessions, Colorado, Indiana, South Dakota, Texas, Virginia, Georgia, Kansas, Montana and Washington have passed bills that – while varying in specifics – would follow the Sunshine State's lead in centralizing, computerizing and cleansing voter rolls. Senator Christopher S. Bond (R-Mo.) has introduced a bill in which certain conditions in any state would trigger mandatory voter list purges.

To a large extent, these bills are a response to "motor voter" legislation, which has added millions of citizens, particularly minorities, to voter registries. Since minority voters tend to be Democratic, it is not surprising that "motor voter" laws are popular among Democrats, and most of the bills attempting to purge the rolls are sponsored by Republicans.

But many factors go into the ill-advised rush to reform. Take the case of Georgia. The day before the November 2000 election, the Atlanta Journal-Constitution and WSB-TV jointly reported that records indicated that deceased Georgians had voted 5,412 times over the last 20 years. They specifically cited one Alan J. Mandel, who apparently cast his ballot in three separate elections after his demise in 1997. Subsequently, a very live Alan J. Mandell (note the two L's) told the secretary of state that local election workers had accidentally checked off the wrong name on the list. That may or may not explain what really happened – but in the midst of the chad mania that dominated the headlines last autumn, details became less important than the newly energized drive for so-called reform.

If the reformers succeed, look out. Florida's Black-hunt purge began under the cover of the voting "reform" law passed by the state in 1998.

Here I wanted to include that the law was promoted in Florida, and pushed nationwide, by the Voter Integrity Project of Washington DC, founded by a Republican operative. Just before Bush's election, VIP presented its special Voter Integrity Award to DBT, the ChoicePoint company – at a VIP conference sponsored by: DBT. But the Post *preferred not.*

I wrote more in the Washington Post *about voting reform, which I won't bother you with here, because, at bottom, this story of a stolen election – the last one, the next one – is not about machines, nor computers, nor database management.*

Democracy and the people who count

If the theft of the US election came down to fixing our voting machines or procedures, we could solve our problems by the means suggested last year by the Russian Duma: "Taking into consideration the growing influence of the USA upon the affairs of the world community" American presidential elections, like Haiti's and Rwanda's, should be held under the auspices of the United Nations.

The solution to democracy's ills cannot be found in computers or in banning butterfly ballots. All that stuff about technology and procedure is vanishingly peripheral to this fact: the man who lost the vote grabbed the power. I report from Europe, where simple minds think that the appropriate response to the discovery that the wrong man was elected would be to remove him from office.

So where do we turn? The Democrats' employing William Daley, son of Chicago's old Boss Daley, as their spokesman during the Florida vote count, and Al Gore's despicably gracious concession speech, show that both political parties share, though in different measure, a contempt for the electorate's will.

Two other presidential elections were nearly stolen in the year 2000, in Peru and in Yugoslavia. How ironic that in those nations, not the United States, the voters' will ultimately counted. Peruvians and Yugoslavs took to heart Martin Luther King's admonition that rights are never given, only asserted. They knew: when the unelected seize the presidential palaces, democrats must seize the streets.

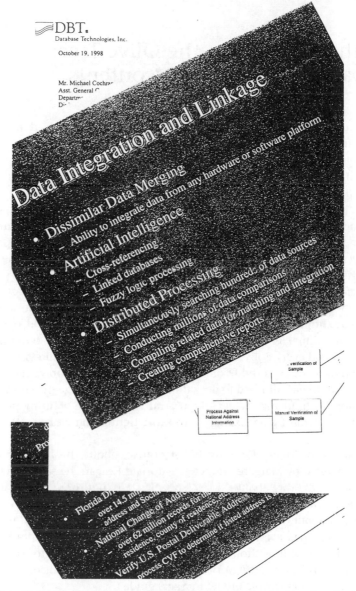

Figure 6. Artificial Intelligence! Fuzzy Logic! Simultaneously searching hundreds of data sources! Process Against National Address Information! Manual Verification! Over 62 million records!

With those capabilities and promises, Florida could justify replacing a firm charging $5,700 for DBT's $2.3 million plan. But, at the direction of the Republican Secretary of State's functionaires, DBT never bothered with the "hundreds of data sources" nor any of the myriad promised protections. On one listing of DBT's databases, a state official had written, *"DON'T NEED."* More accurate would have been, "don't want." Result: thousands lost their vote, mostly Democrats.

2

Sell the Lexus, Burn the Olive Tree: Globalization and its Discontents

I was getting myself measured for a straitjacket when I received an urgent message from Bolivia.

First let me tell you about this jacket. It was Thomas Friedman's idea. He's the *New York Times* columnist and amateur economist who wrote *The Lexus and the Olive Tree*, which is kind of a long, deep kiss to globalization.

I was about to debate with Friedman in Cleveland at a Council on World Affairs meeting last May. Globalization, he said, was all about the communications revolution. It was about the Internet. You could sit in your bedroom, buy shares in Amazon.com and send e-mails to Eskimos all at the same time, *wearing your pajamas.*

We were "*connected*" and "*empowered*" and "*enabled*". And if that wasn't cool enough by itself, globalization made economies grow. Any nation on the planet that simply took the pledge and followed the map could open the hidden gold mine. Poverty would end, and so would the tyrannies of government and every Bolivian would get their own e-mail address.

The end of world poverty! Eskimos! E-mail! I wanted this brave new future and I wanted it *now*! All I had to do, said Friedman, is change into something a little more form-fitting. "The Golden Straitjacket is the defining political-economic garment of globalization." And, the tighter you wear it, "the more gold it produces".

Friedman was talking figuratively, of course, about the latest *economic* fashion, "tailored by Margaret Thatcher". Ronald Reagan, he said, "sewed on the buttons". There are about a dozen specific steps, but the key ones are: cut government, cut the budgets and bureaucracies and the rules they make; privatize just about everything; deregulate currency markets, capital markets, free the banks; open every nation's industry to foreign trade, without tariffs, and foreign ownership without limit; wipe away border barriers to commerce; let the market rule, on setting prices, on investments; cut pensions, welfare, subsidies; let politics shrink and let markets guide us.

Selling the rules is easy work; there is no dissent. OK, there were green-hairs in Seattle and Genoa and so on. As Tony Blair said, "The protests and people who indulge in the protests are completely misguided. World trade is good for people's jobs and people's living standards. These protests are a complete outrage."

But we have to forgive youth its lack of sophistication. What the kids in the street didn't know is that history's over with, done, *kaput*. Friedman tells us: "The historical debate is over. The answer is free-market capitalism." And whether Republicans or Democrats, Tories or New Labour, Socialists or Christian Democrats, we're all signed on, we're all laced up in our straitjackets, merely quibbling about the sleeve length.

I was about to say, "Strap me in." But, I had just received this note – an e-mail – from Cochabamba, Bolivia. It was about Oscar Olivera, a community leader I knew through my work with Latin American labor unions. It said:

Close to 1,000 heavily armed members of the Bolivian security forces dispersed peaceful marchers with tear gas, beating them and confiscating their personal possessions.

What was the problem? Maybe the Internet was down and they couldn't unload their Amazon.com shares.

The message ended: *"Oscar* is missing. His whereabouts are unknown."

Something else bothered me. A large cache of documents had fallen into my hands. They came from the deepest files of the International Monetary Fund, from the desk drawers of officials at the European Commission and the World Trade Organization: Country Assistance Strategies, an Article 133 diplomatic letter, the GATS committee memos – the real stuff of globalization – from inside the organizations that dream up, then dictate, the terms of the new international economics.

In the deep pile, there was nothing about Eskimos on cell phones, but I found an awful lot about cutting Argentine pensions by 13 per cent, breaking up unions in Brazil ... and raising water prices in Bolivia, all laid out in chilling techno-speak and stamped "for official use only".

The spiky-haired protesters in the streets of Seattle believe there's some kind of grand conspiracy between the corporate powers, the IMF, the World Bank and an alphabet soup of agencies which work to suck the blood of Bolivians and steal the gold from Tanzania. But the tree-huggers are wrong; the details are far more stomach-churning than they imagine. In March 2001, when Ecuador's government raised the price of domestic gas and hungry Indians burned the capital, I was reading the World Bank's confidential plan issued months before. The bank, with the IMF, had directed this 60 per cent increase in the price of domestic fuel, predicting coldly this could set the nation alight. It's as if the riots were scheduled right into the plan.

And they were, at least according to one of the only inside sources I can name, Joseph Stiglitz, former chief economist of the World Bank. "We called them the IMF riots." The riots were programmed as well as the response, what the document called "resolve" – the police, the tanks, the crackdown.

And that's what you'll find in this chapter: explication of the lists of "conditionalities" (167 for Ecuador) required by the World Bank and IMF for their loans, the unpublished proposed terms for implementing article VI.4 of the GATS treaty under the World Trade Organization; intellectual property rules under something called the "TRIPS" agreement and how this determines everything from breast cancer treatment to Dr Dre's control of rap music; and all the other dirty little facts of globalization as it is actually practiced. And you can read it in your pajamas.

Friedman ended his talk – he won't debate face-to-face, so we had to speak on separate days – by quoting with joyous approval the wisdom of Andy Grove, the chairman of Intel Corporation: "The purpose of the new capitalism is to shoot the wounded."

That day, for Oscar's sake, I was hoping Friedman was wrong.

Dr Bankenstein's Monsters: The World Bank, The IMF and the Aliens Who Ate Ecuador

So call me a liar. I was standing in front of the New York Hilton Hotel. It was during the big G7 confab in 2000, when the limousine carrying IMF director Horst Kohler zoomed by, hit a bump and out flew a report, "Ecuador Interim Country Assistance Strategy". It was marked, "Confidential. Not for distribution." You suspect that's not how I got this document, but you can trust me that it contains the answer to a very puzzling question.

Inside the Hilton, Professor Anthony Giddens explained to an earnest crowd of London School of Economics alumni that "Globalization is a *fact*, and it is driven by the communications revolution."

Wow. That was an eye-opener. The screeching green-haired freakers outside the hotel demonstrating against the IMF had it all wrong. Globalization, Giddens seems to say, is all about giving every villager in the Andes a Nokia Internet-enabled mobile phone. (The man had obviously memorized his Thomas Friedman.) What puzzled me is why anyone would protest against this happy march into the globalized future.

So I thumbed through my purloined IMF "Strategy for Ecuador" looking for a chapter on connecting Ecuador's schools to the world wide web. Instead, I found a secret schedule. Ecuador's government was *ordered* to raise the price of cooking gas by 80 per cent by November 1, 2000, it says. Also, the government had to eliminate 26,000 jobs and cut real wages for the remaining workers by 50 per cent in four steps in a timetable specified by the IMF. By July 2000, Ecuador had to transfer ownership of its biggest water system to foreign operators, then Ecuador would grant British Petroleum's ARCO unit rights to build and own an oil pipeline over the Andes.

That was for starters. In all, the IMF's 167 detailed loan conditions looked less like an "Assistance Plan" and more like a blueprint for a financial *coup d'état*.

The IMF would counter that it had no choice. After all, Ecuador is flat busted, thanks to the implosion of the nation's commercial banks. But how did Ecuador, an OPEC member with resources to spare, end up in such a pickle? For that, we have to turn back to 1983, when the IMF forced Ecuador's government to take over the soured private debts Ecuador's elite owed to foreign banks. For this bail-out of US and local financiers, Ecuador's government borrowed $1.5 billion.

For Ecuador to pay back this loan, the IMF dictated price hikes in electricity and other necessities. And when that didn't drain off enough cash, yet another "Assistance Plan" required the state to eliminate 120,000 workers.

Furthermore, while trying to pay down the mountain of IMF obligations, Ecuador foolishly "liberalized" its tiny financial market, cutting local banks loose from government controls and letting private debt and interest rates explode. Who pushed Ecuador into this nutty romp with free market banking? Hint: the initials are I - M - F – which made liberalization of the nation's banking sector a condition of another berserker Assistance Plan. The facts of this nasty little history come from yet another internal IMF report that flew my way marked "Please do not cite." Pretend I didn't.

The IMF and its sidekick, the World Bank, have lent a sticky helping hand to scores of nations. Take Tanzania. Today, in that African state, 1.3 million people are getting ready to die of AIDS. The IMF and World Bank have come to the rescue with a brilliant neoliberal solution: require Tanzania to charge for hospital appointments, previously free. Since the Bank imposed this requirement, the number of patients treated in Dar Es Salaam's three big public hospitals has dropped by 53 per cent. The Bank's cure must be working.

The IMF/World Bank also ordered Tanzania to charge fees for school attendance, then expressed surprise that school enrolment dropped from 80 per cent to 66 per cent.

Altogether the Bank and IMF had 157 helpful suggestions for Tanzania. In April 2000, the Tanzanian government secretly agreed to adopt them all. It was sign or starve. No developing nation can borrow hard currency without IMF blessing (except China, whose output grows at 5 per cent per year by studiously following the reverse of IMF policies).

The IMF and World Bank have effectively controlled Tanzania's economy since 1985. Admittedly, when they took charge they found a socialist nation mired in poverty, disease and debt. Their neoliberal experts wasted no time in cutting trade barriers, limiting government subsidies and selling off state industries. The Bank's shadow governors worked wonders. According to Bank-watcher Nancy Alexander of Globalization Challenge Initiative (Washington), in just 15 years, Tanzania's GDP dropped from $309 to $210 per capita, literacy fell and the rate of abject poverty jumped to 51 per cent of the population.

Yet, despite this neoliberal effort, the World Bank failed to win the hearts and minds of Tanzanians for its free market game plan. In June 2000, the Bank reported in frustration, "One legacy of socialism is that most people continue to believe the State has a fundamental role in promoting development and providing social services."

It wasn't always thus. The World Bank and IMF were born in 1944 with simple, laudable mandates – to fund post-war reconstruction and development projects (the World Bank) and lend hard currency to nations with temporary balance-of-payments deficits (the IMF).

Then, beginning in 1980, the Banks seem to take on an alien form. In the early 1980s, Third World nations, haemorrhaging after the five-fold increases in oil prices and a like jump in dollar interest payments, brought their begging bowls to the IMF and World Bank. But instead of debt relief, they received Structural Assistance Plans listing an average of 114 "conditionalities" in return for capital. While the particulars varied from nation to nation, in every case the roll-over of debts dangled from edicts to remove trade barriers, sell national assets to foreign investors, slash social spending and make labor "flexible" (read, "crush your unions").

Some say the radical and vicious change in the Banks in 1980 resulted from Ronald Reagan's election that year as president, the quickening of Mrs Thatcher's powers and the beginning of the "neoliberal" (free market) ascendancy in policy. (My own information is that the IMF and World Bank were taken over by a space alien named Larry. It's obvious that "Larry" Summers, once World Bank chief economist, later US Treasury Secretary, is in reality a platoon of extraterrestrials sent here to turn much of the human race into a source of cheap protein.)

So what have the aliens accomplished with their structural assistance free market prescriptions? Samuel Brittan, *Financial Times* columnist and globalization knight errant, declares that new world capital markets and free trade have "brought about an unprecedented increase in world living standards". Brittan cites the huge growth in GDP per capita, life expectancy and literacy in the less developed world from 1950 to 1995.

Now hold on a minute. Until 1980, virtually every nation in his Third World survey was either socialist or welfare statist. They were developing on the "Import Substitution Model" by which locally-owned industry built through government investment and high tariffs, anathema to the neoliberals. In those dark ages of increasing national government control (1960–80) and new welfare schemes, per capita income grew 73 per cent in Latin America and 34 per cent in Africa. By comparison, since 1980, under the Reagan/Thatcher model Latin American growth has come to a virtual halt, growing by less than 6 per cent over 20 years – and African incomes have *declined* by 23 per cent.

Now let's count the corpses. From 1950 to 1980, socialist and statist welfare policies added more than a decade of life expectancy to virtually every nation on the planet. From 1980 to today, life under structural assistance has got brutish and shorter. Since 1985, in 15 African nations the total number of illiterate people has risen and life expectancy fallen – which Brittan attributes to "bad luck, [not] the international economic system". In the former Soviet states, where IMF and World Bank shock plans hold sway, life expectancy has fallen off a cliff – adding 1.4 million a year to the death rate in Russia alone. Tough luck, Russia!

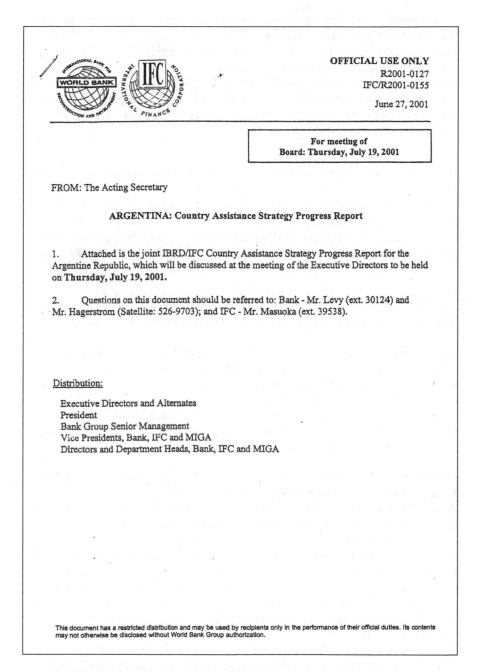

Figure 7. IMF and World Bank documents
Several stacks of documents walked out of the IMF and World Bank which dictate everything from the price of cooking oil in Ecuador to a $40 cut in the monthly pay of Argentines on a public works program.

Admittedly, the World Bank and IMF are reforming. No longer do they issue the dreaded "Structural Assistance Plans". They now call them "Poverty Reduction Strategies". Doesn't that make you feel better?

In April 2000, the IMF reviewed the fruits of globalization. In its "World Outlook" report, the Fund admitted that, "in the recent decades, nearly one-fifth of the world population have regressed. This is arguably," the IMF concedes, "one of the greatest economic failures of the 20th Century."

And that, Professor Giddens, is a fact.

It annoys me something fierce when I expose some institution and they don't respond with a complaint, comment or a lawsuit. But from the IMF and World Bank honchos – nothing. But I hadn't looked on the right continent: in fact, the World Bank wrote a long response to this exposé and published it in an African newspaper. That was odd, but odder still, as to the wacko, destructive plan for Ecuador, they simply denied the documents existed. Figure 7 shows a page from one of the documents that don't exist.

The Globalizer Who Came in from the Cold:
The IMF's Four Steps to Economic Damnation

"It has condemned people to death," the former apparatchik told me. This was like a scene out of Le Carré. The brilliant old agent comes in from the cold, crosses to our side and in hours of debriefing, empties his memory of horrors committed in the name of a political ideology he now realizes has gone rotten.

And here before me was a far bigger catch than some used Cold War spy. Joseph Stiglitz was chief economist of the World Bank. To a great extent, the new world economic order was his theory come to life.

I "debriefed" Stiglitz over several days, at Cambridge University, in a London hotel and finally in Washington in April 2001 during the big confab of the World Bank and the International Monetary Fund. Instead of chairing the meetings of ministers and central bankers, Stiglitz was kept exiled safely behind the blue police cordons, the same as the nuns carrying a large wooden cross, the Bolivian union leaders, the parents of AIDS victims and the other "anti-globalization" protesters. The ultimate insider was now on the outside.

In 1999 the World Bank fired Stiglitz. He was not allowed quiet retirement; US Treasury Secretary Larry Summers, I'm told, demanded a public excommunication for Stiglitz having expressed his first mild dissent from globalization World Bank-style.

Here in Washington we completed the last of several hours of exclusive interviews for the *Observer* and *Newsnight* about the real, often hidden, workings of the IMF, World Bank and the bank's 51 per cent owner, the US Treasury.

And here, from sources unnamable (*not* Stiglitz), we obtained a cache of documents marked "confidential", "restricted" and "not otherwise [to be] disclosed without World Bank authorization".

Stiglitz helped translate one, a "Country Assistance Strategy", from bureaucratese. There's an Assistance Strategy for every poorer nation, designed, says the World Bank, after careful in-country investigation. But according to insider Stiglitz, the Bank's staff "investigation" consists of close inspection of a nation's five-star hotels. It concludes with the Bank staff meeting some begging, busted finance minister who is handed a "restructuring agreement" pre-drafted for his "voluntary" signature (I have a selection of these).

Each nation's economy is individually analyzed, then, says Stiglitz, the Bank hands every minister the exact same four-step program.

Step 1 is Privatization – which Stiglitz said could more accurately be called "Briberization". Rather than object to the sell-offs of state industries, he said national leaders – using the World Bank's demands to silence local critics – happily flogged their electricity and water companies. "You could see their eyes widen" at the prospect of 10 per cent commissions paid to Swiss bank accounts for simply shaving a few billion off the sale price of national assets.

And the US government knew it, charges Stiglitz, at least in the case of the biggest "briberization" of all, the 1995 Russian sell-off. "The US Treasury view was *this was great* as we wanted Yeltsin re-elected. We *don't care* if it's a corrupt election. We *want* the money to go to Yeltsin" via kick-backs for his campaign.

Stiglitz is no conspiracy nutter ranting about Black Helicopters. The man was *inside* the game, a member of Bill Clinton's cabinet as chairman of the president's Council of Economic Advisers.

Most ill-making for Stiglitz is that the US-backed oligarchs stripped Russia's industrial assets, with the effect that the corruption scheme cut national output nearly in half, causing depression and starvation.

After briberization, Step 2 of the IMF/World Bank one size-fits-all rescue-your-economy plan is "Capital Market Liberalization". In theory, capital market deregulation allows investment capital to flow in and out. Unfortunately, as in Indonesia and Brazil, the money simply flowed out and out. Stiglitz calls this the "hot money" cycle. Cash comes in for speculation in real estate and currency, then flees at the first whiff of trouble. A nation's reserves can drain in days, hours. And when that happens, to seduce speculators into returning a nation's own capital funds, the IMF demands these nations raise interest rates to 30 per cent, 50 per cent and 80 per cent.

"The result was predictable," said Stiglitz of the hot money tidal waves in Asia and Latin America. Higher interest rates demolished property values, savaged industrial production and drained national treasuries.

At this point, the IMF drags the gasping nation to Step 3: Market-Based Pricing, a fancy term for raising prices on food, water and domestic gas. This leads, predictably, to Step 3½: what Stiglitz calls "The IMF riot."

The IMF riot is painfully predictable. When a nation is "down and out, [the IMF] takes advantage and squeezes the last pound of blood out of them. They turn up the heat until, finally, the whole cauldron blows up" – as when the IMF eliminated food and fuel subsidies for the poor in Indonesia in 1998. Indonesia exploded into riots, but there are other examples – the Bolivian riots over water prices in April 2000 and, in February 2001, the riots in Ecuador over the rise in domestic gas prices imposed by the World Bank. You'd almost get the impression that the riot is written into the plan.

And it is. Stiglitz did not know about the documents the BBC and the *Observer* obtained from inside the World Bank, stamped over with those pesky warnings "confidential", "restricted", "not to be disclosed". Let's get back to the "Interim Country Assistance Strategy" for Ecuador. In it the Bank several times states – with cold accuracy – that they expected their plans to spark "social unrest", to use their bureaucratic term for a nation in flames.

That's not surprising. The secret report notes that the plan to make the US dollar Ecuador's currency has pushed 51 per cent of the population below the poverty line. The World Bank "Assistance" plan simply calls for facing down civil strife and suffering with "political resolve" – and still higher prices.

The IMF riots (and by riots I mean peaceful demonstrations dispersed by bullets, tanks and tear gas) cause new panicked flights of capital and government bankruptcies. This economic arson has its bright side – for foreign corporations, who can then pick off remaining assets, such as the odd mining concession or port, at fire sale prices.

Stiglitz notes that the IMF and World Bank are not heartless adherents of market economics. At the same time the IMF stopped Indonesia "subsidizing" food purchases, "when the banks need a bail-out, intervention [in the market] is welcome". The IMF scrounged up tens of billions of dollars to save Indonesia's financiers and, by extension, the US and European banks from which they had borrowed.

A pattern emerges. There are lots of losers in this system, but one clear winner: the Western banks and US Treasury, making the big bucks from this crazy new international capital churn. Stiglitz told me about his unhappy meeting, early in his World Bank tenure, with Ethiopia's new president in the nation's first democratic election. The World Bank and IMF had ordered Ethiopia to divert aid money to its reserve account at the US Treasury, which pays a pitiful 4 per cent return, while the nation borrowed US dollars at 12 per cent to feed its population. The new president begged Stiglitz to let him use the aid money to rebuild the nation. But no, the loot went straight off to the US Treasury's vault in Washington.

Now we arrive at Step 4 of what the IMF and World Bank call their "poverty reduction strategy": Free Trade. This is free trade by the rules of the World Trade Organization and World Bank. Stiglitz the insider likens free trade WTO-style to the Opium Wars. "That too was about opening markets," he said. As in the nineteenth century, Europeans and Americans today are kicking down the barriers to sales in Asia, Latin American and Africa, while barricading their own markets against Third World agriculture.

In the Opium Wars, the West used military blockades to force open markets for their unbalanced trade. Today, the World Bank can order a financial blockade that's just as effective – and sometimes just as deadly.

Stiglitz is particularly emotional over the WTO's intellectual property rights treaty (it goes by the acronym TRIPS, of which we have more to say later in this chapter). It is here, says the economist, that the new global order has "condemned people to death" by imposing impossible tariffs and tributes to pay to pharmaceutical companies for branded medicines. "They don't care," said the professor of the corporations and bank ideologues he worked with, "if people live or die."

By the way, don't be confused by the mix in this discussion of the IMF, World Bank and WTO. They are interchangeable masks of a single governance system. They have locked themselves together by what are unpleasantly called "triggers". Taking a World Bank loan for a school "triggers" a requirement to accept every "conditionality" – they average 111 per nation – laid down by both the World Bank and IMF. In fact, said Stiglitz, the IMF requires nations to accept trade policies more punitive than the official WTO rules.

Stiglitz's greatest concern is that World Bank plans, devised in secrecy and driven by an absolutist ideology, are never open for discourse or dissent. Despite the West's push for elections throughout the developing world, the so-called Poverty Reduction Programs "undermine democracy". And they don't work. Black Africa's productivity under the guiding hand of IMF structural "assistance" has gone to hell in a handbag.

Did any nation avoid this fate? Yes, said Stiglitz, identifying Botswana. Their trick? "They told the IMF to go packing."

So then I turned on Stiglitz. OK, Mr Smart-Guy Professor, how would *you* help developing nations? Stiglitz proposed radical land reform, an attack at the heart of "landlordism", on the usurious rents charged by the propertied oligarchies worldwide, typically 50 per cent of a tenant's crops. So I had to ask the professor: as you were top economist at the World Bank, why didn't the Bank follow your advice?

"If you challenge [land ownership], that would be a change in the power of the elites. That's not high on their agenda." Apparently not.

Ultimately, what drove him to put his job on the line was the failure of the banks and US Treasury to change course when confronted with the crises – failures and suffering perpetrated by their four-step monetarist mambo. Every time their free market solutions failed, the IMF simply demanded more free market policies.

"It's a little like the Middle Ages," the insider told me. "When the patient died they would say, 'Well, he stopped the bloodletting too soon; he still had a little blood in him'."

I took away from my talks with the professor that the solution to world poverty and crisis is simple: remove the bloodsuckers.

Joe Stiglitz survived his sacking from the World Bank and complaints about our interviews. In September 2001, he was awarded the Nobel Prize in Economics.

A version of this story was first published as "The IMF's Four Steps to Damnation" in the Observer *and another version in the* Big Issue – *that's the magazine that the homeless flog outside London tube stations.* Big Issue *offered equal space to the IMF, whose "deputy chief media officer" wrote:*

> *... I find it impossible to respond given the depth and breadth of hearsay and mis-information in [Palast's] report.*

Of course it was difficult for him to respond. The so-called "misinformation" came from the unhappy lot inside the Deputy Chief's own agency and the World Bank; unhappy whistleblowers who also quietly provided me with key intelligence for the next story.

New British-American Empire of the Dammed

In April 2000 the front pages of British newspapers were splattered with photos of two dead white farmers in Zimbabwe. The news from Bolivia – "Protests claim two lives" – was pushed into a teeny "World in Brief" in the Guardian. *(In US papers Bolivia vanished, replaced by Monica Lewinsky's dress.) What a shame. The Zimbabwe murders merely exercised a suppressed nostalgia for England's imperial past. But Bolivia is the story of Britain (and America's) imperial future.*

First, let's correct the arithmetic. The count in Bolivia was six dead, 175 injured including two children blinded after the military fired tear gas, then bullets, at demonstrators opposing the 35 per cent hike in water prices imposed on the city of Cochabamba by the new owners of the water system, International Waters Ltd (IWL) of London.

Following the Cochabamba killings, Hugo Banzer (once Bolivia's dictator, then the elected president) declared a nationwide state of siege, setting curfews and abolishing civil liberties. On April 12, 2000, just after the martial law declaration, World Bank Director James Wolfensohn took time out from his own preparations against protests in Washington to comment to reporters, "The riots in Bolivia, I'm happy to say, are now quieting down."

I contacted Oscar Olivera, leader of the Cochabamba protests, to ask him how he organized the riots. On April 6, following the first protests against the price increases, Olivera, a trade union official, with a coalition of 14 economists, parliamentarians, lawyers and community leaders, accepted a government invitation to discuss the IWL price hikes. After entering the government offices in Cochabamba, Olivera and his colleagues were arrested. With Olivera in chains, the riot outside the building could only have been directed by the leader of the 500 protesters, Cochabamba's Roman Catholic archbishop.

There is, of course, the possibility that the World Bank's Wolfensohn had it wrong, and that what he calls rioters were in fact innocent victims of deadly repression. Olivera, one of five protest leaders released (the government banished the 17 others to internal exile), flew to Washington to try to speak with Wolfensohn. But the director is a busy man and Olivera left without a meeting.

Never heard of International Water Limited (IWL)? Like many of Britain's multinationals, it is controlled by a larger US corporation – in this case, construction giant Bechtel of San Francisco.

From its US headquarters, Bechtel issued a statement flatly denying the upheaval in Bolivia had anything to do with its water price hikes. Rather, IWL's American owner hinted darkly that the revolt was partly the work of those opposing a "crackdown on coca-leaf production". Olivera responds that neither he nor the archbishop traffics in narcotics.

The price hikes that triggered the water war were driven by IWL's need to recover the cost of the huge Misicuni Dam project. Water from the Misicuni Dam system costs roughly six times that of alternative sources. Why would IWL buy water from a ludicrously expensive source? Just possibly because IWL owns a part of the Misicuni Dam project.

The public had one other objection with IWL's charging for the dam project: there is no dam. It has not yet been built.

Now, it is a basic tenet of accounting that investors, not customers, fund capital projects. The risk-takers then recover their outlay, with profit, when the project produces a product for sale. This is the heart, soul and justification of the system called "capitalism". That's the theory. But when a monopoly operator gets its fist round a city's water spigots, it can pump the funds for capital projects (even ones that cost 600 per cent over the market) from captive customers rather than its shareholders.

Samuel Soria, the Bolivian government's former consultant on the water projects, said he was unable to extract from IWL evidence it had put in any funds at all into the operation. Soria, chairman of Cochabamba's Council of Economists, was told the water system's purchasers had deposited $10 million into a Citibank account in New York, but Soria found no evidence of its transfer to Bolivia. Water prices, he fears, could eventually rise 150 per cent under IWL management.

"No money was shelled out by anybody" for the water company, Luis Bredow, the editor of Cochabamba's newspaper *Gente* [*People*], told me. Bredow's own investigation concluded that the operators grabbed the entire system for nothing. He attributes these exceptionally favorable terms to IWL's partnering with former Bolivian president Jaime Pasamora, leader of a political party allied to Banzer.

I contacted IWL's London spokesman who said little more than, "How did you find out that IWL was involved in Cochabamba?" (The company's Bolivian group is called Aguas de Tunari.) In fact, the British company's involvement is getting to be, to use Bredow's term, "misterioso". President Banzer, to quell the spreading demonstrations, announced cancellation of the water privatization on April 5.

A day later, word leaked that IWL was back in the saddle at the water company and people took to the streets again, nationwide. On April 10, the panicked government declared that the foreign consortium had "abandoned" their franchise when its British CEO supposedly fled the country. But I was able to track down the IWL executive to a La Paz hotel where, his associates told me, they were about to open negotiations with the Banzer government.

It can't be said that the British-American operators brought misery to Cochabamba; they found plenty already there. Intestinal infections leading to diarrhoeal illness is Bolivia's number one disease and child killer, the result of water hook-ups and sanitation reaching only 31 per cent of rural homes.

World Bank Director Wolfensohn has a solution to the lack of water: *raise the price*. So pay up, Wolfensohn demanded of the protesting Bolivian water users in his extraordinary April 12 diatribe against the "rioters" .

Wolfensohn's shut-up-and-pay-up outburst contradicts the internal counsel of his own experts. In July 1997, at a meeting in Washington, the Bank's technocrats laid out to the Bolivians the case against Misicuni and even warned about social upheaval if prices rose. According to World Bank insiders (I won't get them fired by using their names), the Bank's hydrologists and technicians devised a water plan for Cochabamba at a fraction of Misicuni's bloated cost. This alternative could be paid off without raising prices on current customers. Water supply and distribution would be divided between two companies to avoid the kind of self-dealing inherent in IWF's Aguas de Tunari set-up.

So why did Wolfensohn attack protests against a project the World Bank itself found dodgy and damaging? There are larger plans not discussed with the Bank's low-level minions. Long before ministerial limousines clogged the US capital for the April 2000 World Bank "Ministerial" meeting, the big policy decisions were settled in far-flung "sectoral" meetings. In the case of water, nearly 1,000 executives and bureaucrats gathered in The Hague in March 2000 to review and refine a program to privatize the world's water systems.

But these private operators who carved up the planet into "market segments" in March can only turn in profits if prices rise radically and rapidly. IWF secured from Bolivia a 16 per cent real guaranteed return. This profit boost itself was enough to account for the initial 35 per cent hike in rates. The ransacking of Bolivia's water supply would not have occurred without a bit of helpful arm-twisting by the World Bank.

The IMF, World Bank and Inter-American Development Bank have written water system sell-offs into what they modestly term "master plans" for each Latin American nation. Consortia such as IWL were formed to capture these cast-off public assets.

The IMF and World Bank justify the sell-offs by claiming that privateers are committed to deliver capital for desperately needed water system repairs and expansion. But like a gigolo's flowers, the promises rapidly wilted. Cochabamba's protest organizers knew that just across the border in Buenos

Aires, the region's first privatization consortium eliminated 7,500 workers, the system bled from lack of maintenance and prices jumped, repeating the story of virtually every water privatization from the Philippines to East Anglia. In Argentina, the new owners of the Buenos Aires system include, notably, the World Bank itself.

Britain is re-establishing imperial reach, albeit in the shadow of Americans, through rapid low-capital takeovers of former state assets, concentrated in infrastructure where monopoly control virtually guarantees outsized profit. From the British Gas takeover of the São Paolo, Brazil, gas company to United Utilities' buy-out of the Manila water company, it all seemed a riskless romp – until a few thirsty, angry peasants in the Andes decided they could stop the New Imperium in the streets.

Bolivia vanishes: see Style section

You didn't read this story about the killings in Bolivia in your newspaper? Come now, it was right there in the *Washington Post* ... in paragraph 10 of the story on page 13 of the Style section. I kid you not: the *Style* section. It dangled from the bottom of a cute little story on the lifestyle of some local anti-WTO protesters.

And so one of the most extraordinary international stories of the year just went PFZZZT! – and disappeared from sight.

Some vital stories get buried because they fail the "sex" test of hot photos or have no domestic news hook. But Bolivia had it all. Networks could obtain high-quality video footage of the military gunning down civilians. At the center of this story were huge American and British corporations, including Bechtel of San Francisco. Most important, this general strike in South America offered a dramatic and bloody parallel to protests in Washington occurring on the very same days. By any normal news measure, this was a helluva story of globalization stopped dead in its tracks ... all while the McDonald's burned in Washington.

When Wolfensohn, president of the World Bank, called the massacred protesters "rioters" he was hoping to discourage the press from writing sympathetically about the Bolivians. He need not have worried. There was nothing on the tube; and aside from the mention in the *Post*'s Style section and a few news wire paragraphs in the *New York Times*, for the mainstream media, the Bolivians simply vanished.

However, the little bit of coverage obtained was actually worse than none. The *Financial Times* sent a reporter to Bolivia. The lead paragraph of his report informed us that on the wall of the protesters' headquarters hung "faded portraits of Che Guevara and Fidel Castro". There was no mention at all that six people had died.

The *FT* reporter, who should know better, picked up the line that drug traffickers were somehow behind the water protests. The fanciful accusation was

Figure 8. From February through April 2000, Bolivians, including this Quechua woman, took to the streets of Cochabamba to protest huge increases in the price of drinking water. Prices rose when, under pressure from the IMF, Bolivia privatized and sold its water system to the Anglo-American consortium, International Water Limited. On those same days, thousands took to the streets of Washington to protest at the Spring Ministerial meeting of the IMF and World Bank. US news pundits blasted the American protesters as just a bunch of naive, privileged white kids protesting without a cause. Coverage of the Bolivia protests in major US press: zero – except a passing mention in the *Washington Post*'s fashion and lifestyle section. (© Tom Kruse)

put out on a Bechtel Corporation news release, but hey, a corporate press release is better than a fact.

Bolivians themselves were also denied the full story, but by more direct means. The courageous editor of the Bolivian newspaper *Gente* published an investigative series exposing the sweetheart deals between the US-European investors and politically connected Bolivians. At the end of April, *Gente's* publishers, admitting to threats of financial ruin by the water system's Bolivian partners, demanded that their editor, Luis Bredow, print a retraction of his reports. Instead, Bredow printed his resignation.

As to the Cochabamba protest leader Oscar Olivera, his release was secured by an international campaign (more than once – he has been arrested three times). That was good news, then I received this.

IN A MESSAGE DATED 9/5/00 9:29:32 AM EASTERN DAYLIGHT TIME, SENDER WRITES:

SUBJECT HEADING: BOLIVIA DEAD

ON THE AFTERNOON OF SATURDAY APRIL 8TH 17 YEAR OLD VICTOR HUGO DAZA WAS KILLED BY A SHOT THROUGH HIS FACE. A FRIEND OF MINE KNOWS HIS FAMILY AND SAYS HE WAS IN TOWN RUNNING AN ERRAND FOR HIS MOTHER.

Who Shot Argentina? The Fingerprints on the Smoking Gun Read "IMF"

In August 2001, I received the sad news that Argentina had died, or at least its economy. Officially, unemployment hit a grim 16 per cent – unofficially another quarter of the workforce was either unpaid, locked out or getting too little to survive on. Industrial production, already down 25 per cent halfway through the year, fell into a coma induced by interest rates which, by one measure, have jumped to over 90 per cent on dollar-denominated borrowings.

This was an easy case to crack. Next to the still warm corpse of Argentina's economy, the killer had left a smoking gun with his fingerprints all over it. The murder weapon: "Technical Memorandum of Understanding", dated September 5, 2000. It was signed by Pedro Pou, president of the Central Bank of Argentina for transmission to Horst Kohler, Managing Director of the International Monetary Fund.

I received a complete copy of the "Understanding" along with attachments and a companion letter from the Argentine Economics Ministry to the IMF from ... well, let's just say the envelope had no return address.

Close inspection leaves no doubt that this "Understanding" fired the fatal bullets into Argentina's defenseless body. To begin with, the Understanding required Argentina cut the government budget deficit from US$5.3 billion in 2000 to $4.1 billion in 2001. Think about that. That September, Argentina was already on the cliff-edge of a deep recession. Even the half-baked economists at the IMF should know that holding back government spending in a con-tracting economy is like turning off the engines on an aeroplane in stall. Cut the deficit? As my four-year-old daughter would say, "That's stooopid."

Later, as the economy's wings fell off, the IMF brains trust ordered the *elimination* of the deficit, causing the economy to implode.

The IMF is never wrong without being cruel as well. And so we read, under the boldface heading "Improving the Conditions of the Poor", agreement to drop salaries under the government's emergency employment program by 20 per cent, from $200 a month to $160.

But you can't save much by taking $40 a month from the poor. For further savings, the Understanding also promised, "a 12–15 percent cut in salaries" of civil servants and the "rationalization of certain privileged pension benefits".

In case you haven't a clue what the IMF means by "rationalization", it means cutting payments to the aged by 13 per cent under both public and private plans. Cut, cut, cut in the midst of a recession. Stooopid.

Salted in with the IMF's bone-head recommendations and mean-spirited plans for pensioners and the poor are economic forecasts that border on the delusional. In the Understanding, the globalization geniuses projected that, if Argentina simply carried out their plans to snuff consumer spending power, somehow the nation's economic production would leap by 3.7 per cent and unemployment decline. In fact, by the end of March 2001, the nation's GDP had already dropped 2.1 per cent below the year earlier mark, and has nose-dived since.

What on earth would induce Argentina to embrace the IMF's goofy program? The payoff was an $8 billion aid package put together by the IMF, World Bank and private lenders.

But there is less to this generosity than meets the eye. The Understanding also assumed that Argentina will continue to "peg" its currency, the peso, to the dollar at an exchange rate of one to one. The currency peg doesn't come cheap. American banks and speculators have been charging a whopping 16 per cent risk premium above normal in return for the dollars needed to back this currency scheme.

Now do the arithmetic. On Argentina's $128 billion in debt, normal interest plus the 16 per cent surcharge by lenders comes to about $27 billion a year. In other words, Argentina's people don't net one penny from the $8 billion loan package. None of the bail-out money escapes New York where it lingers to pay interest to US creditors holding the debt, big fish like Citibank and little biters like Steve Hanke.

Hanke is president of Toronto Trust Argentina, an "emerging market fund" which loaded up 100 per cent on Argentine bonds during the last currency panic, in 1995. Cry not for Steve, Argentina. His annual return that year of 79.25 per cent put the fund at the top of the speculation league table.

Hanke profits by betting on the failure of IMF policies. But "vulture" investing is merely Hanke's avocation. In his day job as professor of economics at Johns Hopkins University, Maryland, he generously offers straightforward advice to end Argentina's woe, although his recommendation would put him out of the speculation game: "Abolish the IMF."

To begin with, Hanke would do away with the "peg" – that 1 peso for 1 dollar exchange rate – which has proved a meat-hook on which the IMF hangs Argentina's finances.

But it's not the peg itself that skewers Argentina. The peg causes suffering only when combined with the Four Horsemen of IMF neoliberal policy: liberalized financial markets, free trade, mass privatization and government surpluses.

"Liberalizing" financial markets means allowing capital to flow freely across a nation's borders. Indeed, since liberalization, the capital has flowed freely, with a vengeance. Argentina's panicked rich have dumped their pesos for dollars and sent the hard loot to investment havens abroad. In June 2001 alone, Argentinians withdrew 6 per cent of all bank deposits.

Once upon a time, Argentina's government-owned national and provincial banks supported the nation's debts. But in the mid-1990s, the government of Carlos Menem sold these off to Citibank of New York, Fleet Bank of Boston and other foreign operators.

I spoke with Charles Calomiris, a former World Bank adviser, who describes these bank privatizations as a "really wonderful story". Wonderful for whom? Argentina has bled out as much as $750 million a day in hard currency holdings.

There's more cheer for creditors in the Understanding, including "reform of the revenue sharing system". This is the kinder, gentler way of stating that the US banks will be paid by siphoning off tax receipts earmarked for education and other provincial services. The Understanding also finds cash in "reforming" the nation's health insurance system.

But when *cut cut cut* isn't enough to pay the debt holders, one can always sell "las joyas de mi abuela", grandma's jewels, as journalist Mario del Cavril describes his nation's privatization scheme. The French picked up a big hunk of the water system and promptly raised charges in some towns by 400 per cent.

The Understanding's final bullet is the imposition of "an open trade policy". This puts Argentina's exporters, with their products priced via the "peg" in US dollars, into a pathetic, losing competition against Brazilian goods priced in a devaluing currency. Stooopid.

Still, in the IMF's tiny minds their scheme could work. All that is required is a "flexible" workforce, willing to bend to lower pensions, lower wages or no wages at all. But, to the dismay of Argentina's elite, the worker bees are proving inflexibly obstinate in agreeing to their own impoverishment.

One inflexible worker, Anibal Verón, a 37-year-old father of five, lost his job as a bus driver; his company owes him nine months' pay. Verón joined the "piqueros", the angry unemployed who blockade roads (39 blockades in August 2001 alone). In clearing a blockade in November, he was killed with a bullet to the head, allegedly by the military police.

The death in Genoa of anti-globalization protester Carlo Guiliani was page 1 news in the US and Europe. Verón's death was page 0. It took our top researcher, Oliver Shykles, two days just to find Verón's name. Nor did you read about Carlos Santillán, 27, or Oscar Barrios, 17, gunned down in a church courtyard in Salta Province when the police fired on a protest against the IMF austerity plan.

Globalization boosters like Tony Blair prefer to portray resistance as a lark of pampered Western youth curing their ennui by "indulging in protest, misguided" by naive notions. The media plays to this theme, focusing on the white kids marching in Genoa, but not the 80,000 in the streets of Buenos Aires in May 2000, or the general strike honoured by seven million Argentine workers in June 2000.

In Argentina, President Fernando de la Rua blames violence on the protesters. But the Peace and Justice Service (SERPAJ) charges de la Rua's government with using hunger and terror to impose the IMF plans. I reached SERPAJ leader Adolfo Pérez Esquivel in Buenos Aires. He told me he is documenting cases of torture of protesters by police in the town where Santillán and Barrios died. To Pérez Esquivel (who won the Nobel Peace Prize in 1980) repression and IMF "liberalization" are handmaidens. He told me he has just filed a complaint charging police with recruiting children as young as five into paramilitary squads, an operation he compares to the Hitler Youth.

But Pérez Esquivel, who led protests against the Free Trade Agreement of the Americas, doesn't agree with my verdict against the IMF in Argentina's death. He notes that the economically fatal "reforms" are embraced with enthusiasm by the nation's finance minister, Domingo Cavallo, best remembered as the head of the central bank during the military dictatorship. For the ageing pacifist, that suggests that the untimely demise of the nation's economy wasn't murder, but suicide.

Bad Trips at the WTO

In July 2000, the New York Times *reported that Bill Clinton had saved Africa. That big-hearted lug proposed lending African nations a billion dollars a year for AIDS drugs which – more joy! – the pharmaceutical companies have agreed to just give away at 75 per cent off list price.*

But just when I thought I could announce Christmas in July, I came into possession of a twelve-page document from Argentina. It appears to have originated in the Office of the United States Trade Representative in Geneva (which does not deny the document's authenticity). The confidential official missive threatened Argentina for opening its borders to the drugs trade – not the fun stuff, but sales of legal, licensed medicines. If Argentina does not end its commitment to free cross-border trade in pharmaceuticals, wrote the US

Trade Rep, America would keep Argentina on the "Section 301 Watch List", a kind of death row for trading partners.

If you read the gospels of globalization apostles, you might get the impression that the World Trade Organization is all about doing away with tariffs and trade barriers. *Only in your dreams.* In the real world, the WTO is the mechanism for *privatizing* the tariff system. Once, countries protected their workers and local industry behind taxes at national borders. In the new world trade order, global corporations may demand levies against nations which sell or buy products outside the zones they have marked out by brand names and market segments. The WTO's penal system for prohibited importing and exporting goes under the psychedelic title TRIPS (Trade-Related Intellectual Property Rights).

TRIP-ing, Argentina and Africa – it all fits together. The story begins with this un-fun fact: 25.3 million people in Southern Africa are going to die of AIDS unless medicine arrives *now*. Luckily, Brazil, India and, most aggressively, Argentina can make the drugs dirt cheap and ship them to the dying. But US, British and Swiss pharmaceuticals giants howled about the proposed cross-shipments. The US trade cops, led by then Vice-President Al Gore, backed by Big Pharma, halted the life-saving plan – Nelson Mandela's pleas, Nobel Prize and flowered shirts notwithstanding.

Unfortunately for Gore, running for president at the time, his let-them-eat-aspirin policies resulted in his every campaign stop attracting packs of enraged Gay-mericans, who hollered about his killing more Africans than Michael Caine in Zulu. This did not make good TV for Al. So his buddy President Bill found a few billion to quell the restless natives.

However, the billions come with strings attached or, more accurately, chains and manacles. South Africa must buy 100 per cent of the medicine from the US and pay back all the cash at "commercial interest rates".

The US Trade Rep's poison pen letter to Argentina is the supply side of this scheme to stop South Africa breaking the *de facto* embargo on free trade in pharmaceuticals. South Africa hoped to use a loophole in TRIPS which permits importing of patent drugs in extreme emergencies, even without the patent-holders' approval. Initially, the US retaliated against South Africa by taxing some of its imports to the US – until the anti-Gore demos. The US Trade Rep's threat against Argentina indicates that the Clinton administration re-aimed the sanctions missiles at Argentina to avoid the impolitic Mandela imagery while cutting off South Africa's AIDS drugs supply at the source.

If Argentina didn't back down, this would have happened: after an expected WTO show trial, Argentina's economy would be hung from a pole in Geneva as an example for India and Brazil, other potential exporters.

Maybe I'm not being fair. After all, TRIPS seeks to protect and compensate manufacturers for their risky investments and inventiveness in creating medicines like AZT, Glaxo-Wellcome's anti-AIDS drug.

Glaxo was inventive, all right, but not in discovering AZT. A professor, Jerome Horowitz, synthesized the drug in 1964, under a grant from the US government's National Institutes of Health (NIH). A Glaxo unit bought the formula to use on pet cats.

In 1984, an NIH lab discovered the HIV virus. The government lab urgently asked drug makers to send samples of every anti-retrovirus drug on their shelves. NIH spent millions inventing a method to test these compounds. When the tests showed AZT killed the virus, the government asked Glaxo, as the compound's owner, to conduct lab tests.

Glaxo refused. You can't blame them. HIV could contaminate labs, even kill researchers. So the NIH's Dr Hiroaki Mitsuya, combining brilliance, bravery and loads of public cash, performed the difficult proofs on live virus. In February 1985, NIH told Glaxo the good news and asked the company to conduct human trials.

Glaxo refused again. Here's where Glaxo got inventive. Within days of the notice, the company filed a patent in Britain for its "discovery". Glaxo failed to mention the US government work.

But Glaxo has a heart. The Americo-British behemoth announced it would sell South Africa an AZT-based drug for only $2 a day per patient, more than 75 per cent off the price charged in America and Europe. I called Glaxo USA to say thanks but, after a few questions, it became clear that the $2 price merely matched the Brazilian/Argentine prices, still about triple the cost of production.

Think about that. If $2 is the free market price, then Americans and Europeans pay 400 per cent over the odds, price discrimination explicitly protected by TRIPS. That's the funny thing about the WTO's expansion of so-called intellectual property rights. TRIPS trade barriers are sold in the West on the slick line that *those people*– the dark, unindustrious tribes of the southern hemisphere – are trying to steal *our* inventions. In fact, says expert Jamie Love of the Consumer Project on Technology in Washington, Western patients have as much to lose as Africans under the new regime of thought ownership.

This came to Love graphically in 1997 when Maude Jones, a 30-year-old London woman, called him, begging help to obtain Taxol. The drug could have cured her breast cancer, but the National Health Service did not prescribe it because of its stratospheric cost.

There is no patent on Taxol. The US government discovered it. But pharmaceutical behemoth Bristol-Myers Squibb, because it performed minor work calculating dosage levels, holds the intellectual property rights on dose-related data, even though the data were originally collected by government. Even without a patent, Britain's data protection laws give Bristol-Myers lock-up control on Taxol in the UK for ten years.

Bristol-Myers takes no chances with its cancer monopoly. Taxol comes from the yew tree. While Western drug companies have long argued that Asian rain forest plants are theirs for the taking without paying royalties, Bristol-Myers obtained from Congress the exclusive right to harvest yew trees on US government lands, about the only place it grows on the planet. For these public assets, B-M paid nothing.

But Maude Jones paid. Ultimately, the company was shamed into offering her the medicine for free, if she moved to America. However, doctors concluded the offer was probably too late. As her family already faced bankruptcy, Maude (not her real name) phoned Love to say she had chosen to die.

From her death, Love told me the young woman hoped South Africans, Americans and Europeans would discover "a helpful solidarity". In AIDS and breast cancer, the stricken North and South share a horrific commonality as the new landless peasantry in the apartheid of intellectual property rights.

Dr Dre Guards Sony's Plantation House

The Doctor didn't mince words with me. "Now shut the fuck up and get what's coming to you!" In my exchange with Endre Young, the artist known as Dr Dre, this was the example he gave of his copyright intellectual property, which he fears is reproduced, without compensation, by ne'er-do-wells accessing www.napster.com.

Mr Young filed suit and a California judge, to protect this gentleman beset by copyright pirates, effectively ordered Napster's closure. Mr Young was philosophical about the ruling, "I'm in a murderous mind-state with a heart full of terror."

Yo, what's going on here? Behind the angry black face of the rapper's assault on Napster are the grinning white faces of his co-plaintiffs, Recording Industry Association of America, front for the Big Six record companies – Sony, EMI, BMG, Universal, Warner and Polygram. Together, these six media megaliths distribute over 95 per cent of all music CDs sold in the Western world. Behind their public tears shed for compensating their artists – and since when did *that* become a concern of the music industry? – Is the deeper agenda of protecting this musical OPEC.

According to consent decrees in little noticed cases filed by the US Federal Trade Commission, the Six Bigs have for years bullied retailers to ensure that you get whacked for $36 for that Abba Tribute CD you just had to have.

Now let's look at the B-side of the recording industry combine. As Bill Gates teaches us, a well-functioning monopoly fleeces its customers at one end while simultaneously squeezing suppliers at the other. In the case of the music cartel, the suppliers of raw material – the musicians – have to get through one of six tightly guarded gateways. (The six companies distribute 95 per cent of all CDs in the Western world.) As a result, the only stuff that makes it out the other end of these resistant sphincters onto the airwaves and into the big stores are Spice-bunnies, Eric Clapton de-plugged, pre-fabricated bad boys like Eminem and middle-aged moguls' talent-free trophy wives (which should not be taken as a dig at the gifted Mariah Carey).

In other words, the Big Six don't just control *how* you buy what you want, they tell you *what* you want.

It used to be that industry's inputs, the talent, railed against this closed system. That's where Dre's posse comes in. His tinker-toy "ganstas" give street cred to the moguls' assault on the Internet, the first serious alternative route for distributing music Time-Warner hasn't chosen for you. The system suits rap producer Dre just fine as the cartel allows him and Puff Daddy to jointly lock out musicians that could replace them or the artists in their stable, such as Mr Marshall Mathers (Eminem), author of the "get what's coming to you" lyric. Dre's no fool. He knows that control of his little patch is dependent on his defending his bosses' intellectual property plantation.

Dre v. *Napster* is the musical sideshow of the bigger war over ownership of intellectual property, ranging from ditties to DNA. In my prior story, I described how the Clinton administration blocked South Africa's purchasing of low-cost drugs to stem the spread of AIDS. To protect the right of Glaxo-Wellcome plc to embargo cross-border sales of AZT that did not meet the company's terms, Clinton threatened South Africa with trade sanctions under the World Trade Organization's TRIPS rules.

I am pleased to report that one nation has finally displayed the *huevos* to stand up to America's bully-boy enforcement of WTO diktat: the US Congress voted, and Bush may have to sign, America's unilaterally exempting itself from TRIPS. US retailers will be free to import any cheap drugs they desire from Canada and Mexico though the legal patent holders may howl and bray. Ah, the privileges of empire. And when "intellectual property rights" threatens US privileges, suddenly WTO rules don't apply.

When Nelson Mandela suggested that South Africa could issue "compulsory licences" for local manufacture of cheap AIDS drugs, Al Gore threatened him with the WTO hammer. Yet, at the same time, at the behest of the "Gore-Techs", Al's Silicon Valley billionaire buddies from AOL and Oracle, the US Justice Department compelled Microsoft to divulge its proprietary codes and license Windows software to the Gore-Techs at a government-capped price. Hey, I'm all for the US seizure of Gates's intellectual property, but I can't ignore the rank whiff of hypocrisy.

But then, hypocrisy is the oxygen of the new imperial order of thought ownership. Every genteel landlord of fenced-in intellectual real estate began life as a thief. Under WTO and US law today, how many products built on ideas of others could never have made it to market? (I bet Mr Gates, so quick to shout "piracy!" could name two products that depend heavily on lifting the intellectual discoveries of others: MS-DOS and Windows.) As Isaac Newton would say now, "If I see further than others, it is because I stand on the shoulders of giants *too dumb to patent their discoveries.*"

Not everyone is entitled to compensation. The WTO requires, on penalty of sanctions, that every nation pass laws granting patents on "life-forms", by which Americans and Europeans mean genetically modified Frankenstein seeds or drugs, often remakes of traditional genomes shoplifted from Third World forests. When Thailand mischievously registered traditional medicines as that nation's intellectual property, the US Trade Representative wrote that turning nature's bounty into patent property could "hamper medical research" (reinforcing the notion that Americans are incapable of irony).

WTO is sold as the defender of unfettered markets. But Lori Wallach of Ralph Nader's Global Trade Watch notes that WTO's TRIPS exists to *prevent* free trade. No pharmaceutical or media magnate has to suffer lectures, as do workers who lose their jobs to uncontrolled imports, that sales lost to open borders will benefit them in the long run.

As the Napster case shows, the new expansion of intellectual property rights has little to do with compensation for the creator and everything to do with corporate control.

Still, shouldn't originators receive remuneration? Well, Dr Dre swears his touching soliloquies about his piteous "bitch mama" are taken from The Streets. Has he sent royalty checks to the brothers?

I confess I never interviewed Dre. He didn't return my call. But the words quoted here are, unarguably, his intellectual property, and I wish to compensate him. I want to make sure that you, Dre – and Sony and Microsoft and Glaxo-Wellcome   get what's coming to you.

After I printed this fantasy interview with Dre I received this bitchy little note from record company BMG.

> *You assert that six companies dominate the industry. [Due to] takeovers, there is [sic] currently five, and will soon be four when Warner and EMI merge.*

The industry spokesman avers that my error should convince readers that there is no monopoly control of the market.
I stand corrected.

GATS Got His Tongue

Secret trade treaty documents reveal the shark hidden in the free trade swimming pool ...

When Churchill said, "democracy is the worst form of government except all the others," he simply lacked the vision to see that, in March 2001, the WTO would design a system to replace democracy with something much better – Article VI.4 of GATS.

Some months ago, an extraordinary document, dated March 19, 2001, marked "confidential", came through my fax machine from the WTO Secretariat. This unassuming six-page memo the WTO modestly hid away in secrecy may one day be seen as the post-democratic Magna Carta. It contained a plan to create an international agency with veto power over parliamentary and regulatory decisions.

The memo begins with considering the difficult matter of how to punish nations that violate "a balance between two potentially conflicting priorities: promoting trade expansion versus protecting the regulatory rights of governments".

Think about that. For a few centuries Britain, America and now almost all nations have relied on elected parliaments, congresses, prime ministers and presidents to set the rules. It is these ungainly deliberative bodies that "balance" the interests of citizens and businesses.

Now kiss that obsolete system goodbye. Once nations sign on to the GATS, Article VI.4, called The Necessity Test, will kick in. Then, per the Secretariat's secret program outlined in the March 19 memo, national parliaments and regulatory agencies will be demoted, in effect, to advisory bodies. Final authority will rest with the GATS Disputes Panel to determine if a law or regulation is "more burdensome than necessary". And the GATS panel, not Parliament or Congress, will tell us what is "necessary".

As a practical matter, this means nations will have to shape laws protecting the air you breathe, the trains you ride in and the food you chew by picking, not the best or safest means for the nation, but the *cheapest* methods for foreign investors and merchants.

Let's get down to concrete examples. The Necessity Test had a trial run in North America via inclusion in NAFTA, the region's free trade agreement. The state of California had banned a gasoline additive MBTE, a chemical cocktail that was found to contaminate water supplies. A Canadian seller of the "M" chemical in MBTE filed a complaint saying California's ban on the pollutant fails the Necessity Test.

The Canadians assert, quite logically, that California, rather than ban MBTE, could require all petrol stations to dig up storage tanks and reseal them, and hire a swarm of inspectors to make sure it's done perfectly. The Canadian proposal might cost Californians a bundle and might be impossible to police. But that's just too bad. The Canadians assert their alternative is the *least trade-restrictive* method for protecting the California water supply. "Least trade-restrictive" is NAFTA's Necessity Test. If California doesn't knuckle under, the US Treasury may have to fork out over $976 million to the Canadian pollutant's manufacturer.

The GATS version of the Necessity Test is NAFTA on steroids. Under GATS, as proposed in the memo, national laws and regulations will be struck down if they are "more burdensome than necessary" to business. Notice the subtle change from banning "trade restrictive" rules (NAFTA) to "burdensome rules". Suddenly the GATS treaty is not about trade at all, but a sly means to wipe away restrictions on business and industry, foreign *and* local.

What burdensome restrictions are in the corporate cross-hairs? The US trade representative has already floated proposals on retail distribution. Want to preserve Britain's greenbelts? Well, forget it – not if some bunch of trees are in the way of a Wal-Mart superstore. Even under the current, weaker GATS, Japan was forced to tear up its own planning rules to let in the retail monster boxes.

The government assures us that nothing threatens the right to enforce laws in the nation's public interest. But not according to the March 19 memo. The WTO report that, in the course of the secretive multilateral negotiations, trade ministers have agreed that, before the GATS tribunal, a defense of "safeguarding the public interest ... was rejected".

In place of a public interest standard, the Secretariat proposes a deliciously Machiavellian "efficiency principle". "It may well be politically more acceptable to countries to accept international obligations which give primacy to economic efficiency." This is an unsubtle invitation to load the GATS with requirements which rulers know their democratic parliaments could not accept. This would be supremely dangerous if, one day, the US elected a president named "Bush" who wanted to shred air pollution rules or, say, Britain elected a prime minister named "Blair" with a mad desire to sell off his nation's air traffic control system. How convenient for embattled chief executives: what elected congresses and parliaments dare not do, GATS would require.

Britain's government can brush off the green-haired anti-GATS protester, but can't ignore the objections of the British Medical Association (BMA) jittery about GATS' control over Britain's National Health Service. In its journal, the *Lancet*, the BMA nervously questions Pascal Lamy's assurances that "interpretation of the rules [must not be] settled by disputes procedures," that is, the GATS panel. One defender of GATS calls the BMA's accusation "hysterical".

But after reading the March 19 internal memo, hysteria may be the right prescription. The Secretariat's memo makes no concession to sovereign interpretation of the rules. Under the post-democratic GATS regime, the Disputes Panel, those Grand Inquisitors of the Free Market, will decide whether a nation's law or a regulation serves what the memo calls a "legitimate objective".

While parliaments and congresses are lumbered with dated constitutional requirements to debate a law's legitimacy in public, with public evidence, with hearings open to citizen comment, GATS panels are far more efficient. Hearings are closed. Unions, consumer, environmental and human rights groups are barred from the participating – or even knowing what is said before the panel.

Is the March 19 memo just a bit of wool-gathering by the WTO Secretariat? Hardly. The WTO was working from the proposals suggested in yet *another* confidential document also sent to me by my good friend, Unnamable Source. The secret memo, "Domestic Regulation: Necessity and Transparency", dated February 24, 2001, was drafted by the European Community's own "working party" in which the UK ministry claims a lead role.

In letter to MPs, Trade Minister Dick Caborn swears that, through the EC working party, he will insure that GATS recognizes the "sovereign right of government to regulate services" to meet "national policy objectives". Yet the February 24 memo, representing the UK's official (though hidden) proposals, rejects a nation's right to remove its rules from GATS jurisdiction once a service industry is joined to the treaty. Indeed, this official and officious document contains contemptuous attacks on nations claiming "legitimate objectives" as potential "disguised barriers" to trade liberalization. Moreover, that nasty little codicil borrowed from NAFTA, that regulation must not be "more trade restrictive than necessary", is promoted in the secret EC document, ready for harvesting by the WTO Secretariat's free market fanatics.

Not knowing I had these documents in hand, Britain's Trade Ministry still insisted when I called that GATS permitted nations a "right of to regulate to meet national policy objectives". I was not permitted to question Dick Caborn himself (and in the post-GATS future, I understand, no mortal may gaze directly upon him). But let us suppose, for a moment, that Caborn believes what his press office says on his behalf, that there is nothing to fear from GATS, especially because the UK can opt in or out of clauses as it chooses.

Don't count on it. According to Professor Bob Stumberg of Georgetown University, Washington DC, the WTO is now suggesting that the Necessity Test, the shark in the swimming pool, will be applied "horizontally", that is, to all services. No opt-outs.

A Caborn letter to MPs admits that his pleasant interpretation of GATS has not been "tested in WTO jurisprudence". In other words, *he doesn't actually know* if a GATS panel will rule as in his fantasies. This is, after all, the minister who, with his European counterparts, just lost a $194 million judgment to the US over the sale of bananas.

(Now, I can understand how Caborn goofed that one. Europe argued that bananas are a *product*, but the US successfully proved that bananas are a *service* – try not to think about that – and therefore fall under GATS.)

And note: America doesn't grow bananas – so how did it get in this dispute anyway? Did it have anything to do with the fact that Carl Lindner, Chief of the "Chiquita" Banana Company, is one of the top donors to both Democrats and Republicans?

And that illustrates the key issue. No one in Britain should bother with what some UK trade minister thinks. The only thing that counts is what George W. Bush thinks. Or at least, what the people who think *for* George think. Presumably, the UK's minister won't sue his own country for violating the treaty. But the US might. It has. Forget Caborn's assurance – we need assurance from President Bush that he won't use GATS to help Wal-Mart, Citibank or Chevron Oil beat the hell out of Britain or Canada (or California for that matter).

The odd thing is, despite getting serviced in the bananas case, the Blair government and the European Commission have not demanded explicit language barring commerce-first decisions by a GATS panel. Instead, the secret February 14 EC paper encourages the WTO's Secretariat to use the punitive form of The Necessity Test sought by the US.

Liberalisation of Trade in Services (LOTIS) Committee

Minutes of meeting held on Thursday, 22 February 2001 at Lloyd's, One Lime Street, London EC3

Present:

Chair
Christopher Roberts, Covington and Burling

Secretary
Neil Jaggers, International Finan~

Alistair Aber~~
John ~

~nti-GATS Counter-measures. Alistair Abercrombie introduced IFSL's paper it the "civil society" NGOs campaign against the GATS and what might be done he UK private sector to challenge the criticisms which were being made about ; Agreement. It was hoped that the question and answer part of the paper .uld be agreed quite quickly so that the material could be posted on IFSL's ebsite. It was proposed that, at its meeting on 8 May, the High-Level LOTIS ;roup should discuss private sector strategy, particularly the identification of >pportunities for business leaders to engage in the exercise.

9.2 Matthew Lownde welcomed the private sector's help in countering the anti-GATS arguments. He noted that the campaign by the World Development Movement in particular was leading to a broadening of concerns. If business was to help convince the public, a case was needed based on the need to coordinate benefits which the GATS can bring. He also pointed to the development-related business responses to the NGOs allegations. Malcolm McKinnon said that the pro-GATS case was vulnerable when the NGOs asked for proof of where his firm was economic benefits of liberalisation lay. Christopher Ehrke said that his firm was very willing to be involved in the exercise. He felt that some of the points made in the IFSL paper needed to be more punchy and floated the idea of creating a sub-group to take the work forward. Matthew Goodman said that the exercise should be taken forward in close consultation with the WTO Secretariat, which had already produced some useful material on the matter. Pete Maydon undertook to circulate a recent Finnish paper about the economic benefits of liberalisation, on which the LOTIS paper could draw. He felt that developing countries should be encouraged to refute the arguments put forward by the NGOs. In particular, if every member of the WTO could sign up to the counter-arguments produced by the Secretariat, this would have the broadest impact.
Action Pete Maydon

~~y Manisty wondered how business views could best be communicated ~espect, his company would be most willing to give them ~~an could be involved in his capacity of Chairman ~~e considered that the Committee ne~ ~ coordinate a proactive

Figure 9. Some conspiracy nuts believe that the corporate, business and media honchos meet secretly to set the World Trade Organization's agenda and plot against dissenters. This is a snippet from the minutes of a series of 14 such meetings between Europe's top government trade officials and the world's captains of finance, including Peter Sutherland, former head of the WTO, in this group as Chairman of Goldman Sachs International, the investment bank. The LOTIS group's purpose was to lobby success-fully for radical pro-industry changes to the General Agreement on Trade in Services (GATS) one of the WTO treaties.

Here, the group creates a campaign to counter the anti-globalization arguments of the World Development Movement with an offer by Henry Manisty, an executive with the Reuters news agency, to publicize the pro-globalization propaganda.

So there you have it. Rather than attack the rules by which corporate America whipped the planet, Caborn and the EC are keen on handing George Bush a bigger whip.

To review the confidential WTO documents, visit *http://www.corpwatch.org/issues/wto/featured/2001/gpalast.html*

Tinkerbell, Pinochet and the Fairy Tale Miracle of Chile – Questioning Globalization's Genesis Myth

Cinderella's Fairy Godmother, Tinkerbell and Senator Augusto Pinochet have much in common. All three performed magical good deeds. In the case of Pinochet, he is universally credited with the Miracle of Chile, the wildly successful experiment in free markets, privatization, deregulation and union-free economic expansion, whose laissez-faire seeds have spread from Santiago to Surrey, from Valparaiso to Virginia.

They may be a bit squeamish about the blood on his chariot, but all neoliberal "reformers" must agree, globalization's free market revolution was born from the barrel of his guns. Whatever his shortcomings, they tell us, he was Chile's economic saviour and lit the world's future economic path.

But Cinderella's pumpkin did not really turn into a coach. The Miracle of Chile, too, is just another fairy tale. The claim that General Pinochet begot an economic powerhouse is one of those utterances, like "ethical foreign policy", whose truth rests entirely on its repetition.

Chile can claim some economic success. But that is the work of Salvador Allende – who saved his nation, miraculously, a decade after his death.

In 1973, the year the general seized the government, Chile's unemployment rate was 4.3 per cent. In 1983, after ten years of free market modernization, unemployment reached 22 per cent. Real wages declined by 40 per cent under military rule. In 1970, 20 per cent of Chile's population lived in poverty. By 1990, the year "President" Pinochet left office, the number of destitute had doubled to 40 per cent. Quite a miracle.

Pinochet did not destroy Chile's economy all alone. It took nine years of hard work by the most brilliant minds in world academia, a gaggle of Milton Friedman's trainees, the Chicago Boys. Under the spell of their theories, the general abolished the minimum wage, outlawed trade union bargaining rights, privatized the pension system, abolished all taxes on wealth and on business profits, slashed public employment, privatized 212 state industries and 66 banks and ran a fiscal surplus. The general goose-stepped his nation down the "neoliberal" (free market) path, and soon Thatcher, Reagan, Clinton, Blair, the IMF and the planet would follow.

But what actually happened in Chile? Freed from the dead hand of bureaucracy, taxes and union rules, the country took a giant leap forward ... into bankruptcy and depression. After nine years of economics Chicago-style, Chile's industry keeled over and died. In 1982 and 1983, gross domestic output dropped 19 per cent. That's a *depression*. The free market experiment was *kaput*, the test tubes shattered. Blood and glass littered the laboratory floor.

Yet, with remarkable *chutzpa*, the mad scientists of Chicago declared success. In the US, President Ronald Reagan's State Department issued a report concluding: "Chile is a casebook study in sound economic management." Milton Friedman himself coined the phrase "The Miracle of Chile". Friedman's sidekick, economist Art Laffer, preened that Pinochet's Chile was "a showcase of what supply-side economics can do".

It certainly was. More exactly, Chile was a showcase of deregulation gone berserk. The Chicago Boys persuaded the junta that removing restrictions on the nation's banks would free them to attract foreign capital to fund industrial expansion. (A decade later, such capital market liberalization would become the *sine qua non* of globalization.) On this advice, Pinochet sold off the state banks – at a 40 per cent discount from book value – and they quickly fell into the hands of two conglomerate empires controlled by speculators Javier Vial and Manuel Cruzat. From their captive banks, Vial and Cruzat siphoned cash to buy up manufacturers then leveraged these assets with loans from foreign investors panting to get their piece of the state giveaways.

The banks' reserves filled with hollow securities from affiliated enterprises. Pinochet let the good times roll for the speculators. He was persuaded, to use Tony Blair's words 20 years on, that "Governments should not hinder the logic of the market."

By 1982, the Chilean pyramid finance game was up. The Vial and Cruzat "Grupos" defaulted. Industry shut down, private pensions were worthless, the currency swooned. Riots and strikes by a population too hungry and desperate to fear bullets forced Pinochet to reverse course. He booted his beloved Chicago experimentalists.

Reluctantly, the general restored the minimum wage and unions' collective bargaining rights. Pinochet, who had previously decimated government ranks, authorized a program to create 500,000 jobs. The equivalent in the US would be the government's putting another 20 million on the payroll. In other words, Chile was pulled from depression by dull old Keynesian remedies – all Franklin Roosevelt, zero Margaret Thatcher. The junta even instituted what remains today as South America's only law restricting the flow of foreign capital.

New Deal tactics rescued Chile from the Panic of 1983, but the nation's long-term recovery and growth since then is the result of – *cover the children's ears* – a large dose of socialism. To save the nation's pension system, Pinochet nationalized banks and industry on a scale unimagined by the socialist Allende. The general expropriated at will, offering little or no compensation. While most of these businesses were eventually reprivatized, the state retained ownership of one industry: copper.

For nearly a century, copper has meant Chile and Chile copper. University of Montana metals expert Dr Janet Finn notes, "It's absurd to describe a nation as a miracle of free enterprise when the engine of the economy remains in government hands." (And not just any government hands. A Pinochet law, still in force, gives the military 10 per cent of state copper revenues.)

Copper has provided 30–70 per cent of the nation's export earnings. This is the hard currency that has built today's Chile, the proceeds from the mines seized from Anaconda and Kennecott in 1973 – Allende's posthumous gift to his nation.

Agribusiness is the second locomotive of Chile's economic growth. This also is a legacy of the Allende years. According to Professor Arturo Vasquez of Georgetown University, Washington DC, Allende's land reform, the break-up of feudal estates (which Pinochet could not fully reverse), created a new class of productive tiller-owners, along with corporate and cooperative operators, who now bring in a stream of export earnings to rival copper. "In order to have an economic miracle," says Dr Vasquez, "maybe you need a socialist government first to commit agrarian reform."

So there we have it. Keynes and Marx, not Milton Friedman, saved Chile.

But the myth of the free market miracle persists because it serves a quasi-religious function. Within the faith of the Reaganauts and Thatcherites, Chile provides the necessary genesis fable, the ersatz Eden from which the laissez-faire dogma sprang successful and shining.

Half a globe away from Chile, an alternative economic experiment was succeeding quietly and bloodlessly. The southern Indian state of Kerala is the laboratory for the humane development theories of Amartya Sen, winner of the 1998 Nobel Prize for Economics. Committed to income redistribution and universal social services, Kerala built an economy on intensive public education. As the world's most literate state, it earns its hard currency from the export of technical assistance to Gulf nations. If you've heard little or nothing of Sen and Kerala, maybe it is because they pose an annoying challenge to the free market consensus.

In the year Sen won the prize, the international finance Gang of Four – the World Bank, the IMF, the Inter-American Development Bank and the International Bank for Settlements – offered a $41.5 billion line of credit to Brazil then sinking in its debts. But before the agencies handed the drowning nation a life preserver, they demanded that Brazil commit to swallow the economic medicine that nearly killed Chile. You know the list by now: fire-sale privatizations, flexible labor markets (i.e. union demolition) and deficit reduction through savage cuts in government services and social security.

In São Paulo, the public is assured these cruel measures will ultimately benefit the average Brazilian. What looks like financial colonialism is sold as the cure-all tested in Chile with miraculous results.

But that miracle was in fact a hoax, a fraud, a fairy tale in which everyone did not live happily ever after.

Looking back

I have an advantage over Thomas Friedman. I was there at the beginning, at the moment of conception when the sperm of Milton Friedman's oddball economic theories entered the ovum of the fertilized mind of Ronald Reagan, who was then Governor of California. I witnessed the birth of Thatcherism before Thatcher – there, at the University of Chicago, in the early 1970s, the only American member of an elite group, later known as the "Chicago Boys". Most were Latin Americans, a strange collection in white turtleneck sweaters and dark shades, right out of the movie Z, who would turn Chile into an experiment in torture and free markets.

The group's official title, "Latin American Finance Workshop", was directed by a Professor Arnold Harshberger; Friedman's was the "Money and Banking Workshop". I worked my way in with both of them – even then I was undercover, operating for the electrical and steel workers' union leaders Frank Rosen and Eddie Sadlowski. Frank told me, "Keep your damn mouth shut, put away the childish Mao buttons, put on a suit and *find out what these guys are up to.*"

I wouldn't call Milton Friedman a midget, but what sticks in my mind is that his feet didn't touch the floor in the built-up chair in which he presided. Rhodesia (now Zimbabwe) was a hot topic. The nation was controlled by Whites, 5 per cent of the population, who kept the 95 per cent Black population in virtual slavery, without hope and certainly without the right to vote. Professor Friedman opined from his high chair, "Why are people attacking Rhodesia, *the only democracy in Africa?*" And I remember the professor was driven around in a black limousine by a Black chauffeur.

So, while the other students, the budding bankers and dictators-in-training are drooling in admiration, I'm reporting back, "This Friedman is *one sick puppy*. No one's going to buy this self-serving 'laissez faire' free market mumbo jumbo from some ultra-right wing-nut."

Twenty-five years later, Blair and Bush and Clinton and de la Rua and Putin open their mouths and out comes Milton Friedman. And everywhere I turn, the guys running the show are wearing their Golden Straitjackets and grinning and groping and agreeing with each other. And all I can think of is something another professor of mine, Allen Ginsberg, said: *The soul should not die ungodly in an armed madhouse.*

3

Small Towns, Small Minds

I live 100 miles outside the city, in the sticks. When I published a version of these stories in the New York Times, my village's newsletter printed an editorial suggesting that I pack up and get the hell out of town. It was the second time they'd requested my departure. I can't imagine why.

My Mother Was a Hypnotist for McDonald's

In 1970, one of the corporation's biggest franchisees, moving millions of burgers in Hollywood, California, feared for their crew leaders. Working 15-hour shifts scattered over nights and days for $3 an hour, some of these so-called managers took on that look of insomniac spookiness that could end with one of them "going postal", the colloquialism which describes what happens when the California penchant for self-expression meets the American fascination with automatic weapons. That wouldn't do. So my mother taught them self-hypnosis. "Twenty minutes trance is worth four hours' sleep!" Maybe that's why I don't eat Clown meat anymore. When I look at those grinning, unblinking faces, asking, "Do you want fries with that?" ...

To residents of Montparnasse and Hampstead, the opening of each new McDonald's heralds the Bozo-headed déclassé Americanization of Europe. But to me, McDonald's represents something far more sinister: the frightening Americanization of America.

To understand what I mean, let's begin with this: the US is *ugly*. A conspiracy of travel writers have sold the image of America the Beautiful: Georgia O'Keefe sunsets over New Mexico's plateau, the wide-open vistas of the Grand Canyon. But to get there, you must drive through a numbing repetitive vortex of sprawled Pizza Huts, Wal-Marts, K-Marts, The Gap, Jiffy-Lubes, Kentucky Fried Chickens, Starbucks and McDonald's up to and leaning over the Canyon wall. All America's special tastes – New Orleans jambalaya, Harlem ham hocks, New England crab boil – whatever is unique to a region or town has been hunted down and herded into a few tourist preserves. The oppressive ubiquity of contrived American monoculture has ingested and eliminated any threat of character. The words of McDonald's late CEO Ray Kroc, *"we cannot trust some people who are nonconformists,"* have become our national anthem.

Almost. One hundred miles dead east of New York City, a hamlet of farmers called Southold held out. Southold was the last place in New York State where you could look from a rolling road across an open cornfield uninterrupted by Golden Arches. The town board refused McDonald's request to build as "just not part of our rural character". A group of visiting English land use experts had planted in our village the un-American idea of "stewardship" trumping property rights. In Britain, these battles are common stuff – in 1999, 40 mums and kids in Shaftesbury, Harrow, marched against conversion of the Hungry Horse pub into an Avaricious Clown – but in the US in 1990, Tiny Town Resists was national news. The rebellion lasted six years. Then McDonald's huffed and puffed and threatened law suits, and Southold – my town – bowed down. Today, Southold schools bus students to "instructional" outings at McDonald's.

The story of Mom and McDonald's is my contribution to the Great Bubble debate. A whole gaggle of Chicken Littles in the financial press have been cackling about The Bubble, the allegedly insupportable speculative rise in share prices which had to burst and spew out financial fire, brimstone and bankruptcies.

Yes, we've seen dot-coms vanish like backseat vows of eternal love. But stay calm. The sky is not, I repeat *not*, falling. The Bubble Theorem is the creation of good-hearted souls of the Left made ill by the orgy of monstrous increases in wealth for a few and begging bowls for the many. The world's 300 richest people are worth more than the world's poorest three billion. The stock market could not rise indefinitely on the promises of dot-coms that sell nothing yet lay claim to a large share of the planet's wealth. Brilliant economic analysts like the *Guardian*'s Larry Elliot and complete cranks like Robert Schiller sermonized about the coming "Day of Reckoning". Yet the 2001 "collapse" of the stock market barely dimpled the overall rise in equity values seen over the decade.

The belief that a Price Must Be Paid is religion not economics, Calvinism dressed up in Marxist clothing. What the Bubble-heads fail to accept is that the class war, as Messrs Blair and Bush tell us, is indeed over – but not because we have reached a happy social entente. Let's face it, the working class has been defeated soundly, convincingly, absolutely.

Dr Edward Wolff, director of the Income Studies Project at the Jerome Levy Institute, New York, tells me that between 1983 and 1997, 85.5 per cent of the vaunted increase in America's wealth was captured by the richest 1 per cent. In that time, overall US income rocketed – of which 80 per cent of America's families received 0 per cent. The market's up, but *who* is the market? According to Wolff, the Gilded One Per Cent own $2.9 trillion of the nation's stocks and bonds out of a total $3.5 trillion.

Not coincidentally, the rise in the riches of the rich matches quite well with the wealth *lost* by production workers through the shrinking of their share of the production pie. US workers are producing more per hour (up 17 per cent since 1983) while keeping less of it (real wages are down 3.1 per cent). So there you have it: the market did not rise on a bubble of fictions but on the rock-hard foundation of the spoils of the class war.

What's going on here? Let's start with computers. Forget Robert Reich's sweet notion that computers can make work more meaningful and worthwhile. The purpose of every industrial revolution, from the steam-powered loom to the assembly line, is to make craft and skills obsolete, and thereby make people interchangeable and cheap. And now, computerization is speeding the industrialization of service work.

That brings us back to "Micky D's". While Ray Kroc gets all the kudos for building the company, it was the genius of the brothers McDonald, Richard and Maurice, in 1948, to divide the production of restaurant food into discrete, skill-less tasks. McDonald's ruthlessly and methodically applied to the corner greasy spoon, the working man's café, the techniques of Taylorism, the time-and-motion paradigm which rules factory assembly lines. No more cooks. Any clown can make a hamburger for McDonald's. Their machines are designed so that unskilled employees hired off the street can reach full speed within minutes. Britain's prime minister, mesmerized by the modern, says he is creating a Knowledge Economy. Oh, yeah. At McD's, you can spend all day punching machine-portioned glops of ketchup onto burger buns.

In one of the *Observer*'s undercover investigations, we learned that McDonald's retained the notorious union-busting firm Jackson Lewis of New York. But why should McDonald's bother? Fast food operators report employee turnover averaging 300 per cent per year – and, despite what the industry says, *they love it*. Workers out the door in four months don't demand pensions, promotions, training or unions. In 1996, a British civil court found the company systematically exploited young workers, but that is a temporary situation. It won't be long before the majority of workers of *all* ages will need no more experience than any 17-year-old slacker – and will be paid like one.

The stock market went up because the human market went down. Here in the twenty-first century, Blake's Dark Satanic Mills have been replaced by Bright Demonic Happy Meals as the factory for deconstructing work into a cheap commodity.

It is estimated that one in eight American adults have worked at a McDonald's. This acts as a kind of moral instruction for the working class, as jail time does for ghetto residents. It is one reason behind America's low unemployment rate. As my old professor Milton Friedman taught me, unemployment falls when workers give up hope of higher pay.

Things Like That Don't Happen Here

Last autumn, one of my neighbours, Kenneth Payne, fortified by the courage available at one of our local bars, loaded his shotgun, walked across the road to the trailer home of his best buddy, Curtis Cook, and emptied both barrels into Cook's stomach. While his friend bled to death, Kenneth sat down on his porch and telephoned a local family to say, "No one's going to bother your little girl anymore." Kenneth claimed Curtis had earlier in the evening confessed to molesting the neighbour's eight-year-old child.

The next day, our town's burghers ran out to tell curious metropolitan reporters, "Things like that don't happen here." Really? None of my neighbours mentioned the story of our school principal's daughter, who hid her pregnancy from her parents then drowned her child right after its birth. I thought it worth reporting, so I did, in the Observer *and the* New York Times.

What kind of monstrous hamlet do I live in? While few Americans have heard of it, Britons know it as the congenial, rural town lionized on BBC radio's "Letter from America", broadcast by Alistair Cooke, one of our few unarmed residents.

Like Alistair, I've made shameless use of the cartoon imagery of this convenient exemplar of unspoiled, small town America. In the prior article, I told you about our town's heroic struggle to block McDonald's opening a restaurant, a threat to our quaint rural character. The way I told it, we were gloriously defeated by the corporation's McLawyers who bullied us into bending our preservation laws.

I left out of the story about our defense against the fast food giant being sabotaged from within by that fifth column of small businessmen found in every American town – the local real estate agents, shopkeepers and farmers hoping to turn a quick buck on their properties once the planning rules are breached and broken.

I've written scores of bad-tempered columns about the brutish ways of America's biggest businesses. That viewpoint is admittedly a bit unbalanced. To be fair, we must recognize that for sheer narrow-minded, corrosive greed nothing can beat the US's grasping, whining, *small* businessmen. And within that avaricious little pack, none is so poisonously self-centered and incorrigible as the small town businessman of rural America.

During the presidential debates, Al Gore opened the bidding to win this pampered demographic by promising to slash inheritance taxes, "to save our family farms and businesses". Until President Bush took office, if you inherited a farm or business worth up to $2.6 million you paid no tax at all. But that's just not enough for what the fawning candidates call "local entrepreneurs". Gore promised to raise the exemption to $4 million – only to be trumped by George W. Bush who promised to wipe away inheritance taxes altogether (one of the few promises he kept).

This group of small businessmen and farmers, so deserving of protection of their tax-free millions, is the same that defeated Bill and Hillary Clinton's 1993 proposal to require all businesses to provide bare-bones health insurance for their employees, an expenditure of only 35 cents per hour. Fortune 500 corporations expressed few qualms about the mandatory insurance plan as most big firms already provide some health care coverage for their employees. It was the swarm of Lilliputian entrepreneurs, under the aegis of their National Federation of Independent Businesses, who blocked the Clintons' modest attempt to end medical care apartheid in America.

You name it – maternity leave, minimum wage, even health and safety inspections and rules barring racism in hiring – any meagre proposal to protect the lives and families of working people, and the NFIB's small businesses legions have their swords out to kill it.

But we must never say so. Al Gore can shoot at big tobacco and big oil, Bush can vilify teachers and union workers, but any politician who breathes a word against rural businesses, farmers or the NFIB's Scrooge battalions ends up as electoral road-kill.

Ten years ago, our town convinced a charitable foundation with more money than wisdom to pay for experts from Britain to tell us how to preserve our area's rural character. We held meetings, referenda, elections. It was that active small town American democracy that makes foreign writers like Tocqueville and Jonathan Freedland ga-ga with admiration. At the end, the town voted overwhelmingly to adopt what became known as the "UK Stewardship Plan" to protect our green fields and prevent ugly urban sprawl.

Come by my town today and count the pustules of strip malls and fluorescent signs directing you to Bagels Hot! Cars Like New No Down-Payment! Dog Burger! where cornfields once grew. Sensible British designs and a preservation-minded electorate could not overcome the me-first obstructionism of a hard core of small businessmen and farmers lusting to sell off their land to McDonald's, Wal-Mart and housing speculators.

I didn't equate rural shotgun murders or child molesting to the small town businessman's penchant for despoiling the rural landscape. But they are covered over by the same cowardly silence. No politician, local or national, has the guts to break through the mythology, the legend of the struggling local businessman who cares and sacrifices for his community. This folkloric invention approaches saintliness when the discussion turns to rural, small town America with its treacly images of barbershop quartets, Farmer Brown on his tractor and the Main Street parade after the strawberry harvest.

What makes this myth of happy small town America off-limits to challenge is that it provides pleasant code words for the ugliest corner of the American psyche. When politicians talk about "small town American values", "family values" and the "hard-working small businessman" everyone knows the color of that town, that family and that businessman – white. Pleasantville USA is implicitly placed against the urban jungle populated at the bottom by dark-skinned muggers and pregnant teenagers on the dole, and at the top by Jewish financiers of Hollywood pornography.

It would dangerously undermine this politically useful imagery if the public were reminded that small towns are filled with pale-faced citizens despairing and dangerous as any in the inner cities. Nor could the NFIB win those special exemptions from taxes and planning regulations for small businesses and farms if they were seen, not as struggling defenders of local communities, but as dollar-crazed and duplicitous operators who wouldn't care if McDonald's put a drive-though in the Lincoln Memorial.

Every landscape we build, wrote psychologist Norman O. Brown, is our re-creation of the interior of our mothers' bodies. What does it say about

Americans when we look out over a natural vista we are seized with psychic anguish if we cannot locate a throbbing neon sign flashing PIZZA HOT!

In our little town, it was George, the owner of the local lumberyard, who proudly organized successful business opposition to the UK Stewardship plan. With dollar signs in his eyes, he welcomed McDonald's and the boxy shopping mall that replaced several hundred acres of raspberry fields.

But small-town Georges forget that, when they break down government regulations, it is *big* business that gleefully rushes through the breach. Last time I saw him, George the lumberman was stunned by the announcement that Home Depot, the Wal-Mart of do-it-yourself stores, would replace a nearby cornfield. And that means George is out of business.

In a small town, neighbourly manner, I expressed my sympathy to George. If I were a better person, I would have meant it.

Insane about Asylum

At midnight on May 12, 2000, twelve Mexicans crossed the Rio Grande on the first leg of their journey to Farmingville, Long Island, where my town's tradesmen pick up their laborers. Lost in the fearfully vast Arizona desert, the twelve died of dehydration. I surprised myself by wanting to write something almost kind about my town.

So here's me, using one of the lowest tricks in journalism – asking a London cab driver to give his salt-of-the-earth opinion on one of the great issues of the day: asylum seekers. He couldn't wait.

"Well, it's like you're ashamed to be English today! You're not supposed to be English!"

I had good reason to ask. As an American, I can't get my head around British election time "asylum" hoo-hah. At the last election Prime Minister Blair and his Tory opponent William Hague seemed to be competing for the post of Great White Hunter, stalking "bogus" asylum seekers among the herd of "legitimate" ones.

In America, we don't have asylum seekers; we have immigrants. Lots of them – 29 million by the low-ball official census, with 1.2 million more coming in each year. US cities compete for prime-pick foreign workers as they would for a foreign auto plant.

America certainly has had anti-immigrant politicians. In the nineteenth century we had the appropriately named Know-Nothing Party and in 1988 we had Mike Huffington. Huffington's wife Arianna famously convinced her overly-rich husband to run for the US Senate on a rabid anti-immigration platform.

It was a perplexing campaign for California, where Whites are the minority race and the only true non-immigrants are, if you think about it, a handful of

Shosone Indians. Mrs Huffington herself delivered the most virulent anti-foreigner speeches ... in her thick Greek accent.

After his demolition at the polls, the demoralized Huffington announced he could remain neither a Republican nor a heterosexual.

Huffington's defeat also allowed George W. Bush to convince his party to adopt hug-an-immigrant slogans. Bush would hold open the Golden Door for immigrants, but not out of a weepy compassion for the "huddled masses yearning to breathe free". Immigration is simply good business.

In fact, it's the deal of the millennium, says Dr Stephen Moore of the Cato Institute, a think-tank founded by big-name Republicans. "It's a form of reverse foreign aid. We give less than $20 billion in direct aid to Third World nations and we get back $30 billion a year in capital assets."

By "assets" he means workers raised, fed, inoculated and educated by poorer countries, then shipped at the beginning of their productive lives to the US. (The average age of immigrants is 28.)

The Cato Institute reckons that the US "imports" about $25 billion a year in human "goods". "It is the lubricant to our capitalistic economy," said Moore (as I eschewed thoughts of the film *Modern Times*, where Charlie Chaplin gets squeezed through giant gears), "giving US companies a big edge over European competitors."

Given the US experience, American economists would find the entire British fixation on "bogus" and "legitimate" asylum seekers just wacky. Instead of asking newcomers for a commitment to building Britain, they are asked solely whether they are running for their lives. What an odd standard for choosing new citizens.

American industry saves a bundle due to its access to an army of low-skill, low-wage foreign workers who can be hired, then dumped, in a snap. US industry also siphons off other nations' best and brightest, trained at poor nations' expense.

The habit of siphoning off other countries' high-skilled workers, let me note, permits America's monied classes to shirk the costly burden of educating America's own underclass. (So far, this system hums along smoothly: Bangalore-born programmers in Silicon Valley design numberless cash registers for fast-food restaurants so they can be operated by illiterate Texans.)

To get a closer understanding of the Cato Institute studies, I talked with a piece of imported human capital. His name is Mino (I can't disclose his last name). Mino first tried to get into the US from Guatemala eleven years ago. He paid thousands of dollars to a *gusano* (a "worm") to sneak him across the border. The cash bought Mino a spot in a sealed lorry stuffed with 100 other men. Mino felt lucky: he didn't die. But he did spend three days in jail when La Migra (the Immigration and Naturalization Service) grabbed him.

Back in Guatemala, Mino next bought a plane ticket to JFK airport – and a false visa. This time, no problems. Within days, Mino had a job washing dishes in the local café in my town on Long Island, east of New York.

I asked the chief planner for our region, Dr Lee Koppelman, about the role of "illegal" workers like Mino in our local economy. Koppelman laughed: "There wouldn't *be* an economy without the illegals." He estimates there are more than 100,000 "undocumented" workers in our county alone. Nationwide, undocumented workers total between seven million and eleven million.

Our local businesses, says Koppelman, "turn a blind eye" to the suspect status of the workers stooping in our strawberry fields and clearing our construction sites. One local farmer tells me he gets his field hands from El Salvador – though I know this guest worker program ended more than 20 years ago.

Our business community's "blindness" goes beyond ignoring someone's counterfeit "green card". The local shop paid Mino the legal minimum wage, but worked him twice the legal number of hours.

And that's another advantage to US-style immigration. "The workforce is flexible," says the expert from Cato. "Flexible" means millions of workers too scared of La Migra to blow the whistle on illegal working hours, or to join unions or make a fuss when, at the end of the harvest season (or tourist season or production run) they are told to get lost.

By keeping the Golden Door only slightly ajar, with a third of all immigrants fearful of deportation, America's employers profit from something that works quite a bit like the old South African system of migrant workers. "Workers just materialize," says Koppelman, then are expected to vanish, leaving neither businesses nor communities with any responsibility for their survival nor their families' when work ends.

So why does Britain fear this gloriously profitable scheme of importing valuable worker-assets? The English notion that immigrants drain government resources is a laugh. The US Senate Immigration sub-committee tells me the government turns a nice profit on immigration, efficiently collecting in taxes from migrants roughly double what they get back in services. America approves 2.5 million applications to stay a year; Britain lets in a paltry 129,000.

But what about my cabby's fear of losing his English identity? Face it, Shakespeare's dead. England's cultural exports are now limited to Morris dancing, football hooliganism and Hugh Grant.

I humbly suggest you consider floating Home Secretary David Blunkett into the English Channel dressed like the Statue of Liberty with robe, tiara, torch and a sign reading: "Desperately seeking new material for stagnant gene pool!"

Now for the happy American ending: today, Mino owns a landscaping business, drives a flash pick-up truck, plans to buy a home, get rid of his accent and finish a degree in accounting.

No one here resents Mino's success. His story is every American's story. It's my story. Anna Palast stole across the border in 1920. Luckily, La Migra didn't catch her until a few days before her 100th birthday.

And that's what neither Blair nor the Tories understand. It's not where you come from that counts. It's where you're going.

4

Pat Robertson, General Pinochet, Pepsi-Cola and the Anti-Christ: Special Investigative Reports

Papers fly out of filing cabinets and land on my desk. Voices whisper phone numbers of corporate, government, even church, insiders. People talk and my tape recorder happens to be rolling. I guess I'm a lucky guy.

I've tried to carry over to journalism the techniques of in-depth investigation I used in gathering intelligence for government racketeering cases. While there's the cloak-and-dagger fun stuff (setting up false front organizations as I did for the *Observer* in the Lobbygate sting), most of it involves hours, days and weeks lost in piles of technical and financial papers. Glamorous it ain't. It is expensive and time-consuming – not exactly attractive to editors for whom Quick and Cheap are matters of principle, both professional and personal. Bless those editors who've tolerated my deviant journalistic behaviour.

Almost all the stuff in this book is "investigative", that is, revealing information the subjects of the stories assumed and hoped had been well hidden. These reports were a bit more difficult to tease out, especially when the subject of one, through divine communication, learned that I was a correspondent for a newspaper, the *Observer,* founded by an agent of Lucifer. But I knew that already.

Sympathy for the Banker: Anti-Christ Inc. and the Last Temptation of Pat Robertson

In May 1999, the oldest financial enterprise in the English-speaking world, the Bank of Scotland, decided to launch into the cyber-future with the largest-ever telephone and Internet bank operation, to be based in the US. Their choice of partner and chairman for the enterprise, US televangelist "Reverend" Pat Robertson, scandalized a few Britons.

The United Kingdom's business elite could dismiss objections with a knowing condescension. To them, Robertson was just another Southern-fried Elmer Gantry bigot with a slick line of Lordy-Jesus hoodoo who could hypnotize a couple of million American goobers into turning over their bank accounts to the savvy Scots.

I had a different view of the Reverend Pat. For years, I'd kept tabs on the demi-billionaire media mogul who had chosen one president of the United States and would choose another ... and who left a scent of sulphur on each of his little-known investments from China to the Congo. The Feds were already on his case, but I could speak to insiders in the born-again Christian community, once high in Reverend Pat's billion-dollar religious-commercial-political empire, who would never talk to officialdom.

Most difficult was convincing the Reverend's protectors to let me speak directly to The "Doctor" (as they call him) at his compound in Virginia; and once there, getting my wire through the metal detector. ("Officer, could you please hold my cigarette lighter?")

While some Britons could not fathom why the Bank of Scotland chose Robertson, I was more surprised that Robertson chose the Scots. He had, in fact, written a great deal about that Presbyterian-run finance house. In Robertson's darkly woven universe, the Bank of Scotland was the manifestation on earth of the Spirit of the Anti-Christ.

It's time someone told you the truth. There is an Invisible Cord easily traced from the European bankers who ordered the assassination of President Lincoln to German Illuminati and the "communist rabbi" who is the precise connecting link to Karl Marx, the Trilateral Commission, the House of Morgan and the British bankers who, in turn, funded the Soviet KGB. This is the "tightly knit cabal whose goal is nothing less than a new order for the human race under the domination of Lucifer".

If you don't know about the Invisible Cord, then you have not read *New World Order* by Dr Marion "Pat" Robertson, chairman of the Bank of Scotland's new American consumer bank holding company.

Interestingly, the Scottish bank's biography of Robertson failed to mention *New World Order*, the 1991 bestseller which a *Wall Street Journal* review uncharitably described as written by "a paranoid pinhead with a deep distrust of democracy".

There is so much the Bank of Scotland forgot to include in their profile of Dr Robertson that it is left to the *Observer* to properly introduce this man of wealth and taste. The bank, for example, failed to note that Dr Robertson is best known to Americans as the leader of the 1.2 million-strong ultra-right political front, Christian Coalition. It may seem a bit odd for the Bank of Scotland to choose as their spokesman a man widely feared by many in the target market as America's own Ian Paisley. But the Bank of Scotland says it is not concerned with Dr Robertson's religious beliefs. Nor, apparently, is Dr Robertson concerned with theirs. He has called Presbyterians, members of Scotland's established Church, "the spirit of the Anti-Christ".

What would entice the Bank of Scotland to join up with a figure described by one unkind civil liberties organization as "the most dangerous man in America"? Someone more cynical than me might suspect that the Bank of Scotland covets Dr Robertson's fiercely loyal following of two million conspiracy wonks and Charismatic Evangelicals. A former business partner of Robertson's explained The Reverend's hypnotic pull on their wallets: "These people believe he has a hot-line to God. They will hand him their life savings." Robertson drew believers to his other commercial ventures. "People re-mortgaged their homes to invest in his businesses," the insider told me. If he did use his ministry to promote his business, this would cross several legal boundaries.

In an exclusive interview with the *Observer*, Dr Robertson swore to me he will keep bank commerce, Christianity and the Coalition completely separate. But our look into the Robertson empire, including interviews with his former and current business associates, reveals a hidden history of mixing God, gain and Republican campaign. Not all has been well concealed. Tax and regulatory authorities have tangled for decades with his supposedly non-partisan operations.

The combination of Christianity and cash has made Dr Robertson a man whose net worth is estimated at somewhere between $200 million and $1 billion. He himself would not confirm his wealth except to tell me that his share in the reported $50 million start-up investment in the bank deal is too small for him to have taken note of the sum.

Neil Volder, president of Robertson's financial business and future CEO of the bank venture, emphasizes Robertson's selflessly donating to his church 65–75 per cent of his salary as head of International Family Entertainment. I was surprised: that amounted to only a few hundred thousand dollars yearly, pocket change for a man of Dr Robertson's means. There was also, says Volder, the $7 million he gave to "Operation Blessing" to help alleviate the woes of refugees fleeing genocide in Rwanda. Or did he? Robertson's press operation puts the sum at only $1.2 million – and even that amount could not be corroborated.

More interesting is how the "Operation Blessing" funds were used in Africa. Through an emotional fundraising drive on his TV station, Robertson raised several million dollars for the tax-free charitable trust. "Operation Blessing" purchased planes to shuttle medical supplies in and out of the refugee camp in Goma, Congo (then Zaire). However, investigative reporter Bill Sizemore of the *Virginian-Pilot* discovered that, except for one medical flight, the planes were used to haul heavy equipment for something called the African Development Corporation, a diamond mining operation distant from Goma. African Development is owned by Pat Robertson.

Did Robertson know about the diversion of the relief planes? According to the pilots' records, he himself flew on one plane ferrying equipment to his mines.

One of Robertson's former business partners speaking on condition of confidentiality told me that, although he often flew with Dr Robertson in the minister's jet, he never saw Robertson crack open a Bible or seek private time for prayer. "He always had the *Wall Street Journal* open and *Investors' Daily*." But on the Congo flight, Robertson did pray. The pilot's diary notes, "Prayer for diamonds".

Volder told me that Robertson's diverting the planes for diamond mining was actually carrying out God's work. The planes, he asserts, proved unfit for hauling medicine, so Robertson salvaged them for the diamond hunt which, if successful, would have "freed the people of the Congo from lives of starvation and poverty". None the less, the Virginia State Attorney General opened an investigation of "Operation Blessing".

Volder asserts that Robertson was "not trying to earn a profit, but to help people". As it turned out, he did neither. The diamond safari went bust, as did Robertson's ventures in vitamin sales and multi-level marketing. These disastrous investments added to his losses in oil refining, the money pit of the Founders Inn Hotel, his jet leasing fiasco and one of England's classier ways of burning money, his buying into Laura Ashley Holdings (he was named a director). One cannot term a demi-billionaire a poor businessman but, excepting the media operations handed him by his non-profit organization, Robertson the "entrepreneur" seems to have trouble keeping enterprises off the rocks. Outside the media, Robertson could not cite for me any commercial success.

Undeniably, Dr Robertson is a master salesman. To this I can attest after joining the live audience in Virginia Beach for *700 Club*, his daily television broadcast.

That week, he was selling miracles. Following a mildly bizarre "news" segment, Dr Robertson shut his eyes and went into a deep trance. After praying for divine assistance for his visions, he announced, "There is somebody who has cancer of the intestines ... God is healing that right now and you *will* live! ... Somebody called Michael has a deep chest cough ... God is *healing* you right *now!*"

It is not clear why the Lord needs the intervention of an expensive cable TV operation to communicate to Michael. But more intriguing theological issues are raised by the program hosts' linking miracles to donations made to Robertson's organization. In a taped segment, a woman's facial scars healed after her sister joined the *700 Club* (for the required donation of $20 per month). "She didn't realize how close to her contribution a miracle would arrive." It ended, "Carol was so grateful God healed her sister, she increased her pledge from the *700 Club* to the *1000 Club*."

The miracles add up. In 1997, Christian Broadcast Network, Robertson's "ministry", took in $164 million in donations plus an additional $34 million in other income.

Earlier tidal waves of tax-deductible cash generated by this daily dose of holiness and hostility paid for the cable television network which was sold in 1990 to Rupert Murdoch, along with the old sit-coms that filled the non-religious broadcast hours, for $1.82 billion. Seven years prior to the sale of this media bonanza, the tax-exempt group "spun it off" to a for-profit corporation whose controlling interest was held by Dr Robertson. Lucky Pat.

Robertson donated hundreds of millions of dollars from the Murdoch deal to both Christian Broadcast Network (CBN) and CBN (now Regent) University. That still left Robertson burdened with heavy load of cash to carry through the eye of the needle.

In his younger days, Robertson gave up worldly wealth to work in the Black ghettos of New York. But, says a former Coalition executive, "Pat's changed."

She noted that he gave up his ordination as a Baptist minister in 1988. (He is still called, incorrectly, "Reverend" by the media.) His change in 1988 was accelerated when, says another associate, his former TV co-host Danuta Soderman Pfeiffer, "he was ensnared by the idea that God called him to run for president of the United States".

The 1988 run for the Oval Office began with Robertson's announcing his endorsement by Highest Authority. It was not some quixotic adventure. The losing race generated a mailing list of three million sullen Americans of the heartland whose rage was given voice by Robertson forming, out of defeat, the Christian Coalition. Some say he ran just to generate the list, and Volder offers that this may have been, in fact, the Lord's stratagem. These mailing lists, like the CBN lists, are worth their weight in gold. Robertson swore they would not be used in for the banking business. To dip into the Christian lists uncompensated to promote the new bank would breach the law.

But abuse of these lists lies at the heart of charges by ex-partners with whom I spoke. The IRS opened an investigation of the doctor's use of lists, but had not been able to obtain statements from some witnesses willing to speak with the *Observer*.

Two former top executives in the for-profit operations who have never previously spoken to the media state that Robertson personally directed use of both the tax-exempt religious group's lists and the "educational" Christian Coalition lists to build what became Kalo-Vita, the pyramid sales enterprise which sold vitamins and other products. (Kalo-Vita collapsed in 1992 due to poor management amid lawsuits charging deception.)

A former officer of the company alleges some operations were funded, without compensation, including offices, phones and secretarial help, by the ministry. When insiders questioned Robertson's using viewers' donations for a personal enterprise, Robertson produced minutes of Board meetings that characterized as "loans" the start-up capital obtained from CBN. According to insiders not all Board members were made aware of these meetings until months after they were supposedly held. Dr Robertson's spokesman responds that they are unfamiliar with the facts of the allegation.

The executives were also alarmed about Dr Robertson's preparing to use the 20,000-strong and growing Kalo-Vita sales force as "an organizational structure to back his political agenda" – and partisan ambitions. (US federal investigators never got wind of this alleged maneuver.)

The US Federal Election Commission had already charged Dr Robertson's groups with misusing the Christian Coalition lists. Federal courts are reviewing internal documents including a September 15, 1992, memo from the Coalition's then president, Ralph Reed. The *Observer* obtained a copy of the memo from Reed to the coordinator of President George W. Bush's re-election campaign which says Pat Robertson "is prepared to assist ... [by] the distribution of 40 million voter guides ... This is a virtually unprecedented level of cooperation and assistance ... from Christian leaders." Unprecedented and *illegal*, says the FEC, which sued the Christian Coalition, technically a tax-exempt educational corporation, for channelling campaign support worth tens of millions of dollars to Republican candidates. The action is extraordinary because it was brought by unanimous vote of the bipartisan commission which cited, among other things, the Coalition's favoring Colonel Ollie North with copies of its lists for North's failed run for the US Senate.

Records subpoenaed from the Christian Coalition contain a set of questions and answers concocted by the Coalition and the Republican Party for a staged 1992 "interview" with Bush broadcast on the *700 Club*. This caught my eye first, because it appears to constitute a prohibited campaign commercial and second, because Robertson months earlier claimed Bush was "unwittingly carrying out the mission of Lucifer". With Bush running behind Bill Clinton, Robertson must have decided to stick with the devil he knew.

But the government will never see the most incriminating documents. Judy Liebert, formerly Chief Financial Officer for the Christian Coalition, told me she was present when Coalition President Reed personally destroyed documents subpoenaed by the government. Also, when Liebert learned that the Coalition had printed Republican campaign literature (illegal if true), she discovered that the evidence, contained in the hard drive of her computer, had been removed. Indeed, the entire hard drive had been mysteriously pulled from her machine but not before she had made copies of the files.

When Liebert complained to Robertson about financial shenanigans at the Coalition, "Pat told me I was 'unsophisticated'. Well, that is a strange thing for a Christian person to say to me."

The Coalition has attacked Liebert as a disgruntled ex-employee whom they fired. She responded that she was sacked only after she went to government authorities – and after she refused an $80,000 severance fee that would have required her to remain silent about the Coalition and Robertson. The Feds, notes the Coalition, have never acted on Liebert's charge of evidence-tampering.

Little of this information has been reported in the press. Why? The three-hour dog and pony show I was put through at the CBN-Robertson financial headquarters in Virginia Beach culminated in an hour-long diatribe by his CEO Volder about how Robertson was certain to sue any paper that did not provide what he called a "balanced" view. He boasted that by threatening use of Britain's draconian libel laws and Robertson's bottomless financial treasure chest, one of his lawyers "virtually wrote" a laudatory profile of Robertson in a UK newspaper. As in the days when the Inquisition required recalcitrants to view instruments of torture, I was made to understand in detail the devastation that would befall me if my paper did not report what was "expected" of me. This was said, like all the Robertson team's damning anthems, in a sweet, soft Virginia accent.

Would Dr Robertson use his ministry's following to promote the Bank of Scotland venture? Despite Robertson's protests to the contrary, his banking chief Volder laid out a plan to reach the faithful, including appearances of bank members of the 700 Club, mailings to lists coincident with their own, and "infomercials" just after the religious broadcasts. This is just the type of mixing that has so upset the election commission and the Internal Revenue Service, which in 1998 retroactively stripped Christian Broadcasting of its tax-exempt status for 1986 and 1987.

I met Dr Robertson in his dressing room following his televised verbal intercourse with God. Robertson, though three hours under the spotlight, didn't break a sweat. He peeled off his make-up while we talked international finance. Here was no hayseed huckster, but a worldly man of wealth and taste.

And, despite grimacing and grunts from Volder, Dr Robertson told me he could imagine tying his Chinese Internet firm ("The Yahoo of China," he calls it) into the banking operation. Picking up Volder's body shakes, Dr Robertson added, "Though I'm not supposed to talk about Internet banking."

And he wasn't supposed to mention China. His fellow evangelists are none too happy about his palling around with Zhu Rongi, the communist dictator who gleefully jails Christian ministers. Volder defends Dr Robertson's friendship with Zhu (and association with deposed Congo strongman Mobutu) on the grounds that "Pat would meet with the Devil if that is only way to help suffering people." The fact that the political connections assisted in obtaining diamond (Congo) and Internet concessions (China) is secondary.

The Bank of Scotland will be launched in the US through Dr Robertson's accustomed routes: phone and mail solicitations. But once he hits the Net, with or without the Chinese, this bank deal will make Pat Robertson the biggest financial spider on the world wide web. Yet, his choosing the Bank of Scotland as his partner is surprising because, until this year, Dr Robertson boasted of his *English*, not Scottish, heritage. Moreover, in *New World Order*, he singled out one institution in particular as the apotheosis of Satan's plan for world domination, the British chartered central banks conceived by Scottish banker William Paterson: the Bank of England and Bank of Scotland.

Dr Robertson explains that Rothschild interests carried on the Paterson plan, financing diamond mines in Africa which, in turn, funded the satanic secret English Round Table directed by Lord Milner, editor of the *Observer* (Ah-*Ha*!) a century ago. Furthermore, the Scottish banker's charter became the pattern for the US Federal Reserve Board, a diabolic agency created and nurtured by the US Senate Finance Committee whose chairman was the evil Money Trust's dependable friend, Senator A. Willis Robertson – Pat Robertson's father.

That's right. Pat is the scion of the New World Order, who gave up its boundless privileges to denounce it.

Or did he?

I had done some research on the Anti-Christ. How would we recognize him? How would the Great Deceiver win over God-fearing Christians? What name would he use? As I drove away from the chapel-TV studio-university-ministry-banking complex, I realized I'd forgotten to ask a key question. Why does the ex-Reverend go by the name "Pat" – not his Christian name, Marion? It struck me that "Pat Robertson" is an obvious anagram for the Devil's agent, Paterson of the Scottish bank. My silly thoughts piled higher, fuelled by staying up all night to finish *New World Order*. Suddenly, like Robertson, I too had a vision of an Invisible Cord that went from Lucifer to Illuminati to Scottish bankers to African diamonds to the Senate Finance Committee to Communist Dictators to the world wide web ... Ridiculous, I know, but strangely, though I thought I'd turned off the radio, it continued to play that damned Rolling Stones song,

Pleased to meet you!
Hope you've guessed my name ...

Afterword

The Almighty moves mysteriously, and swiftly. Within a week after the Observer *printed the article, Robertson abandoned the "dark land" of Scotland, as he called it, and the big banking dream went poof! Robertson fled Darkest Scotland. He even resigned from the Board of Laura Ashley, the UK fashion house.*

But our exposure of evidence indicating that Robertson had used the "educational" foundation mailing lists of the Christian Coalition not only for political purposes (as the US government charged) but to promote the failed Kalo-Vita cosmetics pyramid marketing operation opened up whole new possibilities of investigation into whether the pastor sheered his flock. Public interest lawyers with People for the American Way announced they would take our discoveries to the US Federal Elections Commissions and the Internal Revenue Service.

More problems surfaced. The *Observer*, not the Bank of Scotland, announced Robertson's appointment as chairman of the proposed bank venture. Why? Usually such things are announced with fanfare. The answer may be that the US banking authority, the Controller of the Currency, did not know of Robertson's involvement. The "Reverend", though chairman of the *holding* company, could not be found listed as a member of the board of the subsidiary that applied for the banking charter. It seems the Feds have lots of problems granting charters to persons under investigation for misuse of assets. Failure to mention Robertson's chairmanship would not help their chartering cause.

Then there were the allegations of destruction of evidence. The Christian Coalition's CFO told me that Ralph Reed, a big Republican operative even today, "would got through [the subpoenaed documents] and throw everything on the floor – I mean just pitch it – just take it and throw it on the floor". When challenged on the legality (and Christianity) of such actions, Reed reportedly said, "Why don't you just take a gun and blow my brains out."

But Robertson had a better plan. Weirdly, the Christian Coalition's tax-exempt status had been in limbo for an unprecedented ten years, with no US government prepared to take it away nor legally able to grant it. After our story ran, Robertson simply withdrew the application, costing him virtually nothing in cash but thereby pulling the plug on all the investigations of the use or misuse of the Coalition's assets.

Not wanting to leave himself exposed, Robertson within days also announced the shut-down of the Christian Coalition (June 10, 1999). The *New York Times, National Public Radio* and *60 Minutes,* the infotainment flagship of the CBS network, all announced that Robertson and his Coalition were *finis,* his political machine sunk. This was a sure signal that Robertson would rise again, and stronger.

The wily shape-shifter closed Christian Coalition (a Virginia organization) only to establish "Christian Coalition of America". Within a year, his childhood chum, George H.W. Bush, would need his help again. This time, son George W. was in hot water. In January 2000, Senator John McCain beat the Dim Son in the New Hampshire Republican presidential primary. McCain was being hailed as a real American hero, calling for an end to corporate soft-money campaign donations. He looked unstoppable in the race for the Republican nomination ... until the Virginia and South Carolina primaries. This was Christian Coalition turf. A whisper campaign among The Believers tagged McCain, a red-white-and-blue war veteran, as Satan's stand-in. McCain lost those primaries, and that's how Dr Pat chose our president (with a little help from friends in Florida).

The Cola-Nut Coup: Pinochet, Nixon and Pepsi

In 1998, Augusto Pinochet, on one of his many shopping trips to London, was arrested for murder, that is, held for extradition to Spain to face charges. I thought I might track down some of his alleged accomplices. This led to that embarrassing historical factotum, Henry Kissinger – no surprise there – and behind him to the real Mr Bigs of the operation: ITT Corporation, Anaconda Copper and Pepsi-Cola.

When the story hit, my main source screamed bloody murder – not about Pinochet, but about me. Edward Korry, the US ambassador to Chile under Richard Nixon, complained to my editor he'd been had, bamboozled, set-up, conned into talking – six hours of taped revelations. The old ambassador is a fervent anti-communist who thought most highly of the "Chicago Boys", the University of Chicago economic free market shock troops that pillaged and impoverished Chile (my view) or (his view) saved the South American country.

He believed I was one of the "Boys", a student of Milton Friedman and crew, and so the curmudgeon – whose hatred of, and threats against, journalists are notorious – let down his guard. However, I had not lied to him, I really had been one part of the closed little Chicago Boys study group. Just because he convinced himself I was a fellow free market fruitcake, well, there's nothing I could do about that.

And although he attacked me for reporting his words, and his politics gives me the shivers, I look on Ambassador Korry as kind of heroic. Though he hated the Allende government, he would not countenance bribery or bloodshed, not even for Pepsi.

"It is the firm and continuing policy that Allende be overthrown by a coup ... please review all your present and possibly new activities to include propaganda, black operations, surfacing of intelligence or disinformation, personal contacts, or anything else your imagination can conjure ..."

"EYES ONLY" "RESTRICTED HANDLING" "SECRET"
message from CIA headquarters to US station chief in Santiago, October 16, 1970

"SUB-MACHINE GUNS AND AMMO BEING SENT BY REGULAR COURIER LEAVING WASHINGTON 0700 HOURS 19 OCTOBER DUE ARRIVE SANTIAGO ..."
message from CIA, October 18, 1970

You would be wrong to assume this plan for mayhem had anything to do with a cold war between the Free World and communism. Much more was at stake: Pepsi-Cola's market share and other matters closer to the heart of corporate America.

In exclusive interviews with the *Observer*, the US Ambassador to Chile at the time, Edward Malcolm Korry, interpreted these and other chilling CIA, State Department and White House top secret cables obtained by the National Security Archives. Korry literally filled in the gaps, describing cables still classified and providing information censored by black lines in the documents made available under the US Freedom of Information Act.

Korry, an ambassador who served Presidents Kennedy, Johnson and Nixon, gives a picture of US companies, from cola to copper, using the CIA as a kind of international collection agency and investment security force.

Indeed, the October 1970 plot against Chile's president-elect Salvador Allende, using CIA "sub-machine guns and ammo", was the direct result of a plea for action one month earlier by Donald M. Kendall, chairman of the Board of PepsiCo, in two phone calls to Pepsi's former lawyer, President Richard Nixon. Kendall arranged for the owner of the company's Chilean bottling operation to meet National Security Adviser Henry Kissinger on September 15. Some hours later, Nixon called in his CIA chief, Richard Helms, and, according to Helms's handwritten notes, ordered the CIA to prevent Allende's inauguration.

But this is only half the picture, according to Korry. He revealed the US conspiracy to block Allende's election did not begin with Nixon, but originated – and read no further if you cherish the myth of Camelot – with John Kennedy. In 1963, Allende was heading toward victory in Chile's presidential election. Kennedy decided his own political creation, Eduardo Frei (the late father of

Chile's current president) could win the election by buying it. The president left it to his brother Bobby Kennedy to put the plan into motion.

The Kennedys cajoled US multinationals to pour $2 billion into Chile – a nation of only eight million people. This was not benign investment, but what Korry calls "a mutually corrupting" web of business deals, many questionable, for which the US government would arrange guarantees and insurance. In return, the American-based firms kicked back millions of dollars toward Frei's election. This foreign cash paid for well over half of Frei's successful campaign.

By the end of this process, Americans had gobbled up more than 85 per cent of Chile's hard-currency earning industries. The US government, on the hook as guarantor of these investments, committed extraordinary monetary, intelligence and political resources for their protection. Several business-friendly US government fronts and operatives were sent into Chile – including the American Institute for Free Labor Development, infamous for sabotaging militant trade unions.

Then, in 1970, US investments both financial and political faced unexpected jeopardy. A split between Chile's center and right-wing political parties permitted a Communist-Socialist-Radical alliance, led by Salvador Allende, to win a plurality of the presidential vote.

That October, Korry, a hardened anti-communist, hatched an admittedly off-the-wall scheme to block Allende's inauguration and return Frei to power. To promote his own bloodless intrigues, the Ambassador says he "back-channelled" a message to Washington warning against military actions which might lead to "another Bay of Pigs" fiasco. (Korry retains a copy of this still-classified cable.)

But Korry's prescient message only angered Kissinger, who had already authorized the Pepsi-instigated coup, scheduled for the following week. Kissinger ordered Korry to fly in secret to Washington that weekend for a dressing down.

Still clueless about the CIA plan, Korry, now in a White House corridor, told Kissinger that "only a madman" would plot with Chile's ultra-right generals. As if on cue, Kissinger opened the door to the Oval Office to introduce Nixon.

Nixon once described Korry, his ambassador, as "soft in the head", yet agreed with Korry's conclusion that, tactically, a coup could not succeed. A last-minute cable to the CIA in Santiago to delay action was too late: the conspirators kidnapped and killed Chile's pro-democracy Armed Forces Chief, Rene Schneider. The Chilean public did not know of Nixon's CIA having armed the general's killers. Nevertheless, public revulsion at this crime assured Allende's confirmation as president by the Chilean Congress.

Even if Nixon's sense of Realpolitik may have disposed him to a *modus vivendi* with Allende (Korry's alternative if his Frei gambit failed), Nixon faced intense pressure from his political donors in the business community who had panicked over Allende's plans to nationalize their operations.

In particular, the president was aware that the owner of Chile's phone company, ITT Corporation, was channelling funds – illegally – into Republican

Party coffers. Nixon was in no position to ignore ITT's wants – and ITT wanted blood. An ITT board member, John McCone, pledged Kissinger $1 million in support of CIA action to prevent Allende from taking office. McCone was the perfect messenger: he had served as director of the CIA under Kennedy and Johnson.

Separately, Anaconda Copper and other multinationals, under the aegis of David Rockefeller's Business Group for Latin America, offered $500,000 to buy influence with Chilean congressmen to reject confirmation of Allende's electoral victory. But Ambassador Korry wouldn't play. While he knew nothing of the ITT demands on the CIA, he got wind of, and vetoed, the cash for pay-offs from the Anaconda gang.

Over several days of phone interviews from his home in Charlotte, North Carolina, Korry revealed, among other things, that he even turned in to Chilean authorities an army major who planned to assassinate Allende – unaware of the officer's connection to the CIA's plotters.

Once Allende took office, Korry sought accommodation with the new government, conceding that expropriations of the telephone and copper concessions (actually begun under Frei) were necessary to disentangle Chile from seven decades of "incestuous and corrupting" dependency. US corporations didn't see it that way. While pretending to bargain in good faith with Allende on the buy-out of their businesses, they pushed the White House to impose a clandestine embargo of Chile's economy.

But in case all schemes failed, ITT – charges Korry – paid $500,000 to someone their intercepted cables called "The Fat Man". Korry identified The Fat Man as Jacobo Schaulsohn, Allende's ally on the compensation committee.

It was not money well spent. In 1971, when Allende learned of the corporate machinations against his government, he refused compensation for expropriated property. It was this – Allende's failure to pay, not his allegiance to the hammer and sickle – which sealed his fate.

In October 1971, the State Department pulled Korry out of Santiago. But he had one remaining chore regarding Chile. On his return to the US, Korry advised the government's Overseas Private Investment Corporation to deny Anaconda Copper and ITT compensation for their properties seized by Allende.

Korry argued that, like someone who burns down their own home, ITT could not claim against insurance for an expropriation the company itself provoked by violating Chilean law. Confidentially, he recommended that the US Attorney General bring criminal charges against ITT's top brass, including, implicitly, the company's buccaneer CEO Harold Geneen, for falsifying the insurance claims and lying to Congress.

Given powerful evidence against the companies, OPIC at first refused them compensation – and the Justice Department indicted two mid-level ITT operatives for perjury. But ultimately, the companies received their money and the executives went free on the not unreasonable defense that they were working with the full knowledge and cooperation of the CIA – and higher.

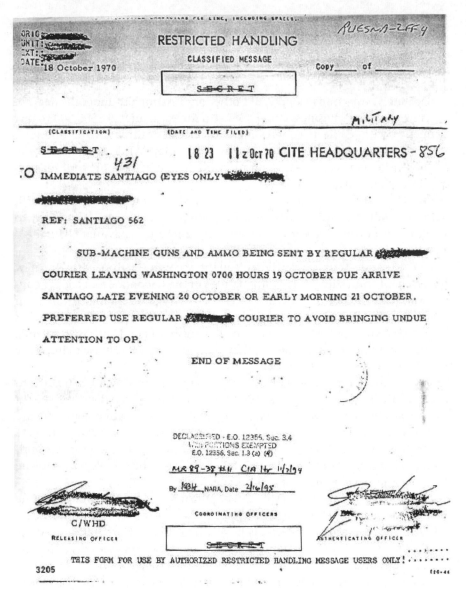

Figure 10. In the fall of 1970, the CIA planned to prevent Salvadore Allende from taking office as President of Chile, by assassinating Allende if necessary. The US Ambassador to Chile, Edward Malcolm Korry, told me he got wind of plot from the British Ambassador, angered by the move to overthrow the democracy. ("All of Latin American probably needed to go through Communism for twenty years," one State Department cable reports the Briton as saying.) Korry blew apart the coup scheme – ordered, he tells me, by Richard Nixon and Henry Kissinger – by Korry's turning in the would-be assassin to the Chilean government. The CIA's attempt, hobbled, went ahead, but backfired, when the plotters killed the democratically-minded head of Chile's armed forces, thereby guaranteeing the Chilean Congress's confirmation of Allende's election. This CIA cable was obtained by the National Security Archive.

In September 1970, in a secret cable to the US Secretary of State, Ambassador Korry quotes Jean Genet, "Even if my hands were full of truths, I wouldn't open it for others." Why open his hand now? At the age of 77, one supposes there is the tempting, though impossible, desire to correct history. The old diplomat himself says only that it is important to take out of the shadows what he calls – a bit optimistically – the last case of US "dollar diplomacy".

And the Ignoble Prize in Chemistry Goes to ...

In May 1999 a cache of documents fell out of a low-flying aeroplane and on to my desk. However they ended up in my possession, they certainly came by an interesting route: from the files of WTO food safety regulators where they had been filched by US functionaries and passed under the table to Monsanto Corporation. This was fresh evidence of a dangerous new epidemic: the infection of science by corporate cash.

Thirty-seven per cent of Americans over the age of 15 find sexual intercourse painful, difficult to perform or plain just don't feel like doing it. Who says so? Doctors Edward Laumann and Raymond Rosen, that's who. And because they said it in *JAMA*, the prestigious Journal of the American Medical Association, the story had enough white-lab-coat credibility to pop up in every US newspaper suffering from Monica Lewinsky withdrawal pains.

Oh, did I forget to mention that the study's authors previously worked for Pfizer, maker of Viagra? *JAMA* forgot to mention it as well.

Maybe you don't care whether Americans are hot or not. But contamination by cash affects research on several other organs. Calcium channel blocking drugs reduce the risk of heart disease. But they may have an unfortunate side-effect: they could give you a heart attack. But don't worry: an avalanche of learned articles in medical journals vouch for the drugs' safety and efficacy. *Now* worry: according to an investigation by the *New England Journal of Medicine*, 100 per cent of the scientists supporting the drugs received financial benefits from pharmaceutical companies, 96 per cent from the manufacturers of these channel blockers. Only two out of 70 articles disclosed drug company ties to authors' bank accounts.

Surreptitiously putting a hunk of the scientific community on its payroll can help a manufacturer win government approval for human and animal drugs. But when suborning conflicts of interest fails to do the trick, one US manufacturer, Monsanto Company, turns to more proactive means of influencing regulators.

The *Observer* had received copies of letters, memoranda and meeting notes indicating that Monsanto obtained crucial restricted documents from a key international regulatory committee investigating the company's controversial bovine growth hormone, called BST. A shot of BST boosts a cow's milk output. But European and American experts say BST has such yummy side-effects as increasing the amount of pus in milk, promoting infection in cow udders and potentially increasing the risk of breast and prostate cancer in humans who drink BST-laced milk.

According to an internal Canadian health ministry memo dated November 1997, Monsanto got its hands on advance copies of three volumes of position papers intended for review in closed meetings of the UN World Health Organization's Joint Experts Committee on Food Additives. This is one valuable set of documents. The European Community's ban on the genetically altered hormone was set to expire in 1999. The Experts Committee advises the international commission which votes whether to add Monsanto BST to something called the Codex Alimentarius, the international list of approved food additives. Codex listing would make it difficult for nations to block imports of BST-boosted foods.

Monsanto's cache included confidential submissions by the EC's Directors General for food and agriculture as well as analysis by British pharmacologist John Verrall.

I spoke with Verrall just after he learned his commentary was passed to Monsanto. Verrall was stunned not just by selective release of reports he believed confidential – participants sign non-disclosure statements about the proceedings – but by the source of the leak. The memo identifies Monsanto's conduit from the UN experts' committee as Dr Nick Weber of the US Food and Drug Administration (FDA). Dr Weber, it turns out, works at the FDA under the supervision of Margaret Miller. Dr Miller, before joining government, headed a Monsanto laboratory studying and promoting BST.

After scouring the purloined Committee documents, Monsanto faxed a warning to company allies in government that one participant on the Experts Committee, Dr Michael Hansen, "is not completely on board". Indeed he was not. Hansen was furious. A BST expert with the Consumers' Policy Institute, Washington, Hansen interprets the memos to mean that some US and Canadian authorities, supposedly acting as objective, unaffiliated scientists, were in fact working in cahoots with Monsanto as advocates for the producer.

Other memos discuss plans by US and Canadian officials sympathetic to Monsanto, to "share their communication strategy" with industry. The plan was to lobby members of the Experts Committee. Monsanto would secretly provide help in preparing a response to critics of BST ahead of the vote of the experts panel scheduled for February 1998. Whether the scheme using inside information affected the outcome, we don't know. We do know Monsanto won that vote.

Because proceedings were confidential, we cannot know how a majority overcame objections of known dissenters. But we can presume Monsanto was not harmed by the late addition of BST defender Dr Len Ritter to the deliberations. An intra-office memo obtained from Canada's Bureau of Veterinary Drugs states that Dr Ritter's name was subtly suggested to the bureau's director in an August 1997 phone call from Dr David Kowalczyk, Monsanto's regulatory affairs honcho.

Of course, there is not much value to Monsanto in obtaining government approvals to sell BST-laden milk if no one will buy the stuff. Luckily for Monsanto, the US FDA not only refuses to require labelling hormone-laced products, but in 1994 published a rule which effectively barred dairies from printing "BST-free" on milk products. This strange milk carton exception to America's Bill of Rights was signed by Michael Taylor, deputy to the FDA Commissioner. Prior to joining the US agency, Taylor practiced law with the firm of King & Spalding, where he represented Monsanto. Taylor, no longer in

Ian Alexander
18/11/97 11:16 AM

To: Ruth Swinimer
cc: Donald Landry, Mansen Yong
Subject: Conversation with Monsanto

I received a call from David Kowalczyk, Monsanto U.S. this morning. He had Keith MacMillan from Monsanto Canada with him.

Dr. Kowalczyk indicated that he had received a copy of the JECFA package for review from Dr. Nick Weber from CVM. He will send a copy to us overnight. He will fax today copies of the AMA positions and various other positions statements.

Dr. Kowalczyk inquired about the meeting with DFC. I indicated that the meeting with DFC was delayed for probably another month. I indicated that the interdepartmental working group on rbST was working on a Communications Strategy and that the group wanted to complete this before meeting with the industry group again.

I explained that the meetings were initiated with DFC as a forum for them to present their position. I explained that there were plans for the Federal government to share a their communication strategy with industry, however, this would come after the various departments of the Federal government had agreed.

I indicated that there was some suggestion that the next meeting would happen on December 16 and that it was the opinion of the interdepartmental group that Monsanto should be invited. Drs Kowalczyk and MacMillan indicated that their interest in attending. They also expressed that they would like to meet with Health Canada prior to that meeting.

I indicated that I hoped to complete the efficacy review shortly and perhaps by that time we might be able to give them an update. It was suggested that we could meet with them sometime during the week of December 8.

I gave them a "heads up" about the request for methodology for measuring rbST in serum. Dr. Kowalczyk indicated that there is no methodology presently for measuring the variants of bst. The method that was developed had too much cross reactivity and was to cumbersome to be reliable and practical. I suggested that they will receive a formal request in the near future and that a full written explanation would be desirable.

Dr. MacMillan asked that we come forward with proposed meeting dates as soon as we are able.

Figure 11. The public rarely gets to see the evidence of the corporate fix in action. Here, Ian Alexander, a Canadian health ministry official, wrote a memo about his call from Dr David Kowalczyk, Monsanto Corporation's lobbyist on genetically-engineered products. "Dr. Kowalczyk indicated that he had received a copy of the JECFA package" – a set of documents, supposedly confidential, of the international health regulatory agency (JECFA), which raised doubts about the safety of Monsanto's genetically modified hormone, BST. The leak to the corporation says the memo, was from none other than Nick Weber of "CVM", an arm of the US Food and Drug Administration.

government, did not return our calls to his office at his current employer – Monsanto Washington.

Monsanto does not just *place* friends in government, it likes to *make* friends. Canadian Health Ministry researcher Dr Margaret Haydon told me Monsanto offered her bureau $1–2 million in a 1994 meeting in return for their authorizing the sale of BST. Monsanto counters the funds were proffered solely to support the cash-strapped agency's research. When asked if he considered the Monsanto offer "a bribe", Haydon's supervisor replied, "Certainly!" though he said he laughed off the proposal.

No one's laughing now. Haydon and five other government scientists filed an extraordinary plea with Canada's industrial tribunal seeking protection for their jobs and careers. They fear retaliation for ripping the cover off long-hidden, highly damaging facts about BST. America's rush to approve the hormone in 1993 rested on a study published in the journal *Science* by FDA researchers, which concluded there were no "significant changes" in BST-fed rats. The rats tell a different tale. Their autopsies revealed thyroid cysts, prostate problems and signs of BST invading their blood. The Monsanto-sponsored US researchers failed to publish these facts and the FDA sealed the full study, saying its public release would "irreparably harm" Monsanto. Indeed it would.

The Canadian scientists, finally winning access to the full study, blew the whistle on the rat cover-up. The facts became public via their labor board action, a decade after the original, misleading report. By then BST had received US FDA approval as safe.

I regret singling out Monsanto if only because I'm left with so little room to honour other corporate nominees for the Ignoble Prize in Chemistry. BST expert John Verrall, a member of the UK Food Ethics Council, says the Monsanto episode only illustrates a trend in which "Multinational corporations have let morals slide down the scale of priorities." He concludes – in what must be a sly reference to Monica Lewinsky – "The white coat of science has been stained."

A Well-Designed Disaster: The Untold Story of the *Exxon Valdez*

On March 24, 1989, The Exxon Valdez *broke open and covered 1,200 miles of Alaska's shoreline with oily sludge.*

The land smeared and destroyed belongs to the Chugach Natives of the Prince William Sound, the last people in America who lived substantially off what they hunt and catch. Within days of the spill, the Chugach tribal corporation asked me to investigate allegations of fraud by Exxon and the little known "Alyeska" consortium. In three years' digging, my team followed a 20-year train of doctored safety records, illicit deals between oil company chiefs and programmatic harassment of witnesses. And we documented the oil majors' brilliant success in that old American sport, cheating the Natives. Our summary of evidence ran to four volumes.

Virtually none of it was reported. The official story remains "Drunken Skipper Hits Reef". Don't believe it.

In fact, when the ship hit, Joe Hazelwood was not near the wheel, but below decks, sleeping off his bender. The man left at the helm, the Third Mate, would never have hit Bligh Reef had he simply looked at his Raycas radar. But he could not, because the radar *was not turned on*. The complex Raycas system costs a lot to operate, so frugal Exxon management left it broken and useless for the entire year before the grounding.

There's more to the *Exxon Valdez* story you've never been told.

- "Alyeska" is the six-company oil group that owns the pipeline and runs the tankers. We discovered an internal memo describing a secret, top-level meeting of the group in Arizona held just ten months before the spill. There, the chief of their Valdez Operations, Theo Polasek, warned executives that it was "not possible" to contain an oil spill in the center of the Prince William Sound – exactly where the *Exxon Valdez* grounded. Polasek needed millions of dollars for spill-containment equipment. The law required it, the companies promised it to regulators, then at the meeting, the proposed spending was voted down.
- Smaller spills before the *Exxon* disaster could have alerted government watchdogs that the port's oil spill-containment system was not up to scratch. But the oil group's lab technician, Erlene Blake, told me that management routinely ordered her to change test results to eliminate "oil-in-water" readings. The procedure was simple, says Blake. She was told to dump out oily water and re-fill test tubes from a bucket of cleansed sea water, which they called "The Miracle Barrel".
- A confidential letter dated April 1984, fully four years before the big spill, written by Captain James Woodle, then the oil group's Valdez Port commander, warns management that, "Due to a reduction in manning, age of equipment, limited training and lack of personnel, serious doubt exists that [we] would be able to contain and clean up effectively a medium or large size oil spill." Woodle told me there was a spill at Valdez *before* the *Exxon* collision, though not nearly as large. When he prepared to report it to the government, his supervisor forced him to take back the notice, with the Orwellian command, "You made a mistake. This was not an oil spill."

The canard of the alcoholic captain has provided effective camouflage for British Petroleum's involvement in the environmental catastrophe that *Exxon Valdez* caused. Alaska's oil is BP oil. The company owns and controls a majority of the Alaska pipeline system. Exxon is a junior partner, and four others are just along for the ride. Captain Woodle, Technician Blake, Vice-President Polasek, all worked for BP's Alyeska.

When it comes to oil spills, the name of the game is "containment" because, radar or not, some tanker somewhere will hit the rocks. Failure to contain the *Exxon Valdez* spreading oil is what destroyed the coastline.

Quite naturally, British Petroleum has never rushed to have its name associated with Alyeska's destructive recklessness. But BP's London headquarters, I discovered, learned of the alleged falsification of reports to the US government *nine years* before the spill. In September 1984, independent oil shipper Charles Hamel of Washington DC, shaken by evidence he received from Alyeska employees, told me he took the first available Concorde, at his own expense, to warn BP executives in London about scandalous goings-on in Valdez. Furthermore, Captain Woodle swears he personally delivered his list of missing equipment and "phantom" personnel directly into the hands of BP's Alaska chief, George Nelson.

BP has never been eager for Woodle's letter, Hamel's London trip and many other warnings of the deteriorating containment system to see the light of day. When Alyeska got wind of Woodle's complaints, they responded by showing Woodle a file of his marital infidelities (all bogus), then offered him pay-outs on condition that he leave the state within days, promising never to return.

As to Hamel, the oil shipping broker, BP in London thanked him. Then a secret campaign was launched to hound him out of the industry. A CIA expert was hired who wiretapped Hamel's phone lines. They smuggled microphones into his home, intercepted his mail and tried to entrap him with young women. The industrial espionage caper was personally ordered and controlled by BP executive James Hermiller, president of Alyeska. On this caper, they were caught. A US federal judge told Alyeska this conduct was "reminiscent of Nazi Germany".

BP's inglorious role in the Alaskan oil game began in 1969 when the oil group bought the most valuable real estate in all Alaska, the Valdez oil terminal land, from the Chugach Natives. BP and the Alyeska group paid the natives *one dollar*.

Arthur Goldberg, once a US Supreme Court Justice, tried to help the Natives on their land claim. But the Natives' own lawyer, the state's most powerful legislator, advised them against pressing for payment. Later, he became Alyeska's lawyer.

The Natives, who lived off what they hunted and caught, did extract written promises from the oil consortium to keep the Prince William Sound safe from oil spills. These wilderness seal hunters and fishermen knew the arctic sea. They demanded that tankers carry state-of-the-art radar and that emergency vessels escort the tankers. The oil companies put all this in their government approved 1973 Oil Spill Response Plan.

Yet, when the tanker struck Bligh Reef, the spill equipment – which could have prevented the catastrophe – wasn't there. (An Alyeska honcho said he was afraid the natives would steal it.) The promised escort ships were not assigned to ride with the tankers until *after* the spill. And the night the *Exxon Valdez* grounded, the emergency spill-response barge which carries oil-containment barriers and pumps was sitting in a dry dock in Valdez locked in ice. We found letters to the government from the oil companies swearing, just before the spill, they would not ship oil unless the emergency barge was in the water, ready to go.

When the pipeline opened in 1974, the law required Alyeska to maintain round-the-clock oil spill response teams. As part of the come-on to get hold of the Chugach's Valdez property, Alyeska hired the natives for this emergency work. The Natives practiced leaping out of helicopters into icy water, learning to surround leaking boats with rubber barriers. But the Natives soon found they were assigned to cover up spills, not clean them up. Their foreman, David Decker, told me he was expected to report one oil spill as two gallons when 2,000 gallons had spilled.

Alyeska kept the Natives at the terminal for two years – long enough to help break the strike of the dock workers union – then quietly sacked the entire team. To deflect inquisitive inspectors looking for the spill teams, Alyeska created sham emergency teams, listing names of oil terminal workers who had not the foggiest idea how to use spill equipment, which, in any event, was missing, broken or existed only on paper. When the *Exxon Valdez* grounded, there was no Native spill crew, only chaos.

Nearly a decade ago, a jury ordered Exxon to pay $5 billion, though the petroleum giant stalls payment through legal maneuvers. The BP-led Alyeska consortium was able to settle all claims for 2 per cent of the acknowledged damage, roughly a $50 million pay-out, fully covered by an insurance fund.

The Fable of the Drunken Skipper has served the oil industry well. It transforms the most destructive oil spill in history into a tale of human frailty, a terrible, but one-time, accident. But broken radar, missing equipment, phantom spill personnel, faked tests – all of it to cut costs and lift bottom lines – made the spill disaster not an accident but an inevitability.

I went back to the Sound just before the tenth anniversary of the spill. On Chenega, they were preparing to spend another summer scrubbing rocks. A decade after the spill, in one season, they pulled 20 tons of sludge off their beaches. At Nanwalek village ten years on, the state again declared the clams inedible, poisoned by "persistent hydrocarbons". Salmon still carry abscesses and tumours, the herring never returned and the sea lion rookery at Montague Island remains silent and empty.

But despite what my eyes see, I must have it wrong, because right here in an Exxon brochure it says, "The water is clean and plant, animal and sea life are healthy and abundant."

Today

Go to the Sound today, on Chugach land, kick over a rock and it smells like a gas station. As to my four-volume summary of evidence of frauds committed

Figure 12. Nanwalek, Alaska. Oil from the *Exxon Valdez* destroyed the fish and wildlife on which these Chugach Native Alaskans survived. The village was under attack from Exxon's oil, then Exxon's money. The money disappeared, but the oil remains in the rocky estuaries, more than a decade after the spill. Here, Lisa Moonan, one of the leaders of the women's revolt, performs the Seal Dance. (© James Macalpine)

against the Natives: in 1991, when herring failed to appear and fishing in the Sound collapsed, the tribal corporation went bankrupt and my files became, effectively, useless.

Coda: Nanwalek Rocks

A longer version of the following story was nearly censored out of Index on Censorship. *The magazine had hired a guest editor for the "Tribes" issue, an amateur anthropologist. He'd been to the same group of Alaskan villages where I worked. The Natives performed their special ceremony for him. Among themselves they call it "Putting on the feathers", in which they provide those quaint and expected lines which so please the earnest white men with 16 mm Airflex cameras and digital tape recorders.*

He wrote down "healing poems" about "our friend the bear". I imagined him with helmet and pukka shorts preserving in his leather notebook the words of the ancient, wizened Injuns. Stanley Livingstone meets Pocahontas.

It was my terrible, self-inflicted misfortune to spoil this delicate idyll of the Noble Savage by my reporting that Alaskan Natives are, in fact, very much like us, if not more so.

At the far side of Alaska's Kenai Fjord glacier, a heavily armed and musically original rock-and-roll band held lock-down control of the politics and treasury of Nanwalek, a Chugach Native village, when I first went to work there in 1989.

According to not-so-old legend, rock came to the remote enclave at the bottom of Prince William Sound in the 1950s when Chief Vincent Kvasnikoff found an electric guitar washed up on the beach. By the next morning, he had mastered the instrument sufficiently to perform passable covers of Elvis tunes. Of all the lies the Natives told me over the years, this one, from the Chief himself, seemed the most benign.

We sat in the Chief's kitchen facing an elaborate Orthodox altar. Russian icons spread the length of the wall. It was a golden day, late summer at the end of the salmon run, but the Chief's 18-year-old nephew hung out in the bungalow watching a repeating loop of Fred Astaire movies on the satellite TV.

Fishing was just excellent, the Chief assured me. He'd taken twelve seals that year. I didn't challenge the old man, legless in his wheelchair. Everyone knew he'd lost his boat when the bank repossessed his commercial fishing licence. The village once had eight commercial boats, now it had three. Besides, all the seal had been poisoned eight years earlier, in 1989, by Exxon's oil.

It took an entire month for the oil slick from the *Exxon Valdez* to reach Nanwalek. Despite the known, unrelenting advance of the oil sheet, Exxon had not provided even simple rubber barriers to protect the inlets to the five lakes that spawned the salmon and fed the razor clams, sea lions, bidarki snails, seals and people of the isolated village on the ice. But when the oil did arrive, followed by television crews, Exxon put virtually the entire populace of 270 on its payroll.

"The place went wild," Lisa Moonan told me. "They gave us rags and buckets, $16-something an hour to wipe off rocks, to baby-sit our own children." In this roadless village that had survived with little cash or store-bought food, the Chief's sister told me, "They flew in frozen pizza, satellite dishes. Guys who were on sobriety started drinking all night, beating up their wives. I mean, all that money. Man, people just went berserk."

With the catch dead, the banks took the few boats they had, and Chief Vincent's sister, Sally Kvasnikoff Ash, watched the village slide into an alcohol- and drug-soaked lethargy. Sally said, "I felt like my skin was peeling off." Nanwalek's natives call themselves Sugestoon, Real People. "After the oil I thought, this is it. We're over. Sugestoon, we're gone unless something happens."

Sally made something happen. In August 1995, the village women swept the all-male tribal council from office in an electoral coup plotted partly in the native tongue, which the men had forgotten. Sally, who's Sugestoon name Aqniaqnaq means "First Sister", would have become Chief if Vincent, she says, hadn't stolen two votes. The rockers, Chief Vincent's sons, were out – so was booze (banned), fast food and the band's party nights in accordance with the new women's council cultural revolutionary diktats. The women returned Native language to the school and replaced at least some of Kvasnikoff's all-night jam sessions, which had a tendency to end in drunken brawls, with performances of the traditional Seal and Killer Whale dances.

They put the village on a health food regime. "We're fat," says First Sister, who blames the store-bought diet which, since the spill, must be flown in twice-weekly from city supermarkets. To show they meant business on the alcohol ban, the women arrested and jailed Sally's disabled Uncle Mack for bringing a six-pack of beer into the village on his return from the hospital.

* * *

On Good Friday 1964, the snow-peaked mountains of Montague Island rose 26 feet in the air, then dropped back twelve feet, sending a tidal wave through the Prince William Sound. At the village of Chenega, Chugach seal hunter Nikolas Kompkoff ran his four daughters out of their stilt house, already twisted to sticks by the earthquake, and raced up an ice-covered slope. Just before the wall of water overcame them, he grabbed the two girls closest, one child under each arm, ran ahead, then watched his other two daughters wash out into the Sound.

Chenega disappeared. Not one of their homes, not even the sturdier church, remained. A third of the Natives drowned. Survivors waited for two days until a postal pilot remembered the remote village.

Over the following 20 years, Chenegans scattered across the Sound, some to temporary huts in other Chugach villages, others to city life in Anchorage. But every Holy Week, these families sailed to the old village, laid crosses on the decaying debris, and Kompkoff would announce another plan to rebuild. Over the years, as the prospect of a New Chenega receded into improbability, Nikolas became, in turn, an Orthodox priest, a notorious alcoholic and failed suicide. He survived a self-inflicted gun shot to the head. He was defrocked for the attempt.

In 1982, Nikolas convinced his nephew, Larry Evanoff, to spend his life savings building a boat that could traverse the Sound.

Evanoff has four long scars across his torso. These wounds from Vietnam helped him get a government job as an air traffic controller in Anchorage, but he was fired when his union went on strike. Larry had lost both his parents in the earthquake.

Larry's boat was not finished until the sub-arctic winter had set in. Nevertheless, he sailed to remote Evans Island with his wife and two children, aged 9 and 14. They built a cabin and, for two years, without phone or short-wave radio, 100 miles from any road, lived off nearby seal, bear and salmon while they cleared the land for New Chenega. Over the next seven years, 26 of Chenega's refugee families joined the Evanoffs, built their own homes and, with scrap wood from an abandoned herring saltery, built a tiny church with a blue roof for Nikolas, whom they still called "Father".

On March 24, 1989, the village commemorated the twenty-fifth anniversary of the tidal wave. That night, the *Exxon Valdez* oil tanker ran aground and killed the fish, smothered the clam beds and poisoned all the seal on which Chenegans subsisted.

In mid-century, the average life expectancy for Chugach Natives was 38 years. They had next to nothing by way of cash and the state moved to take even that away. In the 1970s, new "limited entry" laws barred them from selling the catch from their traditional fishing grounds unless they purchased permits few could afford. The Natives did have tenuous ownership of wilderness, villages and campsites. In 1969, America's largest oil deposit was discovered on Alaska's north slope. The Chugach campsite on Valdez harbour happened to be the only place on the entire Alaska coast that could geologically support an oil tanker terminal. Their strip of land grew in value to tens or even hundreds of millions of dollars. In June of that year, Chief Vincent's father Sarjius representing Nanwalek and Father Nikolas representing the non-existent Chenega agreed to sell Valdez to British Petroleum and Humble Oil (later called "Exxon") – for one dollar.

The Alaskan Natives could not afford to hire legal counsel, so they were truly grateful when Clifford Groh, head of Alaska's Republican Party and the most powerful attorney in Alaska, volunteered to represent them without charge against the oil companies. Some months after signing the one dollar sale of Valdez, Groh took on work representing his biggest client yet, "Alyeska", the Exxon-BP oil pipeline consortium.

But before he was done with the Chugach, Groh transformed them utterly and forever. No longer would Chugach be a tribe. Groh incorporated them.

The tribe became Chugach Corporation. The villages became Chenega Corporation and English Bay (Nanwalek) Corporation. The chiefs' powers were taken over by corporate presidents and CEOs, tribal councils by Boards of Directors. The Sound's natives, once tribe members, became shareholders – at least for a few years until the stock was sold, bequeathed, dispersed. Today, only eleven of Chenega's 69 shareholders live in the island. Most residents are tenants of a corporation whose last annual meeting was held in Seattle, 2,000 miles from the island.

I first met the president of Chenega Corporation, Charles "Chuck" Totemoff, soon after the spill when he missed our meeting to negotiate with Exxon. I found the twenty-something wandering the village's dirt pathway in soiled jeans, stoned and hung over, avoiding the corporate "office", an old cabin near the fishing dock.

Years later, I met up with Chuck at Chenega Corporation's glass and steel office tower in downtown Anchorage. The stern, long-sober and determined executive sat behind a mahogany desk and unused laptop computer. Instead of photos of the village, a huge map of Chenega's property covered the wall, color-coded for timber logging, real estate subdivision and resort development. He had penned a multi-million dollar terminal services agreement with the Exxon-BP pipeline consortium. For Chenega island, a 46-room hotel was in the works.

In 1997, I returned to Chenega. It was the worst possible day for a visit. Larry was out on "pad patrol", leading a Native crew cleaning up tons of toxic crude oil still oozing out of Sleepy Bay eight years after the *Exxon Valdez* grounding. They'd already lost a day of work that week for Frankie Gursky's funeral, an 18-year-old who had shot himself after a drink-fuelled fight with his grandmother.

Larry and his team continued to scour the oil off the beach, his family's old fishing ground, but it wasn't theirs any more. The day before, the Corporation had sold it, along with 90 per cent of Chenega's lands, to an Exxon-BP trust for $23 million.

"Corporation can't sell it," Larry said, when I told him about the check transfer. "People really can't own land." He rammed a hydraulic injector under the beach shingle and pumped in biological dispersants. "The land was always here. We're just passing through. We make use of it, then we just pass it on."

Nanwalek also sold. Chief Vincent's son, leader of the rock band and director of the corporate board, arranged, just before his death from AIDS, to sell 50 per cent of the village land to an Exxon trust.

I was in Corporate President Totemoff's office the day Exxon wired in the $23 million. When Totemoff moved out of the village, he announced, "I hope I never have to see this place again." Now he doesn't have to. I asked Chuck if, like some city-dwelling natives, he had his relatives ship him traditional foods. "Seal meat?" He grinned. "Ever smell that shit? Give me a Big Mac any time."

California Reamin': Hunting the Power Pirates from Pakistan to the Golden Gate, the Untold Story of Electricity Deregulation

On April 10, 1989, Jacob "Jake" Horton, senior vice-president of Southern Company's Gulf Power Unit, boarded the company jet to confront his Board of Directors over accusations of illegal payments to local politicians. Minutes after take-off, the plane exploded. Later that day, police received an anonymous call, "You can stop investigating Gulf Power now."

I had just begun my own investigation of Southern Company for a Georgia consumer organization which would lay the foundation for a series of screeds in the Guardian, New York Times, Washington Post, La Republica (Peru) *and* Financial Times *on the deregulation of the power markets worldwide. Here's the latest.*

Just before George W. Bush took office in 2001, the lights in San Francisco blinkered out. Wholesale electricity prices in California rose on some days by 7,000 per cent. San Francisco's power company declared bankruptcy. Within days of his inauguration, the new president declared an "energy crisis" and proposed laws to wipe away all regulation, economic and environmental, on electricity markets. At first, it was billed as the magic potion to end black-outs; then after the horrors of September 11, 2001, Bush's energy plan was remarketed as a weapon against Middle East terrorists. Alternatively, nasty-minded readers may believe the president's energy program is just some pea-brained scheme to pay off his oil company buddies, fry the planet and smother Mother Earth in coal ash, petroleum pollutants and nuclear waste. In truth, it's more devious than that.

Under the polluters' wet-dream of an energy plan lies the mystical economics of "electricity deregulation". And behind the smoke of this odd backwater of market theory is a multi-continental war over the ownership and control of $4 trillion in public utility infrastructure, a story that began a decade earlier, with Jake's exploding jet.

In 1989, I was focused on transcripts of Treasury Department tape recordings made a year earlier by accountant Gary Gilman. Wearing a hidden microphone, Gilman recorded his fellow Southern company executives detailing the method by which the company charged customers for $61 million of spare parts which, in fact, had not been used. Like all good accountants, they kept a careful record of the phantom parts in electronic ledgers found in one executive's car. I spent months decoding the accounts, gaining an insight into what would, a decade later, lead to black-outs in 'Frisco and riots in Pakistan.

What you will read now are pieces from several stories on the theory and practice of electricity deregulation. After having seen deregulation eat Britain's electricity consumers alive, it was a no-brainer to predict what it would do to California and elsewhere.

Since the turn of the century, US state governments have kept tight lids on utility monopolies' profits. This regulatory system – uniquely open and democratic – was the legacy of the Populists, an armed and angry farmers' movement whose struggle bequeathed to Americans just about the lowest power prices, and highest service quality electricity service in the world – which is, of course, anathema to power company shareholders. In the 1980s, Southern Company was an unremarkable regional electricity company dying of a thousand financial cuts. Consumer groups demanded rightly that electricity companies, including Southern, eat their investments on foolish nuclear plants. Southern showed nothing but cash losses for years.

What about poor Jake? "He saw no other way out," laments former Southern chairman A.W. "Bill" Dahlberg. Dahlberg, who took over after Horton's death, conceived an unorthodox way out for Southern from its regulatory and financial troubles. The plan: the near-bankrupt local company would take over the entire planet's electricity system and, at the same time, completely eliminate from the face of the earth those pesky utility regulations which had crushed his company's fortunes.

California black-outs are just a hiccup on the road to the astonishing success of this astonishing program.

While America's papers were filled with tales of the woes of the two California electric companies bleeding from $12 billion in payments for electricity supplies, virtually nothing was said of the companies collecting their serum. The biggest sellers and traders in the new California and Western market were Enron of Houston, Reliant of Houston and Southern.

The success on Southern's and the Texans' plan for world power conquest (or, if you prefer, "vision for globalization of energy supplies") hinged on Britain. As Keynes noted, the mad rants of men in authority have their origins in the jottings of some forgotten professor of economics. The professor in question here is Dr Stephen Littlechild. In the 1970s, young Stephen cooked up a scheme to replace British government ownership of utilities with something almost every economist before him said simply violated all accepted theorems: a free market in electricity.

The fact that a truly free market didn't exist and can't possibly work did not stop the woman in authority, Mrs Thatcher, from adopting it. In 1990, Professor Littlechild's market, the England-Wales Power Pool, went into business. On paper, it was an academic beauty to behold. In this auction house for kilowatt hours, private power plant owners would ruthlessly bid against each other to cut electricity prices for British consumers.

I can't say for certain whether the market scheme failed in minutes or days, but the pool quickly became a playground for what the industry calls "gaming" – collusion, price gouging and all sorts of sophisticated means of fleecing captive electricity consumers. Ten years of hapless fixes by Littlechild and his successor have failed to stem the tide of rip-offs at the heart of this unfixable system. At the same time, "deregulated" regional electric companies expertly vacuumed the pockets of captive customers.

From their besieged Atlanta headquarters, Southern's executives learned they could charge in "deregulated" England double the price permitted in Georgia. In 1995, Southern bought up England's South Western Electricity Board. This was the first purchase ever by a US power company outside the US, or even outside its own local service area. The cash rolled in and American operators – seeing the UK industry earn *five times* the profit allowed in the US – soon grabbed the majority of the British electricity sector.

Although Mrs Thatcher's private power market scheme was a poor idea proved worse in practice, the International Monetary Fund and World Bank adopted it as a requirement of every single structural assistance program worldwide. The World Bank's former chief economist, Joe Stiglitz, who once promoted the privatizations for the Bank, told me how their teams would fly into Russia and Asia, preach the wonders of selling electricity markets, "and you could see the wheels turning in the local officials' minds". Here was a means for their corruption "rents" to multiply a thousand fold. The baksheesh flowed and power systems were privatized from Brazil to Pakistan.

US power buccaneers, led by Southern and Texas companies Enron, Reliant and TXU, grabbed plants and wires on every continent save Antarctica.

But not in the US, not at first. America stubbornly exempted itself from neoliberal "reform", and this rankled the new international players. So the industry's lobbyists, like Columbus bringing back Indians for display from the New World, brought Mrs Thatcher's professors and their wheezing free market contraptions to California. In 1996, the state's legislature, inebriated by long draughts of utility political donations, tossed out a regulatory system which, until then, had provided reasonably cheap, clean, reliable energy to the state. Despite the British disaster, the sun-addled legislators wrote into the law itself the lobbyists' slick line that a "deregulated" market would cut consumer prices by 20 per cent.

My parents sent me their light bill from San Diego. Instead of 20 per cent savings, in the first year of deregulation, their energy charges rose 379 per cent. But before the big bills hit, the new planetary power merchants, using a combination of money muscle and America's penchant to follow first-and-best California, suckered 23 other states into adopting deregulation plans.

SCE and PG&E, California's two big regional electricity distribution companies, wrote a price freeze into the law which permitted them to stuff their accounts with $20 billion in extra revenues as oil prices fell. They sold off their plants to traders and generations who used the games learned in England – "stacking", "cramming" and "false scheduling" – to vacuum SCE's and PG&E's pockets clean. The $12 billion in debt owed to Southern Company and the other deregulated sellers bankrupted PG&E – which immediately came running to the governor for a bail-out. They got it. California consumers will now pony up about $35 billion to pay off the speculators and generating companies.

Before their assault on the California beachheads, the power pirates landed in Rio de Janeiro, South America's City of Light. In 1999, I received a postcard from Rio, which was completely black. "Cariocis" (Rio residents) mailed them in protest against Light, Rio's electricity company, now nicknamed "Dark". The federal government privatized Rio Light, selling it to Electricité de France and Reliant of Houston, Texas. The new owners, who had promised improved service, swiftly axed 40 per cent of the company's workforce. Unfortunately, Rio's electricity system is not fully mapped. Rio Light's electricity workers had kept track of the location of wires and transformers in their heads. When they were booted out by the new Franco-Texas owners, the workers took their mental maps with them. Nearly every day, a new neighborhood went dark. The foreign owners blamed El Niño, the weather in the Pacific Ocean. Rio is on the Atlantic.

But for the new foreign owners' consortium, not all was darkness. The windfall from reduced wages and price increases helped the foreign owners hike dividends 1,000 per cent. Rio Light's share price jumped from $300 to $400.

The terms of this asset sell-off are dictated by a hefty document drafted by the US-UK consulting firm of Coopers & Lybrand (now PriceWaterhouseCoopers). While the term "market" is sprinkled throughout, the blueprint is feudal, not capitalist. PriceWaterhouseCoopers divided the nation's saleable infrastructure into legally enforceable monopolies designed to guarantee new, principally foreign, owners super-profits unimpeded by real government control nor by competition. It is patterned on the medieval system of "tax farming" by which, for a one-time payment, kings permitted private tax collectors to pick the peasants clean.

And to whom had the World Bank turned over our energy future? It came down to no more than half a dozen big players. I've introduced you to Southern. The largest power seller identified by the governor of California as a price gouger, the co-owner of Rio Light, was Reliant, known as Houston Power & Light before it globalized.[9] I knew them from reading records of their South Texas nuclear plant. The plant's construction management drilled tiny holes in the ceiling of the workers' locker room and placed three-inch espionage-style cameras to ferret out the disloyal. If they suspected a worker had filed negative safety reports, they were fired: John Rex for blowing the whistle on forged safety inspection documents; Thomas Saporito for exposing security violations; Ron Goldstein for flagging faked welding records. Nice guys.[10]

9 I should be careful what I say about Reliant. The company maintained a file on me, including a fantasmic profile of my sex life far spicier than the mundane reality. In 1999 Reliant handed this filth file "confidentially" to reporters who dared quote me. Nice guys.
10 Other key internationalized power companies besides Reliant include Enron, the largest lifetime donor to George W. Bush's political career and Entergy International of Little Rock, Arkansas, tied to Bill and Hillary Clinton. Interestingly, all three come up in Britain's "Lobbygate" scandal (Chapter 8).

Another one of the big players was Entergy International of Little Rock, Arkansas, once a division of a struggling regional electricity company, which started landing huge projects, including ownership of London Electricity following the election of their home-town boy, Bill Clinton, to the White House. Entergy used their connections to sign deals in China; and Entergy's chairman Dahlberg found Peru attractive after that nation's president shut down the elected congress. "They've got a good stable situation there," said the pleased executive. "Sort of a benevolent dictator, which means good, responsible leadership."

Pakistan looked like another Entergy jackpot when, in 1992, the government of Benezir Bhutto, in a manner most strange, agreed to increase the amount Pakistan's power agency would have to pay for electricity from plants part-owned by Entergy (10 per cent) and Britain's National Power (40 per cent). Then, in 1998, Bhutto lost the election and the new Pakistan government discovered her secret ownership of posh properties in London. Putting her unexplained riches together with the crazy generous deal with the UK-US power companies, the government in October 1988 charged her and the Western consortium with bribery. Pakistan's new government then ended the high payments to the British-American consortium on the internationally accepted rule of law that contracts allegedly obtained by bribery are unenforceable.

Officially, the IMF and World Bank condemn bribery. Nevertheless, within days of Pakistan's filing corruption charges and cutting payments to the accused British-American power combine, the IMF Bank, at Clinton's and Blair's request, threatened to cut off Pakistan's access to international finance.

Panicked by the threat of economic blockade, Pakistan prepared to collect the cash to pay off the UK-US consortium. On December 22, 1998, Pakistan's military sent 30,000 troops into the nation's power stations. Peter Windsor, National Power's Director of International Operations, told me, "A lot changed since the army moved in. Now we have a situation where we can be paid, they've found a way to collect from the man in the street." Yes, *at gunpoint*, trade union lawyer Abdul Latif Nizamani told me after his arrest and release following mass demonstrations. (Windsor vehemently denied the bribery charges.)

With Pakistan's army in control of the nation's infrastructure, and acting as guarantor of payment to the multinationals, General Musharraf's final takeover nine months later – a "surprise coup" to Western press – was, in fact, a foregone conclusion to the power plant dispute.

In the months before he left office, President Clinton flew to Pakistan. Shocked congressmen could not understand why Clinton would meet a military dictator not recognized by the US State Department. The answer was the real item on the agenda: higher electricity prices to pay the questionable contracts with the British-American power group.

That takes us back to California. I looked into the December 2000 black-outs. That month in Southern California the wholesale price of electricity jumped 1,000 per cent over the previous year and the price of natural gas, fuel for the power plants, jumped 1,000 per cent *in one week*. Power shortage? Nope. The California power grid operator reported that, just over the California border at the "Henry Hub" gas pipeline switching center, you could buy plentiful gas for $1 a therm. A couple miles down the pipeline in California, the price was $10.

It turns out two power merchants, which controlled the biggest pipe into California, simply blocked part of the tube. Result: panic, price spikes, black-outs. Market speculators made a half a billion dollars on that cute little maneuver. In all, says a technical report by Dr Anjali Shiffren of the state's grid system, "monopoly rents", "economic withholding" and "physical withholding" were responsible for artificial shortages and excess charges of $6.2 billion in 2000, more in 2001. In other words, California didn't run out of *energy*, it ran out of supplies of *government*.

California's governor then borrowed the billions to pay the power pirates and save local electric companies from liquidation. Consumers will pay off this debt for decades. And that is the true wisdom of the deregulated market-place in electricity: the brilliant method by which profits are privatized and losses socialized.

5

Inside Corporate America

For two decades, we've known the name of the enemy. No matter whether Democrat or Republican, Tory or New Labour, politicians compete for their chance to lash him at the whipping post: the bureaucrat, that paunchy apparatchik *with the thick rule book, his fat bottom spreading behind a paper-choked desk, scheming of ways to pick the pockets of the productive class and get in the way of business doing business. Even government tells us: the enemy is government. Our only chance of rescue is a cavalry of inventive, creative entrepreneurial private sector samurai, especially the new, can-do American corporate eagles.*

Wackenhut Corporation, Monsanto, Enron, Reliant, Novartis. These are a few of the knights errant of the New Order. But as Butch said to Sundance, "Who *are* these guys?" Before we put humanity entirely into their hands and their corporate brothers', it might be wise to better acquaint ourselves with how these organizations, who would govern us better than government, conduct themselves when left to their own devices.

In 1998, I was hired by the *Observer* to do just that in an ongoing series of investigative and analytical reports titled "Inside Corporate America". My mission was to enter the bodies and souls of US-based multinationals, many you've never heard of, who may soon have extraordinary control of your health, your culture and your freedom.

Gilded Cage: Wackenhut's Free Market in Human Misery

New Mexico's privately operated prisons are filled with America's impoverished, violent outcasts – and those are the guards. That's the warning I took away from confidential documents and from guards who spoke nervously and only on condition their names never appear in print.

In 1999, New Mexico rancher Ralph Garcia, his business ruined by drought, sought to make ends meet by signing on as a guard at the state prison at Santa Rosa run by Wackenhut Corporation of Florida. For $7.95 an hour, Garcia watched over medium security inmates at the Wackenhut's complex. Among the "medium security" were multiple murderers, members of a homicidal neo-Nazi cult and the Mexican Mafia gang. Although he had yet to complete his short training course, Garcia was left alone in a cell block with 60 unlocked prisoners. On August 31, 1999, they took the opportunity to run amuck, stab an inmate, then Garcia, several times.

Why was Garcia left alone among the convicts? Let's begin with Wackenhut's cut-rate Jails'R'Us method of keeping costs down by packing two prisoners into each cell and posting one guard to cover an entire "pod" or block of cells. This reverses the ratio in government prisons – two guards per block, one prisoner per cell. Of course, the state's own prisons are not as "efficient" (read "cheap") as the private firm's. But then, the state hasn't lost a guard in 17 years – where Wackenhut hadn't yet operated 17 months.

Sources told me that just two weeks prior to Garcia's stabbing, a senior employee warned corporate honchos the one-guard system is a death-sentence lottery. The executive's response to the complaint, "We'd rather lose one officer than two."

How does Wackenhut get away with it? It cannot hurt that it put Manny Aragon, the state legislature's Democratic leader, on its payroll as a lobbyist and used an Aragon company to supply concrete for the prison's construction. Isn't that illegal? I asked State Senator Cisco McSorley. The Democratic Senator, a lawyer and vice chairman of the legislature's Judiciary Committee, said, "Of course it is," adding a verbal shrug, "Welcome to New Mexico."

Wackenhut agreed to house, feed, guard and educate inmates for $43 a day. But it can't. Even a government as politically corroded as the Enchanted State's realized Wackenhut had taken them for a ride. New Mexico found it had to maintain a costly force of experienced cops at the ready to enter and lock-down prisons every time Wackenhut's inexperienced "green boots" lost control. A riot in April required 100 state police to smother 200 prisoners with tear gas – and arrest one Wackenhut guard who turned violent. The putative savings of privatization went up in smoke, literally.

The state then threatened to bill Wackenhut for costs if the state had to save the company prison again. In market terms, that proved a deadly disincentive for the private company to seek help. On August 31, during a phone check to the prison, state police heard the sounds of chaos in the background. Wackenhut assured the state all was well. By time the company sent out the May Day call two hours later, officer Garcia had bled to death.

Why so many deaths, so many riots at the Wackenhut prisons? The company spokesman told me, "New Mexico has a rough prison population." No kidding.

We have obtained copies of internal corporate memos, heartbreaking under the circumstances, from line officers pleading for life-saving equipment such as radios with panic buttons. They begged for more personnel. Their memos were written just weeks before Garcia's death.

Before the riots politicians and inspectors had been paraded through what looked like a fully staffed prison. But the inspections were a con because, claim guards, they are ordered to pull 16- and 20-hour shifts for the official displays.

One court official told me with low pay for dangerous work, Wackenhut filled the hiring gap, in some cases, with teenage guards, some too young to qualify for a driver's licence. And because of lax background checks, some ex-cons got on the payroll.

A few kiddie guards and insecure newcomers made up for inexperience by getting macho with the prisoners, slamming them into walls. "Just sickening," a witness told me in confidence. Right after the prison opened, a pack of guards repeatedly kicked a shackled inmate in the head. You might conclude these guards needed closer supervision, but that they had. The deputy warden stood nearby, arms folded. One witness to a beating said the warden told the guards, "When you hit them, I want to hear a *thunk*." The company fired those guards and removed the warden – to another Wackenhut prison.

Conscientious guards were fed up. Four staged a protest in front of the prison, demanding radios – and union representation. Good luck. The AFL-CIO tagged Wackenhut one of the nation's top union-busting firms. The guards faced dismissal.

Senator McSorley soured on prison privatization. New Mexico, he says, has not yet measured the hole in its Treasury left by the first few months of Wackenhut operations. After the riots, the company dumped 109 of their problem prisoners back on the government which then spent millions to ship them to other states' penitentiaries.

Still, let's-get-tough pols praise Wackenhut's "hard time" philosophy: no electricity outlets for radios, tiny metal cells, lots of lock-down time (which saves on staffing). And, unlike government prisons, there's little or no schooling, job training, library books, although the state paid Wackenhut for these rehab services. The company boasted it could arrange for in-prison computer work, but the few prisoners working sewed jail uniforms for $0.30 an hour. Most are simply left to their metal cages. Brutality is cheap, humanity expensive – in the short run. The chief of the state prison guards' union warns Wackenhut's treating prisoners like dogs ensures they lash out like wolves.

Wackenhut Corporation does not want to be judged by their corrections affiliate only. Fair enough. Following the *Exxon Valdez* disaster in Alaska, an Exxon-British Petroleum joint venture wiretapped and bugged the home of a whistleblower working with the US Congress. This black bag job was contracted to, designed by and carried out by a Wackenhut team.

Wackenhut did not have a very sunny summer in 1999. Texas terminated their contract to run a prison pending the expected criminal indictment of several staff members for sexually abusing inmates. The company was yanked from operating a prison in their home state of Florida. Mass escapes in June, July and August threatened Australian contracts. In New Mexico, Wackenhut's two prisons, which had barely been open a year, experienced numerous riots, nine stabbings and five murders, including Garcia at Santa Rosa. Wackenhut's share price plummeted.

But there was a ray of hope for the firm. At the end of Wackenhut's sunless summer, between the fourth and fifth murder in New Mexico, the office of

Britain's Home Secretary announced he would award new contracts to the company including one to build and operate a prison at Marchington. Wackenhut has become the leading operator of choice in the globalization of privatized punishment based on its stellar experience in the US.

With state after state handing Wackenhut walking papers, what could have motivated Her Majesty's Prison Service to invite the company to operate a UK prison? The Home Office at first denied they offered new work to the company, noting huffily that Britain too cancelled a Wackenhut contract, ending their operations at Coldingley Prison by "mutual agreement". (In fact, it was not so "mutual". A confidential audit leaked into hands of a prison expert and passed to me accused Wackenhut of dubious accounting and "total disregard for fundamental tenets of Prison Services financial policy".)

When the Home Office spokesman said they had given no new contract to Wackenhut, I suggested he look under the corporate alias, "Premier". I received a breathless call the next morning: Yes, we have several contracts with Premier, including operation of the Doncaster Prison (aka "Doncatraz") and the planned Marchington prison. Wackenhut, said the flak, "is a part of the Premier consortium". That's one way of putting it. Wackenhut owns 50 per cent of Premier and controls Premier's UK prison operations.

The prison service checks the backgrounds of its prison guards, but what about companies applying to run the entire operation? Did the UK Prison Service contact US authorities? No. Did they even enquire of Wackenhut an explanation of the deaths, riots, criminal indictments and contract terminations in the US? "Uh, we have no reason to contact Wackenhut." This eyes-wide-shut indifference has a purpose: it permits the Blair government's born-again free market faith in prison privatization to remain undisturbed.

The Home Office has also paid Wackenhut to open a new Child Prison in County Durham. The prison opened one month after American prosecutors charged Wackenhut executives and guards of a Texas juvenile center with "offensive sexual contact. Deviant sexual intercourse and rape were rampant and where residents were physically injured, hospitalized with broken bones."

It wasn't a convict but an employee who told me, "My 15 months in the prison were hell on earth. I'll never go back to Wackenhut." Those sentiments need not worry the company so long as they are not shared by governments mesmerized by the free market in human misery.

Following my initial report on Wackenhut, I was flooded with whistleblowers, insiders and professionals in the incarceration "industry" who piled papers on me: internal company and government documents from three continents, pleading that I keep their names concealed.

To be honest, I hated it. I felt weighed down, responsible and guilty as hell because I couldn't report it. There was the story of Wackenhut's juvenile center in Louisiana where guards beat a 17-year-old boy so severely that part of his intestines leaked into his colostomy bag. But that's not exactly attractive television. Editor after editor said, "No sale."

Nevertheless, I spent nights going through technical documents. One thing is clear to me from reviewing the confidential bid documents leaked to me from Her Majesty's Prison Service: Wackenhut's bid to operate Doncaster Prison was clearly higher in cost to the government than a competing proposal from the civil servants and union employees already operating the prison. But the government jiggered with the bidding analysis to reach the conclusion that somehow higher was lower, less qualified was more qualified. As the Blair government is in love with privatization and love is blind, it chose Wackenhut to do the job.

In the meantime, more Wackenhut guards were indicted in Texas and Louisiana for brutality and illegal use of gas grenades inside a detention center for youth, yet Britain's Home Secretary gave the company approval to open a jail for juveniles near Bristol. I mentioned this to New Mexican State Senator McSorley, who said, "That's bordering on the bizarre."

No senator, it's award-winning. It earned the UK Home Secretary, Jack Straw, one of my annual Golden Vulture awards, which I promised to send him mounted, manacled and beaten black and blue.

What Price A Store-Gasm?

At Wal-Mart's 1992 general meeting, company founder Sam Walton asked his share-holders to stand and sing "God Bless America". The 15,000 Wal-Martians responded emotionally to Sam's call, even though Mr Walton had been dead for two months.

Walton's request to the stockholder-cum-revival meeting in rural Arkansas – channelled through an executive, spot-lit and on bended knee, speaking to the departed Deity of Retail – was not surprising. Wal-Mart is the most patriotic, flag-waving company in America.

Until you look under the flags. Stores are decked out like a war rally, with Stars and Stripes hung from the ceiling and cardboard eagles shrieking, BUY AMERICA! But one independent group sampled 105,000 store items and found only 17 per cent made-in-the-USA items, many on sales carts marked "Made in America!"

Wal-Mart Store's annual sales far exceed the GDP of the old Warsaw Pact. Where does all that stuff come from? Avid Wal-Mart shopper Wu Hongda can tell you.

"Harry" Wu is famous in the US. Although he escaped China after 19 years in a prison camp for "counter-revolutionary" views, Wu conned his way back into the prisons to document *laogai*, the misery of forced labor. In 1995, Wu was caught and re-jailed.

But Wu told me another part of the tale. Just before his last arrest, he set up a fake commercial front and sent a confederate to Guandong Province posing as a wholesale clothes buyer looking to contract with Shantou Garment Trading Company. The Trading Company uses factories in both Shantou town and within nearby Jia Yang prison. Shantou gave Wu's operatives "references" from another customer: Wal-Mart.

I asked Wal-Mart directly if they used incarcerated gangs in Guandong to stitch T-shirts, breaking US law. The company responded, inscrutably, that its contracts prohibit slaves, prisoners or little children from making its products. How does Wal-Mart know if company contractors with plants in China's gulag use captive labor? They can't know. Wu's associate was told Chinese authorities prohibit monitoring production inside the prison.

Of course, asking Wal-Mart if shirts are made by workers shackled or "free" is merely playing China's game. To the workers, whether inside or outside the barbed wire enclosures, China is a prison economy. What wage can a worker expect when competing prison factories pay an effective wage of zero – and when the price for complaining about the system is made so starkly visible?

Wu, now back in the US, continues to shop at Wal-Mart, just to check labels. He has discovered bicycles, condoms and other necessities manufactured by the Peoples' Liberation Army under the aptly named brand "New Order".

Outside China, who makes the dirt-cheap clothes? The answer depends on how you define "children". When reporters confronted CEO David Glass with photos of 14-year-old children locked in his Bangladesh factories, he said, "Your definition of children may be different from mine." But those were the bad old days, back in 1992, before Wal-Mart published its Code of Conduct, which ended contractor abuses.

Or maybe not. According to the highly reliable National Labor Committee of New York, Wal-Mart contractor Beximco is listed as paying teenage seamstresses in Bangladesh 18 cents an hour and their helpers 14 cents working an 80-hour seven-day week. That's half the legal minimum wage and way beyond the legal work week of 60 hours.

Wal-Mart told me this could not happen. But the company has a bad habit of trying to put one over on reporters. In 1994, former *Wall Street Journal* reporter Bob Ortega, author of the fearsome exposé, *In Sam We Trust,* was taken on a dog-and-pony show of Wal-Mart's Guatemalan contract factories filled with smiling adult workers. But Ortega had arrived secretly two weeks earlier to speak with the child seamstresses hidden from the official tour. Later, human rights activists flew Guatemalan Wendy Diaz to the US where she testified about the sweatshop where, as a 13-year-old, she earned $0.30 an hour making Wal-Mart label clothes.

Regarding abuse of child workers, Wal-Mart's former lawyer, Senator Hillary Clinton, the "little lady" Sam appointed to his Board of Directors, did not return my calls.

Despite the bothersome gripes of a few skinny kids from Guatemala, Wal-Mart maintains a folksy image based on Sam Walton's aw-shucks Joe Bloke manner. Joyous clerks, say the company, chant pledges of customer service, which end with shouts of *"So help me Sam!"* The multi-billionaire took time to go into his shops and warehouses, put on a name tag and chat with employees over doughnuts. An employee told me about these folksy chats. In 1982, well on his way to becoming America's richest man, Sam dropped by an Arkansas distribution center and told the loaders, as one regular guy to another, if they voted to join a union in a forthcoming representation ballot, he would fire them all and shut down the entire center.

The words, corroborated by eight witnesses, may have been in violation of US labor law, but they were darned effective. The workers voted down the union, keeping Sam's record perfect. Out of 2,450 stores in America today, exactly none is unionized.

Who needs a union anyway? Arkansas headquarters would not tell the *Observer* the company's wage rate for clerks. So our volunteers called Wal-Marts nationwide to apply for cashier jobs. Openings averaged $6.10 an hour (a hair above Britain's minimum wage), though in deference to an old American tradition, Wal-Mart offered only $4.50 near Indian reservations.

But these wages are before Wal-Mart deducts for health insurance "co-payments". Because the deductions could wipe out their cash pay checks, most workers cannot accept this "benefit".

There is a pension plan and profit sharing. But Sam Walton didn't make his billions by sharing profits. Wal-Mart invented the disposable workforce. About a third of the workers are temporary and hours expand, shift, contract at whim. The workforce turns over like the shoe inventory, so few ever collect full pensions or profit shares.

But Wal-Mart does provide free meals, sort of. Most workers' salaries are near or below the official US poverty line, so those without second jobs qualify for government food stamps. With 780,000 workers, Wal-Mart has the nation's largest payroll, if you call that pay. Taking over the care and feeding of the Wal-Martyred workforce is a huge government welfare program. It could have been worse, but the courts rejected Walton's plea for exemption from the US minimum wage.

Wal-Mart does respond to workers who plead for an extra bowl of porridge. When employee Kathleen Baker handed her store manager a petition from 80 workers hoping for a little raise, she told me, she was fired on the spot for *theft* of the use of the company typewriter to write up the petition. The charge ruined her ability to get another job.

In 1994, Linda Regalado was threatened with loss of her job if she continued to talk to fellow "associates" about their right to join a union. She persevered and Wal-Mart made good on its illegal threat. Shortly thereafter, her husband Gilbert, working at the same store, was seriously injured and Wal-Mart refused to pay for surgery. The government sued the company, but the United Food and Commercial Workers, which backed Linda's cause, threw in the towel. The Commercial Workers' organizer told me that "the Fear Factor had become so widespread" that the union had no choice but to abandon all hope of signing up any Walton operation.

Now Wal-Mart has come to Britain's happy realm. Will Wal-Mart megaliths chew up England's greenbelts and bleed rural high streets? Tony Blair's government denies reports that it has loosened the ban on giant out-of-town stores. Britain's Trade Ministry says its preservation policy remains unchanged (and will announce that policy as soon as industry lobbyists tell them what it is).

A Wal-Marted Britain is not an inevitability. US towns "are wising up," says Al Norman, head of Sprawl-Busters, which helped 88 communities slam the door on the Beast in the Box.

Down the road from my home, 60 miles from New York City, Wal-Mart has built a "Sam's Club". It is one of the company's smallest shops. Still, it could fit three of Britain's Tesco supermarkets plus a football field inside the one building. Entering for the first time, reason cannot withstand 70,000 Standard Commercial Product Units under the fluorescent sun moaning *you want me, take me, have me*, fulfilling my nastiest human desire for Cheap and Plenty.

But my store-gasm has a cost. I step out of the Big Box and into the Pine Barrens, the last scrap of woodland left on Long Island's suburban moonscape, which Wal-Mart, despite a thousand urban alternatives, insisted on cutting up for its car parking lots.

Thirty miles east in my small farming hamlet, one in four shop windows on Main Street say, For Rent. Maybe we'll end up like Hudson Falls, once called "Home Town USA". Planning theorist James Howard Kunstler told me, "That town's main street is now a pitiful husk of disintegrating nineteenth-century buildings." After Sam Walton's Big Boxes landed outside the town, Hudson Falls was "sprawled into extinction".

No more cheap commercial thrills for me. I'm staying out of the Box, *so help me Sam.*

How the Filth Trade Turned Green

Long before George W. Bush killed the global warming treaty, it was mortally wounded by industry lobbyists – and the richest environmental group in America.

Up in the hills of Tennessee, they just *love* air pollution. Can't get enough of it. In fact, they'll spend hard cash for more of it.

In May 1992, the Tennessee Valley Authority paid a Wisconsin power company for the "right" to belch several tons of sulphur dioxide into the atmosphere, allowing the TVA to bust above-contamination limits set by law. Wisconsin cut its own polluting to offset Tennessee's. This was the first ever trade in emissions credits, an experiment in using market mechanisms to cut nationwide pollution overall.

Why should you care if Billy Hill is paying good money to suck soot? Because trading rights to pollute (first tried on Tennessee) was the cornerstone for implementing the Kyoto Protocol, the global warming treaty, which proposed rules for industrial production worldwide for the next three decades.

The Kyoto Protocol aimed to slash emissions of "greenhouse gases" which would otherwise fry the planet, melt the polar caps and put Blackpool and Los Angeles under several feet of water. (It will also have negative effects.)

As you can imagine, industry's big lobbying guns lined up against the Protocol. Leading the charge against the treaty is Citizens for a Sound Economy, an ultra-right pressure group chaired by corporate super-lobbyist Boyden Gray.

Squaring off against CSE is the influential Environmental Defense Fund of Washington DC. So committed are EDF's greens to the treaty that they set up a special affiliate to help implement the protocol's trading system. EDF's new Environmental Resource Trust is chaired by Boyden Gray.

Huh?

How did Gray, top gun of big industry's anti-treaty forces become chief of a respected environmental group? Did he have a deathbed conversion? No, Mr Gray's in fine health, thank you. Someone far more cynical than me might suggest that Mr Gray and his polluting clients, unable to halt the clean air treaty during the Clinton administration, perfected a new way to derail the environmental movement: If you can't beat 'em, buy 'em. By covering themselves in the sheep's clothing of a respected green organization, polluters can influence treaty talks to make darn certain they do not have to change their dirt-making ways.

That's where the Tennessee model comes in. By insinuating into the protocols a company's right to meet pollution targets by buying unused emissions allotments, US industry can blow up the treaty from the inside. Fronting the filth-trading scheme is the Environmental Defense Fund. The idea of contamination credits originated with the corporate lobby Business Roundtable. We know this because the Roundtable left a memo to that effect in a photocopy machine at a Kyoto follow-up meeting in Buenos Aires.

Other than the plain creepiness of selling rights to pollute, what is wrong with such trades if they painlessly cut emissions overall? Well, keep your eye on that "if". I haven't yet found a single trade that took an ounce of pollution out of the atmosphere. The free market fix for dirty air was rotten from the first deal. In the 1992 Wisconsin "sale" of pollution to Tennessee, the Wisconsin company's right to sell sulphur dioxide was based on their agreement not to build another power plant. But state authorities in Wisconsin would never have permitted building the new plant. Therefore, the seller's supposed reduction in pollution was a sham; however, the additional spume of poison from the Tennessee mountains is real and deadly.

Despite this sorry record, US negotiators have pushed emissions trading as a take-it-or-leave-it condition of America's participation in the global warming treaty. Emissions trading, as a so-called "market mechanism" for saving the biosphere, is the pride and joy of the Third Way, the means by which New Democrats hoped to replace those nasty old rule-by-command laws – "THOU SHALT NOT POLLUTE" – with efficient, retail transactions, possibly at your local TOXINS'R'US. (America already has a "stock exchange" where 15 million tons of sulphur dioxide are traded each year.)

Under US treaty proposals, any US or European manufacturer who wants to crank up their earth-baking discharges will have to buy up rights from a green-minded company which has cut emissions. But where in the world will they find earth-friendly industries willing to sell their rights to pollute? You'll never guess: Russia and Ukraine.

In case you were on vacation when Russia became an eco-paradise, I'll fill you in. The treaty's rights to pollute are allocated based on the level of air trash pumped out in 1990. Up to that year, remember, Russians were under communist rule, forced to work in grimy, choking factories. Now they are free not to work at all. The post-communist Russian industrial depression has cut that nation's emissions by 30 per cent. Thus, the bright side of starvation on the Steppes: a bountiful supply of pollution "credits", enough to eliminate 90 per cent of US industries' assigned reduction in pollution.

Is anyone fooled? Did tree-hugging Al Gore, vice-president when the scheme was proposed, jump up and holler "Fraud!" Not a chance. To corporate applause, the VP has blessed the bogus trading in filth credits. Gore even used the pollution trading scam to enhance his green credentials by posing for photo ops surrounded by members of that most revered environmental organization, the Environmental Defense Fund.

It gets worse. The Clinton–Gore administration, before taking its final bow, announced a scheme to give "early credits" to US companies that cut emissions before any treaty takes effect. So, for example, if a chemical company shuts a plant to bust its trade union, they get credits. A dozen top environmental groups are up in arms about this windfall for phantom reductions in pollution – but not EDF, which takes pride in crafting the proposal's details.

How did EDF come up with this bizarre idea? Apparently, under the tutelage of some of America's most notorious polluters, at least according to internal documents faxed to my newspaper from a source (whom, as you undoubtedly understand, I cannot name) from inside the Environmental Resource Trust, the EDF unit chaired by Boyden Gray.

One memorandum, dated October 21, 1997, states: "At the present time, most of the major utilities have been regularly meeting with EDF staff to discuss this concept." Another memo indicates the group could cash in on the credits, opening the door to an environmental group profiting by selling rights to increase pollution. An EDF staffer admitted the plan was drafted with Southern Company and American Electric Power, notorious polluters, "looking over our shoulders".

Why do some enviros appear to act like Rent-A-Greens for the Boyden Grays and corporations they once blasted? It's not just the loot. Rather, genteel alliance with industry is the ticket that lets them hang out with Gore or Bush and the industry Big Boys in the deal-making loop. They believe that, from the inside, talking the "market" lingo, they can change policy. They certainly are allowed to *feel* important. Unfortunately, the collaborationists have confused proximity with influence.

The filth trade is the ugly stepchild of the new mania to replace regulation with schemes that pose as "market" solutions. We know the attractions of the filth trade to politicians of any party: it provides a pretence of action to the public while giving winking assurance to industry that the status quo is not disturbed.

The sale of crud credits is chopping the legs off America's anti-pollution laws and it will be used to sabotage any new global warming treaty.

Marketing-not-governing gimmicks spread like Tennessee kudzu. And it's not limited to the trade in pollution. Don't be surprised when General Pinochet claims to have purchased unused bone-cracking rights from Pol Pot.

Neither Bodies to Kick nor Souls to Damn

Here's something to put your mind at ease. In the US, the federal government payroll includes 150 bureaucrats whose job is measuring the space between a mattress and the railings on a bunk bed.

While the rest of America is busy making things people can use, these ruler-armed squadrons launch surprise raids on shopping malls and furniture stores hunting for the latest threat to society: the killer kiddy bed. If a railing is even a half inch off the specifications in their little rule books, the bed is put under arrest and removed. Altogether the bureaucrats have saved us from 513,000 criminal beds, costing manufacturers nearly $100 million. Never mind that the industry issued its own strict safety standards voluntarily without help from the little men with rulers.

That's Version A. Now try Version B.

One evening in May 1994, James Mayernick's wife put their visiting young nephew, Nicholas, into the top cot of a brand new bunk bed. Ten minutes later, hearing her own son's screams, she rushed to the children's room to see Nicholas hanging. When the boy struggled to free himself, the railing pushed his head into the mattress. The gap between rail and mattress, an inch more than allowed by regulation, permitted his body to slip through, but not his head. Nicholas suffocated, the fifty-fourth child to die trapped in bed rails before the government sweep.

So which version tickles your fancy? In the Version A world-view, the US has become America the Panicked, where self-serving lawyers and journalists have created a lucrative industry of scaremongering, hunting down dangers rare or non-existent. The result of all this misguided hysteria, say the Version A advocates, the Deregulators, is the mushrooming of giant bureaucracies whose sole effect is to hog tie business with red tape and maddening, nit-picking regulations.

America, which touts itself as the land of free enterprise cowboys, John Wayne individualism and capitalism unfettered, has the most elaborate, pervasive, rule-spewing system of regulating private industry on the face of the earth. US government agencies such as the Consumer Product Safety Commission – the bed police – have exploded to a scale unimagined in Europe. For example, in 1999 the UK had 265 nuclear plant inspectors. The US, with not many more operating plants than Britain, had *4,000*.

And for good reason. America tried it the other way, hoping the marketplace would reward enlightened producers and drive out the rogues. Not a chance. The Mayerniks' bed, which smothered their nephew, was manufactured by El Rancho Furniture of Lutts, Tennessee long after the industry published its "voluntary standards" for bed designs.

How did America become international headquarters for corporate capitalism and, at the very same time, the society with the world's tightest constraints on private industry? It all goes back to the beginning of the nineteenth century when Andrew Jackson ran for president on the platform of outlawing that dangerous new legal concoction called, the "Corporations".

Jackson and his ally, Thomas Jefferson, feared this faceless, heartless creature made of stock certificates. Before the advent of the stockholder corporation, business owners had names and faces. They could be personally held accountable for their evils before courts or mobs or the Lord in His Heaven or at society dinners. But, ran Jackson's manifesto, "Corporations have neither bodies to kick nor souls to damn."

President Jackson could not stop the corporate Dreadnought. Instead, as historian Arthur Schleisinger put it, Jackson established government regulation as the means by which the democracy would impose a sense of morality upon these amoral entities.

The regulatory reform gang argues that in the twenty-first century we no longer need the reams of rules and the phalanx of agency inspectors. Enlightened corporations now understand the long-term advantage of protecting the public interest voluntarily. *Oh, please.* Catalina Furniture of California resisted the government order to recall 5,000 of its bunk beds despite a report that, as happened to the Mayerniks' nephew, a three-year-old child was caught between mattress and rails on the thin beds. The company protested at the recall on the grounds that the first trapped child survived.

Recently, I was nauseated by a full-page advert run by Mobil Oil (soon to be Exxon-Mobil) topped with the banner: "Two of the Safest Ships Ever Built". It announced the launch of a new, double-hulled oil tanker which, trumpeted Mobil, would "have prevented most of history's collision caused oil spills". Indeed, it would have. However, the Exxon-Mobil PR people, preening and prancing in their double-hulled self-congratulations, failed to mention that in the 1970s the oil giants successfully sued the government of Alaska, blocking a law requiring they use double hull ships when moving oil out of the port of the Valdez. As a direct consequence, the single-hulled *Exxon Valdez* destroyed 1,200 miles of Alaska's coastline. Mobil-Exxon now sees the light – but only because, after the great spill, Congress, under public pressure, rammed the double-hull rule down Big Oil's corporate throats.

Today, the Jacksonian compact is under assault, and not just from the Republicans – we expect them to be craven toadies to business interests – but from that Democratic coulda-been Al Gore. As vice-president, he pushed a program called "Re-Inventing Government", which all but dynamited Jefferson's head off Mt Rushmore.

Gore's "Re-Inventing Government" program repackaged in Democratic sheep's clothing all the hate-the-government blather which once spewed from moss-back Republicans. Gore's cute anecdotes about red tape and goofy rules mask a treacherous proposal for industry to "peer review" any new government regulation. This would *add* new levels of bureaucracy, procedural delay and red tape. But it would accomplish the goal of General Motors and Alliance USA, a business lobby which devised the plan for Gore, to choke off tougher safety and environmental rules.

I spoke with one of the little bureaucrats with a ruler, Consumer Product Safety Commission inspector Robin Ross. Measuring bed rails "is one of the things I like best" about the job, she says. It is a nice break from her main chore, taking evidence from families of children hung, sliced, drowned and burned. Sometimes, when her day is done, "I just sit in my car and cry."

I asked her about the best-selling book called *The Death of Common Sense: How Law is Suffocating America*. The author, Philip K. Howard, Al Gore's deregulation guru, is especially fond of jokes about government agents "who even measure the number of inches surrounding a railing". Robin acknowledges the need for a second look at rule-making, but she notes that it wasn't the law that suffocated Nicholas Mayernick.

Heartbreaker

No, there aren't a million lawyers in America. Only 925,671. But that's not nearly enough, according to Elaine Levenson.

Levenson, a Cincinnati housewife, has been waiting for her heart to explode. In 1981, surgeons implanted a mechanical valve in her heart, the Bjork-Shiley, "the Rolls-Royce of valves," her doctor told her. What neither she nor her doctor knew was that several Bjork-Shiley valves had fractured during testing, years before her implant. The company that made the valve, a unit of the New York-based pharmaceutical giant, Pfizer, never told the government.

At Pfizer's factory in the Caribbean, company inspectors found inferior equipment, which made poor welds. Rather than toss out bad valves, Pfizer management ordered defects ground down, weakening the valves further, but making them *look* smooth and perfect. Then Pfizer sold them worldwide.

When the valve's struts break and the heart contracts, it explodes. Two-thirds of the victims die, usually in minutes. In 1980, Dr Viking Bjork, whose respected name helped sell the products, wrote to Pfizer demanding corrective action. He threatened to publish cases of valve strut failures.

A panicked Pfizer executive telexed, "*ATTN PROF BJORK. WE WOULD PREFER THAT YOU DID NOT PUBLISH THE DATA RELATIVE TO STRUT FRACTURE.*" The company man gave this reason for holding off public exposure of the deadly valve failures: "*WE EXPECT A FEW MORE.*" His expectations were realized. The count has reached 800 fractures, 500 dead – so far. Dr Bjork called it murder, but kept public silence.

Eight months after the "don't publish" letter, a valve was implanted in Mrs Levenson.

In 1994, the US Justice Department nabbed Pfizer. To avoid criminal charges, the company paid civil penalties – and about $200 million in restitution to victims. Without the damning evidence prised from Pfizer by a squadron of lawyers, the Justice Department would never have brought its case.

Pfizer moans that lawyers still hound the company with more demands. But that is partly because Pfizer recalled only the *unused* valves. The company refused to pay to replace valves of fearful recipients.

As you've learned from watching episodes of *LA Law*, in America's courtrooms the rich get away with murder. Yet no matter the odds for the Average Joe, easy access to the courts is a right far more valuable than the quadrennial privilege of voting for the Philanderer-in-Chief. This wee bit of justice, when victim David can demand to face corporate Goliath, makes America feel like a democracy.

Some Britons appreciate the US system. Several British heart valve victims sued Pfizer in US courts.

In Britain itself, Pfizer has little to fear. As a London solicitor for the pharmaceutical industry told me, "US legal excesses are not visited upon defendants here." And the drug companies want to keep it that way. If you happened to be in Blackpool during the 1998 Labour Party Conference, you could have dropped by Pfizer's booth. (For more discreet approaches to Downing Street, Pfizer used GPC Access, Derek Draper's former lobby firm.) Pfizer had two reasons to cuddle up to New Labour. First, Pfizer was pushing the National Health Service to pay a stiff price for its love potion, Viagra. Second, to protect Viagra super-profits, Pfizer needed to prevent a toughening of UK products liability law demanded by the European Union.

Back in the US, the heart valve victims' rights were under attack. Waving the banner of "Tort Reform", corporate America had funded an ad campaign portraying entrepreneurs held hostage by frivolous lawsuits. But proposed remedies stank of special exemptions from justice. A ban on all lawsuits against makers of parts for body implants, even those with deadly defects, was slipped into Patients' Rights legislation by the Republican Senate leader. The clause,

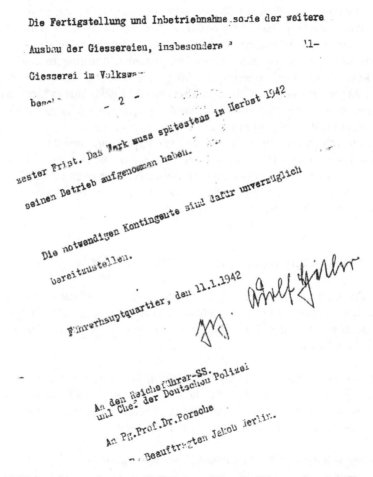

Figure 13. Hitler taking orders from Volkswagen. Here the Führer agrees to Volkswagen's request for more slave laborers from concentration camps. This evidence would never have come to light were it not for law suits filed by blood-sucking lawyer leeches (as the corporate lobby would like to characterize class-action plaintiffs' attorneys). In this case, the firm of Cohen, Milstein, Hausfeld & Toll, Washington DC, outed this document in a suit on behalf of slave workers whose children died in deadly "nurseries" run by the automakers VW, Ford, Daimler and others. If Hitler had been captured, he might have used the defense, "I was only taking orders … from Volkswagen."

killed by exposure, was lobbied by the Health Industries Manufacturers Association supported by – you guessed it – Pfizer.

At their best, tort lawyers are cops who police civil crime. Just as a wave of burglaries leads to demand for more policemen, the massive increase in litigation has a single cause: a corporate civil crime wave.

Six years ago, after 18 buildings blew up in Chicago and killed four people, I searched through the records of the local private gas company on behalf of survivors. What I found would make you sick. I saw engineers' reports, from years earlier, with maps marking where explosions would be likely to take place. The company, People's Gas, could have bought the coffins in advance. Management had rejected costly repairs as "not in the strategic plan". It's not planned evil at work here, but the enormity of corporate structures in which human consequences of financial acts are distant and unimaginable.

I admit, of the nearly one million lawyers in the US, you could probably drown 90 per cent and only their mothers would grieve. But as Mrs Levenson told me, without her lawyer who worked for a percentage of her settlement, Pfizer would not have paid her a dime of compensation.

The tort reformers' line is that fee-hungry lawyers are hawking bogus fears, poisoning American's faith in the basic decency of the business community, turning us into a nation of people who no longer trust each other. But whose fault is that? The lawyers? Elaine Levenson put her trust in Pfizer Pharmaceutical. Then they broke her heart.

War on Corruption? Not Quite, Minister

In July 2000, I had a very interesting conversation with one of Britain's top corporate barristers, who told me about an enlightening conversion he'd had at a Trade Ministry reception. It was just after Tony Blair took over the government. As the free drinks flowed at the Ministry bash,

> ... I was introduced to somebody who identified himself as the chairman of the company you just mentioned [Balfour Beatty] and we were talking about corruption. He announced with enormous pride that he personally had handed over the check to the government minister for the Pergau Dam bribe.

And it just so happened that I had my tape recorder turned on.

There's still one bargain left in Rip-Off Britain: the price of a UK minister remains way below the cost of purchasing officials in the US, even below traditional influence shopping centers in the developing world.

Case in point: last year, it was disclosed that the US Justice Department had sought Swiss help in tracking $60 million from British Virgin Island bank accounts which Justice contends was paid to the current president and former prime ministers of Kazakhstan. The account was funded by US giant Exxon-Mobil, British Petroleum and Phillips Petroleum. (There was no accusation of criminal intent by the oil firms who, we assume, had legitimate reasons to send their millions on holiday to the Caribbean.)

By contrast, in 1989, prior to its merger with Exxon, Mobil paid a mere £10,000 ($15,000) to Neil Hamilton MP, following his attempt to scupper a tax on North Sea oil. During the trial of Hamilton's libel suit against Mohamed Al-Fayed and the *Guardian*, a Mobil executive testified that Hamilton, then sitting on the Finance Committee in Commons, demanded cash for defending the oil company's positions in the committee. The Mobil executive was "horrified"; nevertheless, the company suggested the payment be invoiced as a consulting fee, although "the reality was we were buying off Mr Hamilton for what he had done, in connection with this tax issue".

In what must be the most stunning – and never reported – statement during the trial, Mobil's lawyer informed his executive, *"This was the normal course of things for some MPs who did ask for payment."*

Really? *Which* other MPs? And how much? And which other companies received bills from Parliamentarians'R'Us?

Most important, is this "normal course of things" still business as usual? At first blush, it appeared the game was over. Tough-guy Home Secretary Jack Straw published "Upholding Integrity: the Prevention of Corruption". Extortionists and bribers beware. No more Hamiltonian fees for favors.

Well, *not exactly*, explained a Home Office spokesperson. The Home Office would not call a payment to a Member of Parliament a bribe if the cash is "remuneration" for services performed. Furthermore, the government's proposal states that "offering a bribe" will *not* constitute an offense unless the pay-off is *"primarily"* the reason for a public servant's actions. If a future Hamilton simply hates taxes on oil companies deep in his heart and oil company payola merely stiffens his resolve, the cash is his to keep.

Then bribery is legal? Don't be cynical. A £10 pay-off, says the Home Office, would be a "gratuity", but a £1,000,000 pay-off is corrupt. It depends on the amount the fixer believes would influence the politician's decision. How about £10,000? The functionary told me, either as a warning or an advertisement, "Ten thousand would influence *me*, but maybe not some of our wealthier MPs." (The Home Office declines, however, to publish the legal price list for each member of government.)

I was assured that the normal course of things would remain undisturbed. "We are not trying to *change* the law, just *clarify* it." New Labour, promised the Home Office, had simply repackaged current common law and three old codes into a single new statute.

So why had Mr Straw bothered at all with this legal shuffling? Because there was a need for one change. For the first time, the anti-corruption rules, such as they are, will now apply to British corporations bribing *foreign* officials. This was not a courageous advance toward a moral foreign policy. Rather, PM Tony Blair has been dragged kicking and screaming into action by the Organization for Economic Cooperation and Development's declaring Britain out of compliance with the Organization's Anti-Bribery Convention.

Thus, as a result of the government's belated and grudging move to adhere to international regulations, UK companies that oblige requests for gratuities from Col. Mustaffa Hamilton of Fanatistan are now subject to the same diligent lack of prosecution as in dealings with the domestic Mr Hamilton.

The real test of Blair's commitment to shutting down the worldwide kasbah for favors is not whether the Home Office puts English executives into leg irons but an action far less dramatic: cutting off public subsidies to companies found guilty of corruption. The World Bank has adopted this simple rule: if you pay off a potentate (and get caught), you lose your loan guarantees and your government contracts.

The Government of Lesotho has charged a consortium including construction giant Balfour Beatty (along with several European and American operators) with paying at least 22 million rand to government agents to grease approval of lucrative contract amendments in the building of the Highlands Dam. It looks grim for Balfour Beatty. The Swiss government has obliged prosecutors with details of bank accounts traceable to some of the accused.

While Balfour Beatty's consortium is in the dock in Lesotho, the company is drawing down funds backed by the British taxpayer through the Export Credit Guarantee Department (ECGD) for the company's work on the Ilisu Dam project in Turkey – and Tony Blair wants to sell the London Underground to Balfour Beatty.

The ECGD says it is looking into the Lesotho case. I called Lesotho's Chief Prosecutor about any evidence he had passed to Britain's government. He told me no one from the Home Office, the Department of Trade and Industry (DTI) or the British government had contacted him. That does not mean there has been no UK investigation. The DTI told one watchdog organization that officials asked Balfour Beatty if the charges had merit and the company said "No." Well then, case closed.

"Government is so hypocritical," says Jeremy Carver, head of international law with the firm Clifford Chance. Carver, adviser to the anti-corruption campaign Transparency International, cited the government's predilection for strong press releases and weak enforcement. It was Carver to whom the Balfour Beatty executive boasted he "personally had handed over the check to the government minister for the Pergau Dam bribe" in Malaysia. Carver noted that a Tory trade minister, learning of the pay-off, publicly congratulated Balfour Beatty on its patriotic competitiveness.

Carver looks longingly at the US Foreign Corrupt Practices Act, the oldest, toughest such statute, the grounds for the US Justice Department's foray into Kazakstan. But he may not want to look *too* closely at the US experience.

Where, after all, did the Kazakhs get the idea of paying off a president? In 1995 and 1996, Roger Tamraz, an investor promoting US backing for an oil pipeline in Kazakhstan, secretly provided $300,000 to the Democratic Party, a violation of US election law. This did not surprise Johnny Chung, who pleaded guilty to funnelling money from Red Chinese military industries to Clinton's campaign. Chung, who earned several meetings with the president, explained: "I see the White House is like a subway – you have to put in coins to open the gates."

These and hoarier tales suggest American politicians' zeal to prevent payments of bribes abroad is motivated primarily by a jealous desire to keep all the baksheesh at home.

Not unexpectedly, the week after I reported this story, the mail brought a note from Balfour Beatty.

A company spokesman, Mr Tim Sharp, wrote that he spoke to my source who, according to the company, "denies absolutely having said what is attributed to him". The company demanded a retraction.

There was something odd about this complaint. The company seemed to challenge only the words of the accusation, not the substance. For clarification, I wrote to the company asking for an answer to a simple, and far more relevant, question: "Did Balfour Beatty pay bribes in Malaysia – yes or no?"

I received no reply.

This was a difficult time for Balfour Beatty. A consortium to which the company belongs faces new charges of bribery, this time over another dam project in Lesotho in Southern Africa. Adding insult to indictment, the FBI raided Balfour Beatty's American offices in response to other allegations. I thought the company deserved an extra chance to clear its name.

So I called Mr Sharp:

Question: *Was a payment made to a government official by Balfour Beatty, its chairman or an agent for its chairman regarding the Pergau Dam project, yes or no?*
Balfour B: *I TELL YOU I'VE WORKED WITH SOME JOURNALISTS IN MY TIME!*
Question: *Did you pay a bribe?*
Balfour B: *I LIKE YOUR APPROACH.*
Question: *I just want to know if you bribed the Malaysians.*
Balfour B: *WE COULD SPEND THE REST OF THE AFTERNOON!*
[We nearly did. This continued for almost an hour.]
Question: *I'm worried about the issue of bribery and corruption.*
Balfour B: *AREN'T WE ALL? ....*
Question: *I'm happy to print "Balfour Beatty states unequivocally that no payment was made to a Malaysian official."*
Balfour B: *I SUGGESTED TO YOU THAT YOU MIGHT HAVE MISLED PEOPLE.*
[How had I led my readers astray?]
Balfour B: *THE THING YOU WROTE HAS BEEN DENIED FLATLY BY YOUR ALLEGED SOURCE!*

[Odd this: I had a tape-recording, but Balfour Beatty claimed to have received a letter from the lawyer I had quoted. Twice, I asked Sharp to read it during our interview. Only on the second reading did he include this]:
Balfour B: *[reading from the letter]* "I DO NOT DENY THE ACCURACY OF THE WORDS ATTRIBUTED TO ME IN THE ARTICLE."
Oh.

For their helpful clarification, Balfour Beatty won a Golden Vulture Award, which I offered to deposit in a numbered Swiss account. And the *Observer* printed the following correction:

We hereby retract the statements made regarding Balfour Beatty's alleged boasting of corrupt practices on the grounds that our article was wholly accurate.

When You're Hot, You're Hot

Here's an idea: Why don't we send 10,000 tons of high-level uranium waste to Russia? You'd rather not? Not until you buy your lead suit?

OK then, how about we send 10,000 tons of radioactive garbage to Russia *and* throw in $15 billion for Vladimir Putin. For the cash, Putin must solemnly promise to store the bomb-making material safely and not let any of it slip into the hands of the Iranians or the IRA.

Just when I thought the Bush administration had adopted every crack-brained idea that could threaten Mother Earth, along comes another. This send-uranium-to-Russia scheme is the creation of something called the Non-Proliferation Trust (NPT Inc.), a Washington group which says it "grew out of extensive dialog with ... the arms control community and the environmental community".

If by "arms control community" you were thinking of Greenpeace, you'd be a bit wide of the mark. The chairman of NPT Inc. is Admiral Daniel Murphy, once Deputy Director of the CIA and Bush Senior's chief of staff. The other seven listed board members and executives include former CIA chief William Webster, two nuclear industry executives, one former Nixon administration insider, the general who commanded the US Marine Corps, one top Masonic official and, indeed, one certified greenie tree-hugger.

It may not be your typical save-the-world line-up, but their idea is worth a hearing. Russia has a huge hot pile of "fissile material" – bomb fixings and old nuclear plant rods – sitting in polluted Siberian towns whose very names, like Chilyabinsk-14, sound radioactive. NPT Inc.'s idea is that if we send them more radioactive garbage, plus cash, Russia will then have the means and obligation to store theirs, and ours, safely.

In July the scheme got a big boost when the Duma, under pressure from Putin, abolished the Russian law which barred the nation's importing most foreign nuclear waste.

NPT Inc.'s assemblage of ex-spooks and militarists (and their lone green compatriot) control the operation through three non-profit trusts. But non-profit does not mean that no one gains.

So after no small amount of digging and several pointed questions by my associate Oliver Shykles, this self-described charity admitted it will pay a British-American wheeler-dealer, Alex Copson, some unidentified percentage of the deal. NPT has been reluctant to give details of Copson's potential gain from the success of NPT, possibly because the polo and sports car afficionado with the posh accent lacks the diplomatic gloss appropriate to this sensitive enterprise. Copson once described the natives of the Marshall Islands as "fat, lazy, fucks" when they nixed one of his nuke dump schemes. Sources tell me Copson also suggested dumping hot stuff under the North Sea.

Contractors will share a few billion from this scheme, including German power consortium Gellschaft für Nuklear-Behaltg mbII (GNB). By the way, Dr Klaus Janberg of GNB is director of "not-for-profit" NPT International.

But the real winner, should NPT succeed, would be the long-dead nuclear industry, which George Bush hopes to bring back from the crypt. There is one huge obstacle to Bush's radioactive dream: disposing of the nuclear waste. If you think about it, the only indispensable appliance for a kitchen is a toilet (presumably in another room); so too, one cannot build a nuclear plant without planning for the end product.

At $15 billion, dumping in Russia is a bargain. Since Russia is already a nuclear toilet, who would notice a little more hot crud?

Russia's own environmentalists have noticed, but objections from their Ecological Union are smothered by the ringing endorsement of the nuclear issues chief of one of America's richest environmental groups, the Natural Resources Defense Council. NRDC's Dr Thomas Cochrane sits on NPT Inc.'s MinAtom Trust board of directors, painting the project with a heavy coat of green.

What on Mother Earth would drive the NRDC man to front for NPT? Bernardo Issel, director of the Washington-based Non-Profit Accountability Project, sent the *Observer* a copy of NPT Inc.'s draft, "Long-term Fissile Materials Safeguards and Security Project". At page 18, one finds arrangements for the NRDC to administer a $200 million Russian "environmental reclamation fund", for which the green group will receive a fee of up to 10 per cent of expenditures, a cool $20 million.

NRDC's Cochrane insists his group would have never taken that role. An NPT spokesman says the clause has been removed from a new draft contract, though they have refused our request to see the document.

Is this another case of greens selling out for greenbacks? It's not that simple. The NRDC's Dr Cochrane is as straight a shooter as you'll ever meet. The problem here is not payola, but philosophy. The NRDC represents the new wave of environmental organization enchanted with the use of market mechanisms. Like the Environmental Defense Fund with its goofy pollution-trading scheme, these groups are mesmerized by can-do entrepreneurs with access to huge mounds of capital and sold on the pleasant if naive idea that the profit motive can be bent to the public good.

The NRDC and other pro-market environmentalists are always on the hunt for what their prophet, Amory Lovins, calls "win–win" cases – deals that aid the environment while making big bucks for the corporate players. To the horror of many consumer advocates, NRDC stood with business lobbyists to push the trade in "pollution credits" and promote deregulation of electricity in California, though the group did a quick flip on deregulation when the scheme flopped.

The NPT scheme is the quintessential public–private partnership that business greens find irresistible. For Dr Cochrane, the uranium-dumping scheme's attraction is NPT Inc.'s promise, which cannot be easily dismissed, to provide billions to clean up Russia's radioactive hell-holes. And NPT also promises to toss in $250 million to a Russian Orphans Fund.

Environmental clean-up, non-proliferation and orphans. Why would Russia's green activists turn away from this obvious win–win? The answer, in a word, is "MinAtom". MinAtom, Russia's ministry of atomic industries, is, of course, the agency that created the nuclear mess in the first place. Can MinAtom be trusted to safely handle both the nuclear fuel and faithfully use the several billion for environmental clean-up, not to mention the orphans?

As soon as I heard "MinAtom", I ran to my notes of my interview with Joseph Stiglitz, former World Bank economist and one-time chief of Bill Clinton's Council of Economic Advisers. The economist told me about an incident involving MinAtom which disturbs him to this day.

In July 1998, the Clinton administration privatized the United States Enrichment Corporation, USEC. According to Stiglitz, the privatized USEC proved inefficient at enriching uranium, but exceptionally efficient at enriching several Clinton associates. Hillary's sidekick Susan Thomases was a USEC lobbyist. The law firm that defended the president in one of Bill's bimbo law suits picked up $15 million for work leading up to USEC's flotation. A federal judge concluded, after reviewing documents USEC tried to conceal, that the privatization decision was influenced by "bias, self-interest and self-dealing".

To sell privatization, Clinton's buddies at USEC promised their corporation would buy up tons of Russia's old warhead uranium from MinAtom. As with NPT, the sales pitch was that, by taking over government enrichment operations, private industry could reduce the amount of bomb ingredients in Russia's hands at no cost to the US Treasury. Another public/private win–win.

But Stiglitz, ever the hard-nosed economist, could not fathom how this new profit-making corporation could pay the Russians above-market price for the uranium.

The answer was, USEC couldn't. In 1996, some unnamed birdie dropped a damning document on Stiglitz's White House desk. It was a memo indicating that MinAtom had demanded USEC take about double the amount of uranium originally expected. Rather than take the costly deliveries, USEC quietly arranged a payment to MinAtom of $50 million. Stiglitz called it "hush money". USEC says it was a legitimate pre-payment for the hot stuff. However one describes it, MinAtom was more than happy to play along, for a price.

Yet NPT Inc. tells us MinAtom and US private enterprise can now form a trustworthy partnership to safeguard nuclear material for the next few thousand years. At first, this puzzled me: NPT Inc.'s board is led by the CIA and military men who pushed Star Wars, which they sold on the premise that Russia has probably let slip nuclear material to unnamed "rogue states".

But I think I've solved this puzzling conundrum. What we have here is the ultimate, and very green, recycling program: NPT ships America's uranium to the Russians ... which then falls into the hands of a rogue state ... which then returns it to the US perched atop an intercontinental ballistic missile ... which is shot down by the trillion-dollar Star Wars defence system. Win win for everyone.

"Two Symbols of American Capitalist Hegemony"

September 11, 2001

There's two people you ought to know: Greg O'Neill and Clinton Davis. They are exceptionally important because, according to the *Guardian*, they are "two symbols of American hegemony". Technically, the paper refers to the two towers of the World Trade Center. But it was not American hegemony that fell 50 floors into horrid, crushing oblivion. Nor was it just some architectural artefact that was a justly deserved "painful lesson" about US foreign policy, as one French columnist wrote with unapologetic glee.

For four years, I've written tales from inside corporate America – from pig swill price-fixing conspiracies ripping off Asians to Texas power pirates turning off the lights in Rio. And when the profit hunt turned from goofy to cruel, I've printed the names of victims from Argentina to Tanzania. Now the victims are from inside America itself, from what US television hair-do Tom Brokaw, also happy to reduce humans to emblems, called "the symbols of American capitalism".

Davis worked in the basement of the Trade Center; O'Neill in Tower One. (And, not so long ago, I worked in Tower Two, Floor 50.)

Here's what O'Neill did on Floor 52. When the *Exxon Valdez* grounded, he fought the oil company to get compensation for the Natives of Alaska. When he learned an electric company had faked safety reports on its nuclear plant, O'Neill, a lawyer, sued them and put these creeps out of business.

Davis worked in the cops' division of the state's Port Authority. Neither Davis nor O'Neill would be my first choice as a symbol of US imperial might, to target for retaliation for "terror by Jewish groups", to use one British commentator's bone-head words.

If anything, the Trade Center was a symbol of American *socialism*. These towers were built by New York State in the 1970s, when "government-owned" became quite unfashionable in Thatcherized Britain. The towers' owner, New York's Port Authority, generates the revenue which keeps the city's infrastructure – subways, tunnels, bridges, and more – out of the hands of the ever-circling privatizers. Convincing capitalists that publicly owned operations are as good an investment bet as General Motors fell to government securities market-makers, Cantor-Fitzgerald (100th floor, 700 workers, no known survivors).

Here's a statistic you might find a bit odd to bring up at this moment. Capitalization of corporations owned by the US federal government exceeds $2.85 trillion. Add to that state and local operations, like water systems, and the total invested in public enterprise eclipses the stock market, making the US one of the most socialized nations left on this sad planet. If you're not American, you wouldn't know that. And if you are, you probably wouldn't know that either. There's a lot you probably don't know about America that would surprise you, that would surprise ourselves.

As I write this, George W. Bush is beating the war drum against Osama Bin Laden, a killer created in our president's very own Cold War Frankenstein factory. During the war in Vietnam, thousands filled jails (including me) to resist it. It would help those of us Americans ready to stop the killing machine if Europeans would stop the smarmy lecturing. In a sickening but not unique commentary, the *Guardian*'s Seamus Milne wagged his finger at Americans still gathering corpses. "They can't see why they are hated." He demands that Americans must "understand" why O'Neill and Davis were the targets of blood-crazed killers. *Hey, if your government backs Israel, well, just get used to it baby.* (And what do you mean "*they* are hated" Seamus? When did the Muslim world fall in love with the British Imperial conquerors of Iraq, Palestine and the Khyber Pass?)

After the IRA bombed London's Canary Wharf, I don't remember Americans suggesting this was a just revenge for the Queen's occupation of Northern Ireland, a time to cuddle up to the berserkers with bombs.

Commentators like Milne have a great advantage over me. While Bin Laden hasn't returned my phone calls, he seems to know exactly the killer's cause. We have to "understand" that the terrorists don't like America's foreign policy. Well, neither do I. But I also understand that the bombers are not too crazy about America's freedom of religion nor equality of women under the law. And they're none too happy about our reluctance, despite televangelists' pleas, to cut off the hands of homosexuals.

On my journalistic beat investigating corporate America, I've heard every excuse for brutality and mayhem: "We met all the government's safety standards"; "We never asked for the military to use force on our behalf." The excuses and bodies pile up. Maybe I just have to accept that killing is in fashion again, for profit, for revolution, to protect American interests or to take vengeance on American interests.

Baroness Thatcher thinks we should understand Pinochet; the Bush family ran their own little *jihad* against communism I was supposed to understand; now some Europeans want us to understand a new set of little Pinochets with turbans. To prevent an unelected US president from ordering up counter-atrocities, grieving Americans don't need nasty admonitions about the causes, just or unjust, of our killers.

That terrible Tuesday evening, I had to call O'Neill's home. He answered the phone. "My god, you're safe!"

O'Neill replied, "Not really." I hope that doesn't disappoint the *Guardian*.

Davis was safe too, in the towers' basement. But he chose to go up into the building to rescue others. Today, this symbol of American capitalist hegemony is listed as missing.

6

The Best Democracy Money Can Buy

Who owns America? How much did it cost? Was the transaction cash, check or credit card? Or a donation to my son who's running for president? Or a consulting contract to my wife's former law partner to comfort him on his way to the federal penitentiary?

And what do you give a billionaire who has everything? That gold mine in Nevada they so covet? Immunity from prosecution?

Then there's the practical difficulty of gift-wrapping the US Congress.

Ah, the Smell of Texas in the Morning

According to LaNell Anderson, real estate agent, what I'm smelling is a combination of hydrogen sulphide and some other unidentifiable toxic gunk. With the crew from BBC's Newsnight, *we've pulled up across from a pond on Houston's ship channel, home of the biggest refinery and chemical complex in America, owned by Exxon-Mobil.*

The pond is filled with benzene residues, a churning, burbling goop. Though there's a little park nearby, this is not a bucolic swimming hole. Rather, imagine your toilet backed up, loaded, churning and ripe – assuming your toilet is a half-mile in circumference.

In May 2001, I flew to Houston to prepare for the official release of President George W. Bush's proposal to end the energy crisis in California. The Golden State was suffering rolling black-outs. The state's monthly electricity bill shot up by 1,000 per cent.

But as soon as I got a whiff of the president's proposals, I knew his plan had nothing to do with helping out the Gore-voting surfers on the Left Coast. Bush's "energy crisis" plan reeks of pure *eau de Texas*, that sulphurous combination of pollution, payola and political power unique to the Lone Star State.

Bush put his vice-president, Dick Cheney, in charge of the committee to save California consumers. Recommendation number one: build some nuclear plants. Not much of an offer to earthquake-prone California, but a darn good deal for the biggest builder of nuclear plants based in Texas, the Brown and Root subsidiary of Halliburton Corporation. Recent CEO of Halliburton: Dick the Veep.

Suggestion number two: drill for oil in Alaska's Arctic Wildlife Refuge. California does not burn oil in its power plants, but hey, committee member and commerce secretary Don Evans gave the Arctic escapade a thumbs-up. Evans most recent employment: CEO of Tom Brown Inc., a billion-dollar oil and gas corporation.

And so on. Former Texas Agriculture Commissioner Jim Hightower told me, "They've eliminated the middleman. The corporations don't have to lobby the government any more. They *are* the government." Hightower used to complain about Monsanto's lobbying the secretary of agriculture. Today, Monsanto executive Ann Venamin *is* the secretary of agriculture.

Well, back to energy. California's electricity watchdog agency claims that speculators and a little club of energy merchants exercised raw monopoly power to overcharge state consumers by a breathtaking $6.2 billion last year. Bill Clinton, before his final bow, issued an order on December 14, halting uncontrolled speculation in the electricity market. You could hear the yowls all the way to Texas where the big winners in the power game – Enron, TXU, Reliant, Dynegy and El Paso corporation – have their headquarters.

These five energy operators, through their executives and employees, ponied up $4.1 million for the Republican presidential campaign cycle, according to the Center for Responsive Politics in Washington. They didn't have long to wait before their investment – excuse me, *donation* – paid off big time. Just three days after his inauguration, Bush swept away Clinton's orders directing controlled power sales to California.

Back in the ship channel, once LaNell picked up the scent of airborne poisons, she hopped from her Lexus, pulled out a big white bucket and opened a valve, sucking in a three-minute sample of air which she'll send off to the US Environmental Protection Agency. She believes the EPA will trace and fine the polluter.

Hunting killer fumes is a heck of hobby. LaNell began after learning she had a rare immune system disease associated with chemical pollution. Her mom and dad died young of lung disease and cancer. She grew up and lives near the ship channel.

I didn't have the heart to tell her that she might as well chuck away her buckets. Quietly tucked into President Bush's new budget is a big fat *zero* for the key EPA civil enforcement team. This has no connection whatsoever to the petrochemical industry dumping $48 million into the Republican campaign.

LaNell stopped to chat with some Chicano sub-teens playing soccer with an old bowling ball. They live in what Exxon-Mobil calls its "vulnerability zone". The refinery released 1,680,000 lb of toxic chemicals into the air and water here in 2000 by accident. According to Exxon-Mobil records, if the pentane on site vaporized and ignited, it would burn human skin within 1.8 miles: 7,300 people live in that zone.

Bush is addressing the problem. He's closing down public access to these reports on the killing zones.

A giant flare suddenly lit up the other side of the channel – and LaNell sped off to investigate. She discovered that a chemical plant blew a hydrogen line –

and the operators, rather than store the ruined batch of ethylene, chose to ignite it. The toxic fireball, big as the Houses of Parliament, burned from the stack for several hours, exhaling a black cloud over Houston.

LaNell said this sickening "sky dumping" procedure is okey-dokey with Texas state regulators. Now Bush proposes moving air quality enforcement away from the tougher feds to these laid-back state agencies. And the Bush energy plan proposes additional loosening of EPA rules on the chemical industry.

On to Dallas, where I met with Phyllis Glazer, founder of a group of bereaved mothers in Winona, Texas. They lost their children to rare diseases which they believe are related to a local hazardous waste "injection well", a big underground chemical dump. Cynthia wore one of those fancy Western dance shirts with the metal bangles and cowhide fringe, so I brilliantly asked her if she enjoys Texas two-stepping. "Actually, I don't do a lot of dancing these days. My bones are deteriorating."

Phyllis and the moms took a bus to Washington DC. But official doors slammed in their faces. "They said someone who's given 200,000 or a couple million, their call goes straight through."

One Texan who made his way through the doors to power is Ken Lay, the chairman of Enron, the electricity speculating outfit which made out so well in Bush's energy program. Lay is a Pioneer, but not the kind that lives in a little house on the prairie, busting the soil. A "Pioneer" designates the big buckaroos who pledged to raise $100,000 apiece for Mr Bush. Four hundred Pioneers – that's $40 million in campaign booty.

Lay wouldn't talk to me, but his fellow Pioneer, Senator Teel Bevins, Texas Panhandle rancher, was right friendly. His office walls in the Capitol in Austin sport a pair of riding chaps, his Pioneer medallion and the head of a deceased Long-Horn. I was assured the back half of the beast ended up on the Senator's barbecue.

Getting the hundred grand for Bush was no problem for the cowboy-politician. Easiest money he ever raised ("Eezist monuh ah eva rayzed"). And Bush never forgets his friends. One unheralded milestone of Bush's first 100 days is his allowing beef packers to zap meat with radiation to kill salmonella, a disinfectant cheaper than non-nuclear methods. (Bush's proposal to permit a bit of salmonella in school lunch meats was withdrawn after the public reacted with loud gagging and retching noises.)

I told the senator about Phyllis Glazer, the cancer victim and pollution fighter, and her complaint that Washington access required big bucks donations.

"Well, it's easy for the press to take some victim and make her a poster girl. The reality is individuals in a country with 300 million people have very little opportunity to speak to the President of the United States."

But what about Pioneer Lay of Enron Corp? His company, America's number one power speculator, is also Dubya's number one political career donor. Lay was personal adviser to Bush during the post-election "transition". And his company held secret meetings with the Energy Plan's drafters. Bush's protecting electricity deregulation has meant a big pay-day for Enron, profit up $87 million in the first quarter of Bush's reign thanks to reversing Clinton orders.

The senator is nothing if not candid. "So you *wouldn't* have access if you had spent two years of your life working hard to get this guy elected president *raising hundreds of thousands of dollars?"*

In case I didn't understand, he translated it into Texan. "*Ya dance with them what brung ya!"*

I couldn't argue with that. If President Bush chose to two-step with Lay of Enron instead of Phyllis Glazer, well, let's be honest, Phyllis ain't much on the dance floor these days.

Check out Senator Biven's riding chaps on the BBC broadcast from the Lone Star State which you can still view in RealVideo at
http://news.bbc.co.uk/olmedia/1315000/video/_1319141_payback_vi.ram

Did Bush spike the investigations of Bin Laden?

During America's days of innocence just before September 11, 2001 our unelected president's favors for his monied buddies appeared as a vaudeville of venality, but not life-threatening. Then, after September and into the new year, darker tales began to seep out of the pus-holes of America's intelligence agencies.

After September 11, the BBC's and *Guardian's* investigation teams, in coordination with the National Security News Service of Washington, set out to find out why the CIA, FBI and other well-funded spooks could neither prevent nor know about the most deadly attack on America since Pearl Harbor. From inside the agencies we heard that government chiefs stopped key investigations into allegations of the funding of Al Quaida and other terrorist organizations by top Saudi royals and some members of the Bin Laden family, not just Osama. Crucially, one top-placed operative told me that, even under Bill Clinton, investigations that implicated Saudis were subject to "constraints". But after the elections, under Bush's control, the agencies were ordered to "back off" from any inquiries into the Saudi royals or the Bin Laden family, except for the supposed lone black sheep, Osama.

As a result, one agent told me, "There were particular investigations that were effectively killed." We learned that the Bush administration's ruling killed the secret hunt for the funding, possibly from Saudi Arabia, for Pakistan's successful manufacture of an "Islamic" atom bomb. Without realizing the black

SECRET (A)
WFO COMMAND POST
SEPTEMBER 13, 2001/6:00pm-6:00pm SHIFT
Prepared by IRS Susan L. Newman, 6:00pm

SIGNIFICANT ACTIVITY

ARAB SEEKING TRANSPORTATION TO CANADA

At approximately 8:00 ~ on 9/12/01, SA Brian McCauley met with a source who had
information about an   ~ who was requested to arrange immediate transportation for an
Arab out of the Un¹   ~ssociate contacted the source on September 4, stating that he
needed help in sm·   ·¹e country on September 11 or 12. The source said
no, as that was n   ~ntacted again on September 5 and September 11
by the associat·   The source was in contact with Agent
McCauley and   for the Arab. It was learned that the
Arab was in   ¹¹~n through and was in need
of an alterr   ~ return to DC and he
would be   ~k to DC, it will
likely be

9/19/01
8:16:52

Case ID .:
Responses :

02/23/1996 and closed on 09/11/1996 on ABL because of his
relationship with the WORLD ASSEMBLY OF MUSLIM YOUTH (WAMY), a
suspected terrorist organization.

1991-WF-213589

View Document Text
SECRET

Serial : 39

On 9
pos
ad
    ~ *information: (S) Investigation do date has determined the following.*
    ~ *Randolph Street, #1230, Arlington, Virginia 22203 since*
    08/29/1997. He has been receiving mail at P.O. Box 8671, Falls
    Church, Virginia 22041 since 03/11/1996 and may also receive
    mail at 10310 Main Street, Fairfax, Virginia 22030. From June
    1994 to August 1997, the captioned subject is believed to have
    lived with ABL at 3411 Silver Maple Place, Falls Church, Virginia
    22042.

mmand . . . >
Help F3=Exit F4=Prompt F7=Bkwd F8=Fwd F12=Cancel
PrevDoc F16=NextDoc F17=PrevWd F18=NextWd

SECRET

Figure 14. FBI confidential. The designation "199" means "national security matter."
This is first of over 30 pages of documentation obtained by the BBC and the National
Security News Service (Washington) indicating that the FBI was pulled off the trail of
"ABL" (Abdullah bin Laden) on September 11, 1996 – and reactivated exactly five years
later. According to agents and higher level sources in the CIA who spoke with us, before
the attack on the World Trade Center, these cases were shut down for political reasons.
While President Clinton "constrained" investigations of alleged Saudi funding of
terror networks and the making of the "Islamic" atomic bomb, Bush "Jr" effectively
"killed" those investigations – until September 2001.

humor of his comment, the insider added that the restrictions on the investigations ended on September 11.

And there was a lot to investigate – or in the case of the CIA and FBI under Bush, a lot to deliberately ignore. One international arms dealer (I'm sorry, but in this business, sinners are better sources than saints) described a meeting of Saudi billionaires at the Hotel Monceau in Paris in May 1996 to decide who would pay, and how much, to Osama bin Laden's operations. (Our information is that this was not an act of support for Osama but protection money to keep the mad bomber away from Saudi Arabia.) At a lower level, FBI agents let slip a document showing that, on September 11, 1996, the FBI closed an investigation on Bin Laden family members – not Osama – and their links to "alleged terrorist" organizations. FBI agents were livid that these investigations were shut down for five years – until September 11, when they were, for sad and obvious reasons, reactivated.

Was the FBI's case closed because there were no grounds to watch these groups and the Bin Ladens? At the time the FBI agents were directed to look away, one organization, the World Assembly of Muslim Youth (WAMY) was accused of connections to terror in India and the Philippines. Maybe they are completely innocent (the FBI targets lots of innocents, too many in fact), but the question was, why was the FBI blocked – then unblocked on September 11? When we asked, the answer came back from several sources: "Arbusto" and "Carlyle". A young George W. Bush made his first million as principal of Arbusto Oil, Texas. The nearly worthless venture ended up as a gold mine for the little Bush ("Arbusto" means "shrub" in Spanish), with financing and contracts from Saudi-linked businessmen and Gulf Arabs.

Carlyle is a holding and investment bank which, through its ownership of United Technologies and other arms makers, has become one of America's top defense contractors. It also has the distinction of having had both Bush *père* and *fils* as paid retainers. In 1999, the elder Bush traveled to Saudi Arabia as a Carlyle representative.

James Baker, Bush the First's pro-Saudi secretary of state, works for Carlyle; its chairman is Frank Carlucci, Bush Sr's former defense secretary. The Bin Laden family held a stake in the secretive private company until just after the September 11 attack. It would be absurd to say that the Presidents Bush spiked investigations of terrorist funding by the Saudis in return for packets of money. The system is not so crude. But it is quite natural to conclude that these smiling billionaires, where associates made your family wealthy, are unlikely to have funded mass murder of Americans, despite the evidence.

Bush Family Finances: The Best Democracy Money Can Buy

Writing in London, I have put up with condescending comments about America's democratic rituals from a nation with an unelected House of Lords occupied by a bunch of cross-dressing genetic fossils. It's easy to knock America, but the world should think of the $3 billion spent in the 2000 US election campaign in positive terms. Think of it as the privatization of democracy – though an outright auction for the presidency would have been more efficient.

George W. Bush may have lost at the ballot box but he won where it counts, at the piggy bank. The Son of a Bush rode right into the White House on a snorting porker stuffed with nearly half a billion dollars ($447 million): my calculation of the suffocating plurality of cash from Corporate America ("soft" money, "parallel" spending, "marketing fund"), a good 25 per cent more than Al Gore's take.

George W. could not have amassed this pile if his surname were Jones or Smith. The key to Dubya's money empire is Daddy Bush's post-White House work which, incidentally, raised the family's net worth by several hundred per cent.

Daddy Bush has many friends who filled up his sonny's campaign kitty while Bush performed certain lucrative favors for them. In 1998, Bush *père* created a storm in Argentina when he lobbied his close political ally, President Carlos Menem, to grant a gambling licence to Mirage Casino corporation.

Bush wrote that he had no personal interest in the deal. That's true. But Bush *fils* did not do badly. After the casino flap, Mirage dropped $449,000 into the Republican Party war chest.

The ex-president and famed Desert Stormtrooper-in-Chief also wrote to the oil minister of Kuwait on behalf of Chevron Oil Corporation. Bush says, honestly, that he "had no stake in the Chevron operation". Following this selfless use of his influence, the oil company put $657,000 into the Republican Party coffers. Most of the loot, reports the Center for Responsive Politics, came in the form of "soft money". That's the squishy stuff corporations use to ooze around US law which, you may be surprised to learn, prohibits any donations to presidential campaigns in the general election.

Not all of the elder Bush's work is voluntary. His single talk to the board of Global Crossing, the telecoms start-up, earned him $13 million in stock. The company also kicked in another million for his kid's run.

And while the Bush family steadfastly believes that ex-felons should not have the right to vote for president, they have no objection to ex-cons putting presidents on their payroll. In 1996, despite pleas by US church leaders, Daddy Bush gave several speeches (he charges $100,000 per talk) sponsored by organizations run by Rev. Sun Myung Moon, cult leader, tax cheat – and formerly, the guest of the US federal prison system.

Take two packets of payments to the Republican Party from ...

CENSORED [11]

The Bush family daisy chain of favors, friendship and campaign funding goes way back to Dubya's "War Years". Junior Bush was a fighter pilot during the war in Vietnam, not in the United States Air Force, where one could get seriously hurt, but in the Texas air force, known as the Air Guard. Texas's toy army, an artefact of Civil War days, is a favorite club for warmongers a bit squeamish about actual combat. Membership excused these weekend warriors from the military draft and the real shoot 'm up in 'Nam. Young George W. tested at 25 out of 100, one point above "too-dumb-to-fly" status, yet leaped ahead of hundreds of applicants to get the Guard slot.

In 1968, an aide to the Lone Star State's lieutenant governor Ben Barnes quietly suggested to Brig. Gen. James Rose that he find a safe spot in the Air Guard for Congressman George H. Bush's son. Neither of our Presidents Bush remember asking for this favor. How Barnes knew he should make the fix without a request from the powerful Bush family remains a mystery, one of those combinations of telepathy and coincidence common to Texas politics.

Fast forward to 1997. A company named GTech operated the Texas lottery. That year GTech's operation faced an unprecedented threat. The state's lottery director was sacked following revelations that GTech had put the director's boyfriend on the company payroll while he was under indictment for bribery. A new clean-hands director, Lawrence Littwin, ordered an audit, ended GTech's contract and put it out for re-bid. Littwin also launched an investigation into GTech's political donations.

Then a funny thing happened. The Texas Lottery Commission fired Littwin. Almost immediately thereafter, the Bush-appointed commissioners cancelled the bidding for a new operator, though the low bidder had already been announced to replace GTech. The commissioners also halted the financial audit, ended the political payola investigation – and gave the contract back to GTech.

---

11 *This part is all about a Canadian gold mining company that Bush Sr worked for after he left the White House. The story's a real page-turner: all about Daddy Bush, the dictator Suharto, Adnan Khashoggi (the arms trafficker pardoned by Bush Sr) and that gold mine in Nevada.*

Well, you won't read about it here. That's because there is some chance that someone may read this book while standing on the soil of the United Kingdom. The gold company's lawyers have demanded and received a promise from *Guardian Newspapers* never again to publish this article. For me to do so here would mean taking a chance that corporate censors might attempt to use libel courts to lock my paper in a financial Tower of London and suck our bank accounts dry. Read Joe Conason's story in *Salon*, "Exporting Corporate Control" which can be found at http://www.salon.com/news/col/cona/2001/07/20/gold/index.html.

So hand me the scissors; out it goes. No games, no coy rewriting of the material. If Britons want to read a free press, they should go to Moscow or Tanzania or Bolivia where this information has been published – or, alternatively, trade in your Queen for a written constitutional guarantee of freedom of the press. In fact, you can borrow America's – we aren't using it.

Why did the Texas government work so hard at saving GTech's licence? An unsigned letter to the US Justice Department points to one lobbyist to whom GTech paid fees of $23 *million* – Ben Barnes. The letter accuses Barnes of using his knowledge of Governor Bush's draft-dodging to lock in GTech's exclusive deal with the state. In court papers filed in a civil racketeering suit brought by discharged regulator Littwin, Barnes confessed that he got Bush into the Guard and took millions from GTech. Littwin asserted that other witnesses can prove the cash bought the governor's influence to save GTech's licence.

GTech responds, irrefutably, that it terminated the contract with Barnes before the 1997 dismissals of the lottery directors – but not before the blackmailing alleged in the anonymous letter. And, although the company denies it maintained the financial connection to Barnes, GTech's chairman Guy Snowden[12] was a partner in a big real estate venture with Barnes's wife.

What did GTech get for their $23 million to Barnes, the man who saved Dubya from the war (to which Bush Sr happily sent other men's sons)? Can't say: in November 1999 GTech paid a reported $300,000 to Littwin. In return, the whistleblower agreed to seal forever Barnes's five-hour deposition transcript about the Bush family influence on the Lottery and the Air Guard.

I'm not complaining, mind you. After all, the Bush family has given us the best democracy money can buy.

Republicans and Democrats, Hand in Hand, to Save the Billionaire Boys' Club

A thoughtful reader found my Texas tales about President Bush a wee harsh:

> *"G'day, asshole! Smelled any good ones lately? That's generally where guys like you have their noses. By the way, it's PRESIDENT Bush to you, numbnuts. Now, have a g'day and may Ireland be free!"*

> *So I resolved to be a bit fairer – and take a look at the strange financial history of the Arkansas Hillary-Billies. I thought it proper to check Special Prosecutor Ken Starr's evidence. He had nothing. Starr, whose mind is as small as it is vicious, spent $40 million investigating the Clintons and turned up with little more than a bucket of dirty "Whitewater", a stained dress and some overwritten soft porn, "So then I pulled down the President's ... ." How could they find nothing? Part of the problem was that Starr and staff were no Sam Spades, just a bunch of right-wing preppy snots from white-shoe law firms who thought they could replace investigative know-how with unlimited meanness.*

---

12 In 1995, Snowden was forced to resign as chairman of GTech when a jury found he tried to bribe British billionaire Richard Branson.

But if Starr was lost in a nutty cavort with Clinton's slick willy, the Senate Governmental Affairs Committee was looking into the serious stuff: six-figure payments to Hillary's former law partners by the Riady family of Indonesia and Entergy International of Little Rock, Arkansas, Hillary's former client. (When it came to foreign policy that suited Entergy, the Clinton Administration could not be more accommodating.) Then, in 1998, just as the Republicans on the Senate Committee were closing in on the evidence that could, if borne out, pull down the Clintons ... the Committee closed its investigation.

Why? In 1998, I found an answer: "Triad."

Clinton was saved from this far more threatening inquiry by two of America's wealthiest industrialists, Charles and David Koch. They had not set out to rescue Clinton. The Koch brothers despise Clinton with a passion.

Koch Industries is the biggest company you've never heard of – and their owners like it that way. Estimates of its annual turnover, at $35 billion a year, make it bigger than Microsoft or Boeing Aircraft. We can only estimate because Koch [pronounced "coke" like the cola] is a private corporation, second largest in the US. David and Charles Koch, who own nearly all of it, are reported to have a combined net worth of $4 billion.

The Koch clan's fortune originated in Russia where daddy Fred Koch built oil refineries for Stalin's regime. In 1946, Koch returned from the Soviet Union to Wichita, Kansas, and founded the ultra-right John Birch Society. David and Charles have rejected their father's politics, preferring to back ultra-*ultra* right-wing causes. In 1980, as a Libertarian Party candidate, David campaigned against Ronald Reagan.

Secrecy is the Kochs' trademark. From headquarters in Wichita, they operate the nation's only private, secure telephone network outside the CIA to control their core business as America's largest purchaser of oil and gas from small farmers and Indian reservations.

As a private company, the Kochs answer to no one about their expenditures. No little old ladies query them at stockholder meetings. Unconstrained, the Koch brothers can indulge their singular dream. Where other US corporations throw a few million dollars into the political arena in the hope of obtaining a few special favors, the Kochs have spent close to $100 million to change the entire tone of political discourse in America.

And they succeeded. With $21 million spent to establish the Cato Institute in Washington DC, $30 million to start the Council for a Sound Economy and tens of millions more for think tanks, political action committees and the like, they constructed a nonpareil policy apparatus which reinvigorated the anti-government movement with a new intellectual legitimacy backed by fearsome political clout. From Cato and the Koch machine came Newt Gingrich's "Contract for America" and the funds to put Gingrich in power in the 1994 elections.

Not that the Kochs don't call in special favors. In 1989, the US Senate Special Committee on Investigations reported that "Koch Oil, a subsidiary of Koch Industries, is the most dramatic example of an oil company stealing by deliberate mismeasurement and fraudulent reporting." FBI agents had watched Koch Industries trucks taking, but not fully paying for, oil from little gathering tanks on Indian reservations. An expert for Indian tribes calculates that $1.5 billion of Koch Industries' wealth comes from pilfered oil. Koch denies all charges.

Action against Koch stalled until 1995 when an FBI agent on the Senate investigation, Richard Elroy, charged in a letter to the Justice Department that criminal prosecution had been declined "for political reasons" during the first Bush presidency. But Clinton's Justice Department followed up on the FBI's evidence and filed civil lawsuits charging Koch Industries with 315 wilful acts of pollution. Clinton also empanelled two grand juries to consider criminal indictments.

The government's case would have collapsed if one clause of the "Contract for America", the Regulatory Reform Act, had become law.

Passage of the legislation depended upon the Republicans holding their majority in Congress. In the 1996 election cycle, Republican control was in jeopardy. Crucial to their ultimate narrow victory in that campaign was a multi-million dollar television advertising blitz in key districts paid for by the Coalition for Our Children's Future, a registered charity. The action was extra-ordinary for a child protection society – as was their choice of candidates to assist. Only weeks before CCF purchased the adverts, every one of the incumbent congressmen they helped, all Republicans, voted to abolish food stamps for children of the poor.

The politicians supported by the "Children's" fund had something in common besides an antipathy to free meals for youngsters. Their districts contained Koch operations.

US law prohibits corporate payments in aid of political campaigns. Investigators with the Senate Governmental Affairs Committee located bank records linking the Children's charity and other political front groups to Triad Management, an operation funded by the Kochs. Democratic senators threatened to subpoena Koch Industries' chiefs to question whether they funded Triad and manipulated its related groups. Democrats could drag the tycoons before the same public tribunal on campaign finances skewering Clinton.

A key Senate insider, who must remain anonymous, says Republicans then offered a straightforward trade: "A truce – you don't do Triad, we don't do Clinton." Other sources inside the Committee confirm that the Republicans, under the direction of Senators Trent Lott and Don Nickles, rather than risk exposure of the Kochs' web of mega-dollar funding operations, agreed to shut down the money probe and let Clinton off the hook.

The true, unreported reason for the collapse of the inquiry most threatening to Clinton – the one that could have knocked him out of office, the Indonesia money chain – reveals the ultimate measure of Koch influence, that Republicans sacrificed their case against the president to keep their secret benefactors under wraps.

Both parties were content with their mutual protection agreement. With the important fundraising allegations off limits, there has been nothing left for Republican investigators to do – except rummage through Monica Lewinsky's dirty laundry and sniff at the president's zipper.

I ran this story in the Observer. *It was, of course, never reported in the US. Why did Democratic insiders give me this information? Because they were spitting mad at the Republicans; the Dems thought they had a cease-fire and the Republicans were playing games with the Monica Lewinsky story. Republicans decided that the deal only barred investigation of campaign finances; and did not include light-weight stuff like the president's playing stinky finger with an intern.*

I discovered the deal not because I was on some kind of hunt for the goods on Clinton or on Newt Gingrich, but because, in my old day-job as an investigator and government adviser, I'd been tracking the Koch brothers, Entergy Corporation and the Riady interests. (See "California Reamin': Hunting the Power Pirates" in Chapter 4.) That both Entergy and Koch, master deal-makers, popped up in the middle of a Senate inquiry which suddenly stopped dead gave off the smell of a bit too much bipartisan cooperation.

The Kochs, by the way, are a real piece of work. FBI agents caught their company skimming oil out of the gathering tanks of poor Indians in Oklahoma in the 1980s. Maybe the top guys at Koch Industries, the billionaire brothers themselves, didn't know about the skimming game; maybe there was a good explanation. But not according to Roger Williams, an executive in the oil-gathering operation.

Williams kept records of the filching – a couple of dollars worth of oil here, a couple there – hardly the kind of petty cash that billionaires would seem to bother with. But Williams (on tape I've obtained) was asked how Charles Koch reacted to a paper that "showed how much overage they had and how many dollars". Williams said, of billionaire Koch and another executive with him at the time, "They would just giggle and nudge each other, you know, it's kind of a fun time."

And that's where I heard the phrase that well explains the success of some of America's wealthiest corporate chiefs. Williams was surprised at the billionaire's concern over these small-change scams, but Williams said Charles Koch told him, "*I want my fair share and that's all of it.*"

7

Cash-for-Access – "Lobbygate":
The Real Story of Blair and the Sale of Britain

On the first Wednesday of July 1998, on the floor of the House of Commons, Britain's prime minister rose to defend himself. According to the news reports, for the first time since his election the year before, Tony Blair's hands were shaking. The PM denounced the American reporter whose exposé of wholesale corruption in his cabinet "had not one shred of evidence". Meanwhile, Blair's spokesman, a former pornographer named Alastair Campbell, grabbed every newsman he could find in the hallway to whisper that they should not trust a "man in a hat", while Peter Mandelson, known as Prince of Darkness, and the power behind the power of the prime minister, hissed a warning about "the man with an agenda".

Unfortunately, I couldn't enjoy any of this. I could hardly keep my eyes open, half-passed-out after 70 sleepless hours in my "safe house" in Crouch End. I had moved in with sympathetic friends in the middle of the night because of a crank bomb scare at my hotel and to avoid camera crews.

But that's not why I didn't get any sleep. My paper, the *Observer*, had run a front-page story with detailed evidence that cronies of the prime minister, including his princeling and other cabinet members, had bartered policies for payola, cash for access. Our *Observer* team described lobbyists' special, secret access to ministers operating a flea market for favors out of 10 Downing Street. *Not a shred of evidence?* My paper announced that I had *tape recordings* of lobbyists explaining exactly how and when and to whom they made the fixes – for Tesco's supermarkets, for American power companies, for friends of Clinton, friends of Bush, friends of Blair and for Rupert Murdoch.

Blair's attack-masters demanded, the radio and TV stations demanded, *I play the tapes*. They said, the tapes are phoney. They don't exist. Palast's a liar. And now the business editor of the *Observer*, the brilliant journalistic fanatic Ben Laurance, was shouting at my friends trying to block him at the door at my Crouch End hideaway that I had to get out of bed, get to the BBC studios and confront with tape the number one New Labour fixer, Derek Draper, on another live *Newsnight* broadcast.

But the truth was, I didn't have the tape.

The day before, I called my wife back home in the States with our one-year-old twins and told her to express to me the tape marked "Draper". It was right in the middle of my desk. Linda said, "I don't see any tape. There's no tape here."

The next day, the entire front page of the *Mirror* was taken up by a photo of a balding, snearing, devious-looking man – me – under a four-inch-high screamer, "THE LIAR".

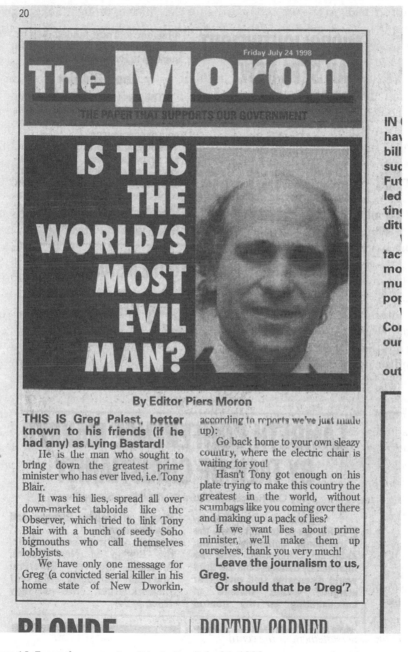

Figure 15. From the magazine *Private Eye*, July 24, 1998

"CASH FOR ACCESS – LOBBYGATE" began innocently enough. Antony Barnett, Britain's best investigative journalist, got a tip that lobbying firms close to Blair's New Labour Party government were getting their hands on inside information to pass on to their clients. Antony who, with the editor, Will Hutton, had just asked if I could write for the *Observer*, thought I might give a couple of these guys a call, maybe hinting to our targets I needed a little influence.

At first, I said no. My idea had been to bring to journalism the full arsenal of weapons used in my official racketeering probes. No more quick and cheap. What I had in mind would take time and it would cost thousands of pounds.

To do this right, we needed a front, for which I enlisted a top US business executive, Mark Swedlund, formerly with Booz Allen Hamilton, who mixes street smarts with boardroom savvy. We added a former Morgan Stanley executive (no name, sorry) and gave ourselves impressive legitimacy by tying up with one of America's white shoe law firms well known to Her Majesty (no names, sorry again).

The most difficult fake-out was to recreate me. All these lobbyists knew me; it was their job to know. They knew I contributed to the *Guardian*, but more important, I was, before the election, one of Blair's much displayed American policy advisers, close in with Blair's Trade and Industry and energy ministers, "that influential American", said a big-shot British industrialist. It was bullshit, but now it would be useful bullshit.

I couldn't wear a false moustache and voice-coder – so I changed from Greg Palast, policy weanie and reporter, to Greg Palast, scuzz-ball, sleaze-o-"consultant" on the take ... *just like them*. I didn't get my beach-front estate and stable of ponies, I told them, by writing good government advice for the *Guardian*. I had a damn successful consulting firm that made *deals*.

At no time did we offer money in return for influence or access or favors (though they would be offered to *us*). I was looking for something else: what had these lobbyists already done for *others*. My line: "The Texans I'm working with don't want a lot of boasting horseshit, *these boys need hard, no-nonsense evidence of exactly what you've done, for whom. Names, dates, deeds, and solid proof, if you want our business.*"

And they delivered ... right to our suite at the London Tower Hotel.

Lobbygate – Cash for Access

Complete and uncut

> *"There are 17 people that count. To say that I am intimate with every one of them is the understatement of the century."*

On the morning of June 8, 1998, I found a surprise in my fax machine, a copy of the Trade and Industry Select Report on Energy Policy. What made it surprising was that the report had not yet been released to the public.

Attached to the fax was a short, hand-written note to me from Karl Milner of GJW Government Relations. Through the 1997 general election, Milner handled internal communications for Gordon Brown, then Shadow Chancellor. Milner wrote, "Thought you may be interested."

I was. In May, the *Observer* received a tip from reliable sources that certain lobbyists had offered clients advance drafts of confidential government papers. But our investigation nearly crashed on take-off. When I first contacted Milner on behalf of two American clients seeking "an influential presence" in Britain, he immediately recognized me as a writer for the *Guardian*. Yet surprisingly, he faxed the restricted government document to my offices at Union Associates in New York, a firm well known for its investigations of corporate corruption.

I called Milner. Maybe he had not filched the documents from the government but rather had committed the lesser offense of lifting a pre-release copy from a journalist. Milner assured me otherwise. His special access to policy papers for his clients was standard operating procedure. "We have many friends in government. They like to run things past us some days in advance, to get our view, to let them know if they have anything to be worried about, maybe suggest some changes." The report contained crucial recommendations sought by another potential client to whom he was pitching.[13]

The managing director of Milner's firm is Andrew Gifford, chairman of the Association of Professional Political Consultants. The Nolan Committee on Standards of Conduct, Britain's ethics watchdog, praised the Association's voluntary Code of Conduct. The government concluded the industry could police itself without government regulation.

"I'm very excited"

June 11: the Chancellor of the Exchequer, Gordon Brown, announced new government spending caps. I was trying to end my third phone call with Derek Draper, top lobbyist with GPC Market Access. Draper had been chief aide to Minister without Portfolio Peter Mandelson. "I'm *very excited*," said Draper, "Very excited."

What had so excited Mr Draper?

"Gordon Brown put the cap on total spending at 2.75 per cent, not 2.5 per cent, like everyone expected! And we said so! We said so last week!"

This one-quarter percentage point difference may seem minuscule, but in the hands of securities traders and arbitrageurs, advance word could be parlayed into quite a windfall. Indeed, the week earlier, Draper had given the

13 I can now say that was Enron, the energy Goliath from Texas, tight in with the Bush family. See, "Ah, the Smell of Texas in the Morning" in Chapter 6.

correct number to his client Salomon Brothers, the US investment banking giant. I complimented Draper on his firm's extraordinary forecasting work. He responded, "No, I'm afraid it's inside information." In a voice crackling with school-boy glee, Draper added, "If they [Salomon] acted on it, they'd have made a fortune!"

Indeed they would have. And under US law, they would have risked jail time.

The *Observer* never asked any lobbyist to produce confidential government documents or information. We did not have to. Milner, Draper and others provided the evidence unrequested, meant to convince us they could deliver the goods from Tony Blair's New Labour government.

Draper too quickly recognized me as a writer with the *Guardian* and *Observer*. Yet, from our first New York-to-London call, Draper gossiped, gushed and ultimately could not resist revealing his special access to the Treasury and Downing Street.

If we retained his firm, what could he deliver for our money? Could he secure a seat on one of the government's task forces? Done! "We just got the Chief Executive of British Gas on the government's Welfare to Work Task Force." Draper emphasized that winning this coveted spot at the elbow of the chancellor was an enormous achievement for a company once known in Labour circles as "the Fat Cats headed by Cedric the Pig" (an unkind reference to former British Gas chairman Cedric Brown).

What if my clients had reputations far less savoury than BG? Not a problem. In fact, Draper was about to sign up such a "challenging" client, US lottery operator GTech Corp (another company close to the Bushes). The company was in hot water. A jury had found them guilty of attempting to bribe the British tycoon Richard Branson (they wanted him to drop his competing bid for Britain's lottery). Blair had committed to oust GTech from the lucrative Camelot consortium, which had exclusive rights to operate the UK lottery. Draper described his scheme-in-progress to waltz GTech around the official watchdogs and lure Labour ministers into a sticky web of agreements with his new client.

"The government needed someone to sell tickets for this ridiculous Millennium Dome thing that my old boss is building. But GTech is offering to do that via the national lottery-selling equipment. Now it doesn't take a lot to work out that if the government thinks that GTech can sell government tickets for the Dome then it's got to be a legitimate firm to sell tickets for the lottery. See what I mean? Our forte, like, is to be *imaginative*."

His "old boss" was Peter Mandelson, minister without portfolio, architect of the New Labour shift to the right. To call Draper and Mandy close would be a grievous understatement. Mandy had dedicated his book, *The Blair Revolution*, to the young man.

In a recent profile in *Business on Sunday* Draper said his friendships with Labour's top office-holders were a "hindrance" to his lobbying business because his former workmates are "all so concerned to be ethical". Nevertheless, Draper assured me that, if we needed to change a law to our liking, "I can have tea with

Geoffrey Robinson! I can get in to Ed Balls!" When Draper spoke of reaching Paymaster General Robinson and Balls, the chancellor's chief adviser, you could hear the exclamation points in his voice. He added, "Once someone pays us."

A kind of schizophrenia

While fielding calls and faxes from Draper and Milner, we reached Lawson Lucas Mendelsohn, a firm less than one year old yet already the hottest lobby group in town, collecting £2 million in billings in one year. LLM lists 20 powerful clients including the RSPCA and Rupert Murdoch's News International. Named for its three founders, LLM is the definition of "inside". Neal Lawson advised Tony Blair on campaign strategy, Ben Lucas conducted Blair's political briefings and Jon Mendelsohn handled the future prime minister's contacts with business.

But LLM is no influence-for-hire operation that can be purchased by anyone with a check-book. To obtain their much-sought services, LLM clients are asked to review and embrace an eleven-page introductory statement of principles and methods, a somewhat chilling mix of Peter Mandelson and Nietzsche. A chart on page 3 displays two columns labelled in bold face, "The Passing World and The Emerging World". To the Passing World belong "ideology", "conviction" and "politicians who lead". These will be replaced in the Emerging World by pragmatism, consumption and "politicians who listen". The sales brochure-cum-manifesto announces that the political terms Right and Left are now "obsolete". LLM promises to guide clients to understand "not only new Labour but more importantly the new world".

Partner Ben Lucas knows what government will do because "we know how they think". But what may seem like telepathic prognosticating comes down to harvesting insider leaks. Lucas knew, for example, that on June 11 Gordon Brown would announce the creation of a new housing inspectorate. "The reason I knew that in advance is that I was speaking to people who were writing the chancellor's speech." He delivered the information to an LLM client and advised them on ways to capitalize on the early warning.

Also, like his competitor Draper, Lucas had several days' notice of details in the chancellor's public spending announcement. Lucas offered up other examples of "intelligence which in market terms would be worth a lot of money".

The inside track on decisions is one thing, influencing the outcome is another. Influence requires access. What could we obtain for our monthly retainer? LLM's Lawson trumped GPC's tea with Geoffrey Robinson by offering, if needed, to "reach *anyone*. We can go to Gordon Brown if we have to." His partner Lucas commented, "We use relationships in a subtle way."

And how were these relationships subtly used? On behalf of Tesco, LLM were about to derail the chancellor's plan for a tax on car parks. LLM was holding secret negotiations that very week with Policy Unit advisers to Blair, the ones who told Deputy Prime Minister John Prescott, nominally in charge of the issue, when to jump and how high. The tax, pushed by environmentalists to discourage excessive auto use, would have cost the supermarket giant more than £20 million annually.

Lawson also took credit for taking the regulatory heat off Anglian Water. The utility had failed to live up to its promises to invest in reducing water leakage, and had run into trouble in mishandling sewer sludge. And LLM successfully lobbied against trade union pleas for easier recognition.

When complimented for avoiding less reputable clients such as GTech, Lawson countered that he had in fact lobbied for the scandal-plagued lottery operator. LLM used Labour's trust in them to "assure the government how [GTech] will behave". GTech does not appear on the LLM's published client list.

Lawson and Lucas were quick to point out that lobbying is not all about calls to the Treasury. Sometimes LLM recommends the indirect route, "placing things with columnists we know the chancellor reads". They called this "creating an environment". In addition, LLM operates a captive think tank, Nexus, to give their views (or their clients' views) the imprimatur of academic legitimacy. Sometimes they make use of the Socialist Environmental Research Foundation, which, Lucas assured me, is a purchased front for retailers.

Lawson explained how LLM plays on what they call politics without leadership. In a milieu in which a lack of conviction is deemed an asset, with no fixed star of principles by which to steer, policy is susceptible to the last pitch heard over cocktails. "The Labour government is always of two minds, it operates in a kind of schizophrenia. On big issues especially, they don't know what they are thinking. Blair himself doesn't always know what he is thinking."

Lunch at Number 10

Draper was now aware that he had competitors for our business, and he determined to display his prowess at opening the doors to power. "I took the chief executive of the House Builders Federation in to see Geoff Norris [Blair's policy adviser] the other day, and that meeting *took place in the Downing Street dining room!* It's not difficult for me to take people into these people."

Sensing I was not impressed with merely breaking bread with ministers, he offered a story certain to leave an impression. Draper's client PowerGen PLC has long hungered to buy a regional electricity company, but even Conservative trade minister Ian Lang had rejected such an acquisition as a naked attempt to create an electricity monopoly controlling a third of England. Lang's successor at the Department of Trade and Industry (DTI), Margaret Beckett, appointed by Blair, had already blasted such competition-killing combinations. PowerGen's case seemed lost. Now Draper told me he'd steered the chairman of PowerGen, Ed Wallis, around Beckett and brought him directly into the Treasury for a confidential meeting with a top adviser to Chancellor Brown. The PowerGen merger deal is now locked. Government rejection "will not happen again". Had Draper pulled off an extraordinary fix or was this merely hard-sell horsefeathers?

I told Draper my own clients, representing US oil shippers and power plant builders, would need exemptions from environmental rules, in effect, a licence to pollute England. Draper had told me, "I don't sell my mates," but in this case, if we retained him, he would go straight "to Number 10 [to] one of my best friends, Liz Lloyd," whom Blair had put in charge of environment matters at the Downing Street Public Policy Unit.

Why would he not take us to the minister of the environment? In response, Draper introduced me to the ways of what he calls "Policy World, the little world of business people and politicians" with true authority. A good lobbyist not only opens doors, he steers his clients away from those who have fallen off the surface of this potent planet. "There is an environmental minister, Michael Meacher. He's *very* weak and basically he's irrelevant and nobody should have to take him into account. To be honest with you, he's a nobody going nowhere, so I wouldn't particularly sort him out. I don't think he'll be in the job much longer. Then the DTI obviously matter, but they're very weak, as people perceive Margaret Beckett to be useless and perceive [energy minister] John Battle to be pretty useless. So if you wanted to change the government's approach, quite frankly, you don't want to advocate to someone in the DTI."

Interestingly, Draper strongly advised against currying favour with Labour through political donations, though he could arrange a sponsorship of a Labour event, in which case, my clients' names could be shielded from publicity.

The Nigerian connection

Shandwick Public Affairs' annual revenues of £2.6 million make it the biggest operator in the influence game. Shandwick's chief operative, Colin Byrne, formerly Blair's press aide, is older than his go-go competitors, more reserved and less given to boasting about a fix. Byrne never offered a stolen document, never tried to sell lunch at Downing Street.

Byrne's new partner is Chris Savage, recently of the Trades Union Congress. The firm advertises his services as "one of the few people on the Left who really understands industry policy". They are joined by Richard Aylard who, says his company profile, "drafted all of HRH's speeches and articles on the environment" from 1989 to 1996. Prince Charles need not lift his pen.

How did Shandwick employ these progressive and green credentials? According to Byrne, their signal accomplishment was what he terms "corporate reputation management" for Shell International. Their prime assignment was to create a political shield for Shell Oil's operations in Nigeria in the wake of the Nigerian dictatorship's execution of Ken Saro-Wira. Saro-Wira had organized indigenous protests against the oil company. Did anyone at Downing Street find Shandwick's defense of Shell in Nigeria a bit offputting? "No, not at all!" Byrne assured me. Indeed, with their reputation under Shandwick's management, "Shell are now perceived as very much being the Good Guys again."

In the entire tour of lobby shops, not one of these former environmentalists and anti-sleaze crusaders signalled qualms about flacking for a Shell or a GTech – with a single exception. A Labour-connected lobbyist handling a big-name corporate account passed me a note asking for help in landing a non-profit organization as a client, "So I can stop working for these pigs."

Part II: To London
Understatement of the century

Monday, June 23. The investigation moved to the Sanctuary building at Westminster Abbey. Within this historic courtyard at Number 7, GPC Access's Derek Draper guides us through the peculiarities of British democracy.

"There are 17 people who count," Draper tells us. "And to say I am intimate with every one of them is *the understatement of the century*." This intimacy is based on a web of favors of which the lobbyist keeps a careful mental inventory. At Gordon Brown's confidential request, he put out a supposedly independent newsletter praising the chancellor's minimum wage proposal. In the *Sunday Telegraph*, he authored a 2,000-word profile of Ed Balls, a Brown aide. He'd given Balls editorial control and the *Telegraph* was none the wiser. As to Jonathan Powell, the prime minister's chief of staff, gatekeeper at Number 10, "I got him the job."

Draper lectures us that one must not call in these chits in a crude manner. In seeking favors from government chiefs, "It is important to reference the New Labour mindset and flatter them into thinking their viewpoint is new. You say to Geoffrey Robinson, for example, that he is very important."

My "business partner", Mark Swedlund, interrogated Draper. We Americans have come for access, not lessons in Labour rhetoric. We needed proof of Draper's insider bona fides.

Draper rose to the challenge, literally. He stood up from his chair, removed a phone pager from his belt and, holding it above his forehead, read off one phone message after another, nearly two dozen, from the powerful and near-to-power. "Ed Miliband – call me, Dave Miliband – please call, Andrew Hackett … that's [deputy prime minister] Prescott's office." The recitation continued. There were several messages from Liz Lloyd of the Downing Street Policy Unit, Balls from the Treasury and others, each pleading for a moment of the lobbyist's time for tea, advice or requests unknown.

The lobbyist was in a cheery mood. His walking the CEO of the Builders' Federation into Downing Street the week before was already paying dividends. Blair's adviser Geoff Norris agreed to resurrect the Builders' plans to dig up several greenbelt areas for houses. "Just a bloody bunch of mud tracts at the edge of town," as Draper described the lands at issue, despite the claims of local councils.

Such favors must be returned. "Tony needed ten environmental gimmicks" for a news release to support the government's green image. Draper rapidly provided a list, "electric cars, silly things like that". Draper rolled his eyes. "They loved it."

Message to Murdoch

Our next stop, Soho. There, in the trendy loft offices of LLM lobbyists Ben Lucas and Jon Mendelsohn, we endured a mind-numbing two-hour lecture on the Third Way, "analytically-driven evidence-based decision-making," a solid wall of New Labour-speak.

But what at first seemed like an aimless think tank seminar had purpose. Lucas and Mendelsohn's point was to introduce us to a world in which, as their manifesto told us, message matters more than content. For their fee of £5,000–20,000 per month, these two Professor Higginses would instruct us in the political grammar of the Emerging World of Tony Blair.

Our cover story was that we needed LLM's help in defeating environmental restrictions, as they had done for Anglian Water. Mendelsohn advised we must recast our plan for new power stations, noisy and polluting, into something that sounded earth-friendly. "Tony is very anxious to be seen as green. Everything has to be couched in environmental language – even if it's slightly Orwellian."

But LLM demands more of their clients than adopting new PR gloss. LLM clients are expected to "reshape their core corporate culture", to get in sync with New Labour's vision, as their client Tesco had done to defeat the car park tax. Part of Tesco's cultural reshaping involved dropping £11 million into Mandelson's Millennium Dome project.

Once we have changed our culture, we asked exactly how does LLM help us get a law changed? Lucas said, "This government likes to do deals."

He gave an example. Labour's anti-monopoly competition bill threatened LLM client Rupert Murdoch's media empire, a little problem with alleged predatory pricing practices. LLM carried the word from Downing Street to Murdoch's News International that, if their tabloids toned down criticism of the bill, the law's final language would reflect the government's appreciation. On the other hand, harsh coverage in Murdoch's papers could provoke problems for the media group in Parliament's union recognition debates. The message to muzzle journalists was not, said Lucas, "an easy one in their culture". However, the outcome pleased all parties.

Unlike his wheeler-dealer partners, Jon Mendelsohn, aloof and intellectual, does not have an obvious ounce of fixer in him. Rather, he is their Big Idea man with a deep understanding of Blair's obsession with corporate and media contacts. "Labour's super-majority in Parliament means the only countervailing force is media and the business community. So when the economy turns soft, as it naturally must, we will make certain they stay with us. If we have business and media, the people will come along."

Given this grand plan, it was not difficult for LLM to secure places for their clients on official task forces. The problem was the opposite: LLM's challenge was to procure a steady supply of executives to feed Labour's insatiable appetite for industry contacts. Clients were complaining about the explosive number of task forces, panels and "quango" meetings that Labour asked them to attend.

Mendelsohn concluded, "'Lobbying' is a misnomer. The fact that you know someone is irrelevant. Friendship accounts for nothing."

But just in case, Lucas reeled off a list of their cronies and favors owed by each: "[Home Secretary] Jack Straw asked us to set up ... Gordon Brown asked us to host ... ." And so on.

Lucas reviewed their awesome fee schedule, and we were on our way.

Over-priced claret

Rush hour in Soho. We walked down the street to the Groucho Club where we would be guests of an operative with yet another lobby shop. He'd got word that these Americans were looking for political help. Over a bottle of over-priced claret, we listened to one more young Blairite make his pitch for our business.

We then detailed what his competitors had on offer: Milner's purloined reports, Draper's deals with Ed Balls, LLM's insider information from the Exchequer.

I waited for him to top their accomplishments. He put both hands over his eyes. "It's appalling," he said, "It's *disturbing*." If that's what we wanted, he'd have none of our business.

This was political consulting's finest hour.[14]

Mr Liddle's offer

The next evening, GPC held its annual bash at the Banqueting Room in Whitehall Palace. Under vaulted ceilings inset with nine canvasses by Rubens, GPC's 200 guests washed down thin canapés with a never-ending supply of champagne (Lambray Brut) poured by discreet waiters. Lords, MPs and

14 I'm withholding the firm's name – exposing a lobbyist's rectitude could cost them. I discovered they had already lost the business of an American power company seeking to get to the Treasury's Ed Balls to reverse another quasi-judicial decision by Minister Beckett. Their *beau geste* was for naught. Our information is that Blair personally stepped in over Beckett after a request from the White House.

Downing Street powers by the dozen mixed with the nation's business elite. It was Derek Draper's phone pager come to life.

At the center of this swirl, Draper held court. Yet, he graciously took the time to offer us free samples of his connections, introducing us to several government luminaries who could be useful to our projects, including more than half the prime minister's Policy Unit. From the chairman of the Select Committee on Trade and Industry we endured an earnest discourse on the development of Parliament's energy review (and we confirmed how lobbyist Milner of GJW received advance information of his committee's report).

We asked Draper to point us to someone who could vouch for his influence with government. He reached out, seeming to pull at random from the crowd the nearest figure. He grabbed a short, balding man with sweat beaded on his forehead. Derek told the official we were potential GPC clients, then walked off.

Roger Liddle is one of the more important men in government, in charge of European affairs for Blair's Public Policy Unit, with an office in 10 Downing Street. After some chit-chat about our electricity generators, we asked Liddle if Draper was as influential as he claimed. Liddle leaned forward. "There is a Circle." Liddle was now whispering. "There is a Circle and Derek is part of the Circle. And anyone who says he isn't is An Enemy." He reassured us that, "Derek knows all the *right* people."

Could Draper introduce us to key policy-makers? In response, Liddle handed us a card with his Downing Street and home phone numbers, and made this extraordinary offer. "Whenever you are ready, just tell me *what* you want, *who* you want to meet and Derek and I will make the call for you."

Derek and I. It was a strange locution. Swedlund remarked that Liddle sounded "more like a member of Derek's outfit than a member of the government". It was not until the next day we learned that Swedlund was not far off. Liddle had, until the general election, been managing director of Draper's firm. Officially, he'd placed his 25 per cent ownership interest in GPC Access into a blind trust when he took the post at Downing Street. Any new business Liddle cooked up for Draper could go right into the Liddle's "blind" piggy bank.

Jail

The next morning I received a call from the persistent lobbyist from the Groucho. He still refused to match his competitors' offers. "If Draper and Lawson delivered half of what they promise *they'd be in jail!* Half of Downing Street would be in jail!"

Phone call from Tony

"What I really am," said Derek Draper the next day, "is a commentator-fixer. Your Mayor Daley has nothing on me." We were sitting in the exclusive Reform

Club on Pall Mall. Draper sipped his trademark champagne and sank into a red leather armchair under a tall painting of an aristocrat from another century. He tossed a copy of *Progress* magazine on the antique table. "I own it," he said of the Blairite journal, "100 per cent of it, all the shares." The funds to launch the magazine came from an unnamed "Labour billionaire",[15] a financial arrangement accomplished by "a single phone call from Tony". In the lobbyists' world, there are no last names.

Draper had just filed his weekly column published in the *Express*. His writings are edited in an unusual manner. "I don't write that column without vetting it with Peter Mandelson. They say, Oh Gordon will be mad at Derek, but he won't because his press secretary has vetted it."

It was June 25. For Draper, it was a day of miracles he had prophesied. Only two hours earlier, the government released its energy review. The coal industry would be saved if PowerGen agreed to sell a few generating plants. Simultaneously, newspapers reported PowerGen would buy Midlands Electricity for £2 billion, if the government approved. The suspicious alignment of the two announcements forced Trade Minister Beckett to deny categorically that a secret deal had been struck. "There has been no wink or nod to anyone about anything." But then, how would she know? Wallis's meeting at the Treasury was a quiet affair, no record of it was kept and, as Neal Lawson informed me, Beckett is "out of the loop".

Draper should have been pleased with his success. But his mood was philosophical. "I don't want to be a consultant," he said. "I just want to stuff my bank account at £250 an hour."

Of all the things Draper told me, the most astonishing is that he was only 33 years old.

Beer at Crouch End

From the Reform Club, Swedlund and I took a cab for a get-together with Will Baker, another lobbyist of sorts.

We joined up with Baker at a friend's flat in Crouch End. Baker works as an anti-poverty campaigner for a large organization based in Liverpool. The group is pleading with Labour to eliminate electricity and gas heating disconnections, and this puts them squarely up against Draper's and Milner's key clients, the utility companies. The anti-poverty group lacks the £8,000 a month to hire an LLM or other professional consultants, so Baker and his colleagues must themselves act as lobbyists on behalf of their low-income constituents.

Over Budweisers at the kitchen table, Baker said his group failed to get a meeting with a single key minister during the government's Utility Review,

15 Later, Barnett, my partner at the *Observer*, would find out the secret billionaire was Lord Sainsbury, rewarded by Blair with a cabinet post most helpful to his business interests in genetically modified food production.

not even contact with junior civil servants. "We can't get in the door. They tell us to submit our comments in writing. We are just totally excluded." He could not imagine an invitation to sit on a Task Force.[16]

The curtain comes down

It's hard not to like Draper, Milner and Lawson. They each have that Bart Simpson charm: mischievous, a bit immature, yet endearing. And they exude New Labour's *enthusiasm* for the New Britain. Do any of these young men harbour misgivings about renting out their contacts? They see no reason for apology. It's their world after all. They are convinced that they crafted New Labour and now, through GPC, GJW and LLM, they are merely charging admission to enter the show they produced.

But even the best players of the game fear for its future. Derek Draper, in an unusually reflective moment, said he had worried thoughts about the inside access to government that goes under the rubric "public–private partnership". Draper said, "I think there will be a scandal here eventually. The curtain is going to come down. I'm sure it will happen." Then he returned to discussion of fees and lunch.

And inside the newsroom ...

Just before the story hit the streets, the *Observer* contacted Roger Liddle for his side of the story.

Liddle was the squat little man who offered to get "what you want and who you want to meet" at Downing Street. This was no small fish in the net. Liddle and Peter Mandelson had co-authored the book *The Blair Revolution* . The three of them were the key architects of that revolution-in-reverse, the program to seize the Labour Party, yank it to the right, and rename it "New" Labour. That was step one; step two was The Project – to merge New Labour with the Liberal-Democrats, Liddle's political bailiwick. Big business would provide the gilded glue, shepherded by the lobbying firm set up by Liddle and Draper, GPC.

Blair moved Liddle right into 10 Downing Street, and made him the real power on European affairs. Liddle's equity in Draper's lobby shop went into a "blind trust". Liddle's wife was a dear friend of the wife of my editor Will Hutton. When Liddle heard the story was about to break, he called Hutton at home, knowing full well that Will was about to turn Liddle's career into

16 Ultimately, the government, despite campaign promises, chose to continue the system permitting private electricity, gas and water companies to disconnect poor customers behind in their bills – a big victory for Draper's and GJW's clients over Baker's group of clerics and poor people. Special access is not a victimless crime.

garbage with a pen stroke. Liddle begged. He claimed he was drunk, and when he's drunk he's a fool, everyone knows that, and he shot his mouth off, didn't mean it, didn't know what he was saying.

Hutton told me this on Sunday morning over croissants at a little bistro in Belsize Park. "Lobbygate" was on the streets, but we talked mostly, as we prefer, about industrial regulation and the political economy of Brazil. He was off that afternoon to São Paolo to meet President Cardoso – reluctantly, because of our influence-peddling story. I said, "Go. Brazil's the future, Britain's history."

In Hutton's view, Liddle was pathetic and sincerely remorseful. So Will gave him the benefit of the doubt and did not call for Liddle's resignation in the editorial leader. And besides, Liddle told him, he couldn't gain from swinging business to Draper: the blind trust had sold off his interest in Draper's lobby firm.

Hutton's as smart, maybe smarter, than his formidable reputation as Britain's leading intellect. So I paused to let him work it out himself. *Liddle knew his interest had been sold?* "So, Will, the blind trust ain't so blind." Hutton, a big man, laughed so hard he almost knocked over the metal table. He'd been had. Liddle was a weasel and a liar. But not a very good one.

In the newsroom the next day, I met the deputy editor. With Hutton away, the wan young corporation man now in charge preferred to meet surrounded by a guard of lawyers and marketing people. By Monday afternoon, the full force of the New Labour government and their running dogs at the other papers were tearing our journalistic flesh. And the deputy wanted to throw them something to chew on. Preferably me.

In the meantime, he'd *hand over our tapes* to the government. I said, "Well, that's nuts, that's just straight fucking insane nuts." But he'd made an Executive Decision. "So give us the tapes."

I explained about my wife. Didn't have 'm. He looked ready to die on the spot. He figured he would lose his job. (He did.)

In the meantime, he had another brainwave: he'd *tell* Alastair Campbell, Blair's press python, which accusations we had on tape, and which were "merely" backed up by witnesses and contemporaneous notes. How brilliant. I opined: "The sleazy little shit-holes will talk away with excuses anything we have on tape then flat-out deny anything from notes, say we made it up." But there was no stopping him from stepping on his own dick.

At 4 am London time, I reached Hutton in Rio. "There's a Concorde leaving São Paolo tomorrow. For Christ's sake, Will, *get on it.*"

Too late. The *Observer* showed our cards to Campbell and immediately, the government's guardians talked away what we had on tape, flat-out denied what we had from notes and witnesses, even though Swedlund – he was with me at the meetings with Draper, in the hugger-mugger with Liddle – gave us a sworn affidavit under penalty of perjury.

Liddle was no longer the pathetic drunk contrite over his corrupt offer. At first, he announced he couldn't remember meeting me, certainly couldn't remember what was said. Once he knew we had "only" a sworn affidavit of a witness, he grew bolder, and in his third version, he suddenly remembered it all clearly. And what he remembered was that I was a liar; I'd fabricated his words.

Then the next morning, a hand-scrawled note came through the *Observer's* fax machine, no signature. "I've got your tape. What's it worth to you?" Linda thought she was quite droll.

Lobbyist Ben Lucas, smugly assured that I had no tape, flatly denied to *Newsnight's* cameras that he had detailed to me passing on advance information from the Treasury to his client, the Government Association. Meirion Jones, one very smart producer at the program, let Lucas swallow that grenade – then played on air my tape of him saying the words he denied.

Then it was Draper's turn to step on a landmine. Assuming I had no tape of our chats, Draper denied the words I attributed to him, but that day, Linda relayed the tape via phone, and anyone could hear Draper's incriminating statements about Downing Street cronies on the *Guardian's* web-site. Draper lost his job, but got a payout which will keep him in Lambray Brut for another decade.

In that first week, while I was The Liar and Blair's hands were shaking, I was sure I'd nailed Liddle. The mendacious little scamp was drunk, was he? Didn't remember me, did he? Never offered to bring me into Downing Street, give me his private numbers? In fact, the next day after his offer, and sober as a deacon, *Liddle called me from 10 Downing Street* to set up a time to get together, to seal the deal. He denied it, and that stunned me. Now I had him! All I had to do was go over the Downing Street phone records and point to my mobile phone number ... when I discovered that, in Great Britain, telephone records of a public servant from a public phone were "private", or confidential or some kind of state secret. I was screwed. Liddle walked away smelling like a rose; and Blair rewarded him with the highest increase in salary awarded anyone in government.

Mandelson was promoted to minister for trade and industry, replacing Margaret Beckett – who knew me and refused Blairite requests to denounce me (as the deputy prime minister, John Prescott, had done, denying, weirdly, that he knew me, and in case he did, he never borrowed any jokes from me. But that's another story.) From his new position, Mandelson would carry out several deals dear to the heart of Bill Clinton's and George Bush's friends, which Beckett had resisted. We'll get to that.

The Politics of Emptiness

From the *New Statesman*

Humiliating Draper and his lobby buddies was a dumb move on my part. The real story, about Treasury and Trade Ministry deals for Murdoch, Tesco's, GTech, Enron – about the corporate powers getting the inside word, the inside track, the inside deal – was all lost. Suddenly, the story became the lobby boy-liars. I shrugged my shoulders and flew home. Two months later, I mailed off this intemperate screed to the New Statesman.

The *Observer* splashed the story "Cash for Secrets" by Antony Barnett and me, on Sunday, July 5. By Thursday, July 9, I knew our three months' investigation had been a waste of my time – and I got the hell out of your country. In the four days between publication and my escape, the media turned the story on its head. Derek Draper, on returning from his Italian vacation, hijacked the spotlight. Suddenly, it was all about Derek's Big Mouth and about other "boastful young men" exaggerating their insider connections. The story was now Lobbygate, or as Derek preferred it, "Drapergate". At Heathrow, I was tempted to write on the departure lounge wall, YOU'VE GOT IT WRONG. IT'S NOT ABOUT LOBBYISTS. The real story was about Tony Blair and his inner circle. I thought we had exposed New Labour's obsessional pursuit of the affection of the captains of industry and media. It was a tale of the highest men in government twisting law and ethics to win the approval of this corporate elite. But by Thursday, the New Labour faithful could take comfort in the conclusion of the *New Statesman* that the *Observer* revelations were merely about Draper's "overselling his product," and therefore, the allegations were "almost trivial".

Trivial pursuit

Indulge my penchant for trivia. Among other discoveries, the *Observer* disclosed lobbyists' revelations that:

... In return for Tony-praising tabloid coverage, the government offered Rupert Murdoch's News International valuable amendments to the competition and union recognition bills

... In secret meetings with the deputy prime minister following an £11 million donation to the Millennium Dome, Tesco won exemption from the proposed car park tax. Value: £20 million annually

... Using confidential government information and special access to Downing Street, American power company Enron reversed a government plan to block their building new gas-fired power stations

... A US investment bank and privileged UK businesses received advance notice of Gordon Brown's exact future spending plans. ("Valuable market-sensitive information," lobbyist Ben Lucas told me. "Worth a fortune," Draper confirmed.)

... PowerGen chairman Ed Wallis met a key Treasury adviser to obtain a *sotto voce* agreement to approve merger plans previously rejected by the Tory government. These deals were worth billions.

The list went on. We had not stumbled on a tawdry little fix or two. It was systemic. New Labour had opened up secret routes of special access to allow selected corporate chiefs to bargain, alter or veto the government's key decisions. Derek Draper was not the story, only my unwitting source. In his role shepherding his industry clients discreetly through back doors at Numbers 10 and 11, Draper, like the other young New Labour lobbyists, was nothing more than a messenger boy, a factotum, a purveyor, a self-loving, over-scented clerk.

Übermensch of the New Labour order

Pouring sherry cocktails at my Tower Hotel suite – this front operation cost the *Observer* a pretty penny – I asked one of Draper's competitors, Rory Chisholm, if he could match Derek's setting up the meeting between PowerGen and Treasury to talk mergers. "Now hold on there!" Chisholm, a Director of GJW, a lobbyist of the old school, put down his drink. "That's getting a bit *illegal*. It's a *judicial process. It's like approaching a judge.*"

Why would New Labour skate so close to the ethics edge? I found my answer in a confidential booklet, "Understanding the World Today", given only to potential new clients of the hot new consultancy Lawson Lucas Mendelsohn. LLM, named for key campaign advisers to Blair, Gordon Brown and Jack Straw, is no influence-for-hire shop that can be purchased by anyone with a checkbook. To obtain their much-sought services, corporations must, Ben Lucas told me, "change their culture" by embracing the statement of principles and methods in LLM's sales brochure-cum-manifesto. On page 3, LLM prophesies apocalyptic transformations: "AN OLD WORLD IS DISAPPEARING AND A NEW ONE EMERGING." LLM then helpfully divides all human thought and emotion into two long columns, one labelled "The Passing World", the other, "The Emerging World". IDEOLOGY and CONVICTION must be left behind in the Passing World. In the Emerging World, PRAGMATISM will replace ideals, and CONSUMPTION will replace convictions – BUYING takes the place of BELIEF. LLM admonishes new clients, "*The emergence of this 'new world' has a profound effect on what is important.*" The listing shows that image is more important than accomplishment. Results from government are an obsolete concern of the Passing World, replaced by reputations. Style is everything. "WHAT YOU DO" is replaced by "HOW YOU DO IT".

Here the investigation led me to the heart of New Labour. And I found nothing there at all. Stripped of ideology and lacking all conviction, nothing remained but ambition. Jonny Mendelsohn, brainy, aloof, bloodless, the perfect *Übermensch* of the New Labour order, explained to me the party's addictive needs. "[Our] super-majority in Parliament means the only counter-vailing force is media and the business community. So when the economy turns soft – as it must – we will make certain they stay with us."

In our hours of humorless discussions, I came to understand what a source told me: "LLM is not a lobby firm, *they are an arm of government.*" Through LLM, New Labour has sent forth its young to scavenge for influential men of business and media and lock them into Labour through a skein of deals. Typical lobby firms bring their client's wish list to government. LLM inverts the process. As

Lucas confided to us, Blair's circle made the initial approach to the Murdoch organization with the offer to trim the government's own union recognition and competition bills – in return for Murdoch's muzzling his papers.

It would be a mistake to view the politics of emptiness – in which ideals and beliefs are suspect – as a New Labour invention. Blair, Cardoso of Brazil, Frei of Chile, are all products of the factory that manufactured Bill Clinton, all bionic election machines who, in Mendelsohn's words, are "not ideologically constrained". LLM's manifesto dismisses "leaders who lead" as antique creatures of The Passing World. Today, markets lead. Industry CEOs lead. In the Emerging World, prime ministers and presidents LISTEN. Without the restraints of conviction, they are free to respond to the requests of the powerful while shifting their media images as the public mood demands.

All during the week after the *Observer* printed the exposé, we received an avalanche of calls of support and congratulations – from high inside the government. "You've got the little bastards. Keep digging." But outside of his long-knifed cabinet, the prime minister had two key protectors, William Hague and Paddy Ashdown, erstwhile leaders of the opposition parties. Six months ago, no one could have imagined the Tory general lecturing Blair, "A government without convictions is a government for sale." But after the thrill of his initial attacks, Hague realized a full-scale investigation of sleaze could do him no good. Ashdown must have calculated that silence would reap more rewards than pestering questions. I waited to be called before a parliamentary committee. No one called. No one investigated. No one wanted to. The opposition seemed to go out of its way NOT to demand the release of Liddle's diaries, phone records or meeting notes, nor to call Gordon Brown's advisers for questioning on their dealings with PowerGen. Other suspect meetings – between Tesco and Prescott, between Liddle client Rio Tinto Corporation and Blair himself – drew no questions.

British commentators were quick to say that Lobbygate was no Watergate. But how would they know? The Watergate break-in was at first derided as a "third-rate burglary". It was the senators of Richard Nixon's own party who asked a hundred times, "What did the president know and when did he know it?" On television, I watched the US Congress grill every White House operative, open the files, play the tapes. But from this Parliament, nothing. I imagined some grand secret council of Britain's betters voting not to permit disclosure of the inner workings of power lest the lower orders become restless. And where were my fellow journalists? These little puppies yapped at the *Observer*'s evidence, but none demanded the government open its records. The *Financial Times* did confirm Draper's passing confidential Treasury figures to a New York bank – but no one asked who in Gordon Brown's office made sure Derek had a steady supply of inside information. Instead, all media eyes turned on Draper's antics. To the government's relief, Derek put on his cap and bells, played the boastful court jester and created a sideshow distraction while all the king's men escaped.

As I slouched toward Blackpool for the Labour Party Conference, I could hear the chant of the party faithful, "At least they're not as bad as the Tories." Said repeatedly, this seems to calm the troubled hearts of believers, even if it isn't true.

The New Statesman *published this story in their special Labour Party Conference issue, flew me back to Britain and announced I'd be their main speaker at their "fringe meeting", where I was to debate with Derek Draper. The boy fixer had enough sense to duck out, but I didn't and won my second front-page* Mirror *headline. I was The Liar again and worse. The Labour Party pulled my press credentials and, as a security threat(!), I was not allowed inside the* cordon sanitaire *of the New Labour faithful.*

The morning after the "Liar II" headline hit, Peter Wilby, editor of the *New Statesman*, called, frantic (or as frantic as the cool, cool Wilby ever gets). It was 30 minutes to press and he was going to retract a key accusation in my story. In the printed version, I'd identified Ed Balls, aide to Chancellor Brown, as the "Treasury aide" who met PowerGen executive Ed Wallis to arrange a secret merger approval, the fix that Chisholm described as "a bit illegal". Wilby printed an apology, accepting Balls's statement that he'd never met any representative of PowerGen.

Though I don't blame Wilby, the retraction was wacky, at least half of it: I had seen the receipt for the luncheon between Balls and Draper, PowerGen's lobbyist. But Balls was right about one thing: he never met Wallis. The name was wrong, but the story was right. Who could have made this complex deal fly and kept it under wraps? Who met Wallis to cut the merger-for-coal-contracts trade? My partner Barnett got the answer to me within the hour: Chancellor Gordon Brown's Paymaster-General, Geoffrey Robinson. Robinson owns the *New Statesman*.[17]

You have to admire these guys. They simply have no shame. Exposure was embarrassing to the policy swapfest, but not an impediment. Three weeks after we revealed LLM's scheme to get Tesco's out of the £20 million a year car parking tax, I reported this for the Observer.

To the surprise of green campaigners, out-of-town shopping centers will be exempted from the car park tax. Congratulations are in order for lobbyists Neal Lawson, Ben Lucas and Jon Mendelsohn, the firm at the center of the cash-for-access.

17 Wilby's a ballsy cat – he was prepared to print that Robinson met Wallis and was the center of the fix even though "This may lead to the unusual situation in which our proprietor will sue his own publication." I spared him the aggravation.

Downing Street has derided the *Observer*'s disclosures as merely "boasting" by the politically connected lobbyists. But in this instance, the outcome is exactly as predicted in a taped telephone conversation on June 11 between an LLM lobbyist Lucas and the *Observer*.

On July 7, 1998, following the publication of the first cash-for-access reports, Blair's spokesman released a statement denying that Tesco's £12 million sponsorship of the Millennium Dome was timed to influence the government's decision on the tax. A government spokesman said that the donation was made in February, whereas "there were no proposals for car parking charges even suggested until April". Both new information obtained by the *Observer* and previously unpublished portions of the recordings of lobbyist Lucas contradict the government's statement.

According to those who took part in the creation of the government "White Paper on Transport", the car park tax was first proposed to Deputy Prime Minister Prescott's Department five months earlier, on November 17, by green activists Transport 2000 in a meeting which included industry representatives.

Lobbyist Lucas claims he informed Tesco even earlier than that. After telling us (while we were under cover) he could obtain "intelligence which in market terms would be worth a lot of money," he offered a "couple of examples," including this: "Our advantage for Tesco, going back to the car parks tax issue, is not that we started work on it now but that we'd warned them about it over a year ago, and we can plot as it were."

In a segment of the recording of the June 11 call, previously undisclosed by the *Observer*, Lucas laid out in detail the bargain he claims to have made with the Labour government. "We've been developing a strategy for [Tesco] to head the government off basically and push them in a different direction in the plans which they're about to announce next month and to get them to effectively do a deal whereby the contribution to community transport which is already made by this company is seen as an alternative to them having to pay this tax." (Lucas warned the *Observer* that this information was "quite sensitive".)

The White Paper released two months after the taped call follows the lobbyist's plan exactly. Tesco and the other supermarkets would be left free of tax. In return, local authorities would "build on the initiatives which some major retailers have already taken" to subsidize bus routes bringing customers to their shopping centers. The White Paper notes that large retailers "already provide" subsidies. For Tesco, new contributions would be small or nonexistent per their lobbyists' plan.

The release date of the government report was delayed from June 23 (the day the *Observer* operatives met Lucas), and shortly after that, the supermarket tax exemption was added to the White Paper.

The wording in the White Paper used to justify the tax exemption followed exactly the language crafted by LLM and revealed to "American businessmen" (the *Observer* team) eight weeks earlier.

"US Businessman" - You have a philosophy, you have tremendous resumes and you know bios, but a little bit about how you've been able to operate or what you've been able to accomplish would be real helpful.

Lucas - It's ... there are some examples which we can give you, some of which are still quite sensitive because the government is still relatively new. There's a lot which is still as it were, in negotiation. An example of this is, to pick an example, the biggest food retailer in Britain is called Tesco, they're a client of ours. They have a concern about the government potentially introducing a tax on all car parking spaces in supermarkets in Britain which would cost them about 20-30 million pounds. We've been developing a strategy for them to head the government off basically and push them in a different direction in the plans which they're about to announce next month and to get th   o effectively do a deal whereby   to community transport   is company is seen   g to pay this tax and represented in th announced in July KPMG a major acco problem that they the big six accoun inadvertently ident particularly anti-L organised some tax Labour government w taxation. So six mon Gordon Brown who was press conference spe black mark had been p on to work for them a refashioned the whole to government and as a that the morning of th   get since the election his   used us and said that he would like to do a special meeting with

Figure 16. From the transcript of the June 11 call between a "US Businessman" (myself) and Ben Lucas, lobbyist. Photo: On June 23, 1998, "Businessman" sets off to meet with Lucas. (Photo: Mark Swedlund)

Blair promised investigation and "reform", put into the hands of Parliament's Committee on Standards of Conduct. After piddling with the topic for over a year, Lord Neill's committeemen reached their conclusions, recommending *against* opening all government diaries and phone records. They'd heard Draper tell them, "I wasn't actually passed any confidential information about a government decision." The fixes, the meetings, the information swap, all denied – without a single probing question from the committee nor, heaven forbid, a demand for his phone logs and diaries, nor, heaven forbid, those of any accused minister.

From the lobbyist's testimony Lord Neill and his committee concluded, as one said, "We may have serious problems but they are not of the gravest nature."

We must not think the committee acted without considering all the facts, although Lord Neill declined an offer to hear crucial new evidence from the *Observer*'s investigations – tapes, faxes, witness statements. Apparently, the evidence was not needed. "The committee," said their official spokesman, "felt the subject matter had been covered completely in the testimony of Derek Draper."

Kissed Not Loved: Tony Blair, Globalization's Toy-Boy

After Lobbygate, I picked up the vibe that Blair and friends no longer felt affection for me. But why the vicious response to any dissent? What drove this man?

As I built the files for "Principles of the Project" for Ecologist *magazine, I began to see Blair in a different light; not the soulless poll-puppet, but a man in love ... with American "entrepreneurialism". In all the creepy little deals, who benefited? GTech corporation of New Jersey, Entergy of Little Rock, Arkansas; Reliant of Houston, Monsanto of St Louis. Lobbygate was less about England than about Clinton, Bush and the projection of American corporate powers onto one tiny, cold island, and their welcome by the always-grinning native chief, Mr Tony. Like Cardoso of Brazil and Vincente Fox of Mexico, Blair is bedazzled by the invitation to board the good ship Globalization.*

Here was Blair's passion.

Principles of the Project

In his heart, Tony Blair hates Britain. This prime minister despises a nation lost in "How Green Was My Valley", weepy over the shutting of filthy coal pits; fossilized trade unions who chain workers to dead industries rather than build new ones. He cringes at the little bell ringing over the door of the hamlet chemist, so quaint and maddeningly inefficient; at the grousing farmers with two little pigs and tiny plots edged with dry stone; and over his right shoulder, at the rabid blue-hairs who demand he keep the Queen's snout on the coinage. For four years, he gazed with an almost erotic envy at Bill Clinton, Chairman of the Board of America, Inc. The prime minister dreams of birthing the Entrepreneurial State but finds himself caretaker of a museum of nineteenth-century glories made somnolent by the lullaby of easy welfare and low ambitions.

Blair's burden is that his nation doesn't understand him. The Left sees in the PM a hypocrite, toady to corporate campaign donors, traitor to Labour Party ideals. Writes a Mr Bob Spooner to stalwart gazette *Left Labour Briefing*: "Tony Blair has betrayed everything that the early socialists believed in!" as if the PM could lose ideals he never had. Even those who merrily voted New Labour have the uncomfortable suspicion that there is no There in Blair, just an empty suit pulled this way and that by focus group puppeteers. One fool wrote, *"Blair is a bionic election machine. He is a box of gears with a smile painted on the front. He could drink a glass of water and smile at the same time. The country is being run by people who are professionals at getting elected – they have no philosophy."*

I was the fool. But one man got it dead right, minister Peter Mandelson. Days before he resigned for fraudulently concealing a loan from Geoff Robinson:

> *New Labour has to be more than a ruthless electoral machine. It has to be a political party of values and ideals.*

Go ahead and laugh. You do so at your own peril. There really is a Project, with a moral design, international in scope, disciplined, principled, evangelical.

Blair's goal is nothing less than the transformation, the *SALVATION*, of his nation's social-economic soul. Blair has been to the Future, and from its source in Washington has taken the Promethean fire back to Bristol and Bournemouth. Tony Blair may be the most idealistic, visionary leader in the non-Moslem world. That should scare you.

Return with me to 1998. Treasury minister Geoffrey Robinson was Tony Blair's Can-Do Man. But taking care of PowerGen Plc *and* their Texas confederates would be a heavy lift. By 1998, PowerGen had managed to dictate 85 per cent of the prices bid for wholesale electricity in the England-Wales "Power Pool". Profits had been astronomical. But PowerGen's CEO, Ed Wallis, wanted more. He wanted East Midlands Electricity. But that seemed out of the question. Even the Tories had turned down his last request to take over a regional electricity company.

And Wallis wanted even more. His ambition was international, and his quick way to cross the globe was to propose a merger to Houston Industries, an unloved group of power pirates just past a brush with bankruptcy. For their part, the Texans were enticed by the invitation to own a piece of the fixed casino that is the UK power market. That too was out of the question: the Tories had killed a nearly identical American buy-out request in their last days in office – in response to the taunts of Labour in Opposition. PowerGen's dual merger scheme looked dead on arrival.

For Geoffrey Robinson to bring it back from the crypt, he would have to overcome two formidable obstacles: the law and Mrs Beckett. The law was clear: only the trade and industry minister, Margaret Beckett, could review and authorize mergers – not even the prime minister could interfere. Beckett was an Old Labour war-horse, and the hell if she was going to go easier on industry than her Tory predecessor. She had already turned down one US power company merger. In Downing Street they called her "Minister No", the Can't-Do Gal.

But Beckett was sorted. PowerGen's lobbyist (Derek Draper) had learned, and unwittingly informed me in June 1998, that Beckett would soon be sent to pasture in a post far away from the delicate levers of competition policy.

The only big problem remaining then was to work the PowerGen requests in a way that would satisfy the wishes and desires of the man with ultimate authority over Britain's energy system: President Clinton.

And Bill Clinton had quite a wish-list. According to internal US Embassy files, Clinton wanted to keep a lid on Britain's windfall profits tax on US companies that already owned half the UK electricity system; to get this Mrs Beckett out of the way of several American merger targets; and to let Clinton's most favored friends, Enron and Entergy corporations, build gas-fuelled power plants.

This last one was trouble. Power plants using gas wiped out coal mining jobs, so Beckett had slapped a moratorium on building new ones. Clinton's top man, Commerce Secretary Bill Daley – son of Boss Daley of Chicago and, like his dad, rarely defied – phoned Beckett to go over the US government's shopping list. He got no satisfaction. The Americans were getting testy, even the US Embassy got into the act, slipping strained communiqués under Beckett's door as a crucial June 4, 1998, Cabinet meeting approached.

For Robinson, crisis was opportunity. He knew exactly how to take care of PowerGen's needs and Bill Clinton's with one stroke. If the government could arrange for the trade secretary to reverse policy and bless the PowerGen/East Midlands merger and, at the same time, PowerGen were to commit to a big contract for British coal, despite its premium price, the Trade Ministry could then grant American companies waivers from the moratorium on building new gas plants without causing the loss of those last beastly jobs in the coal pits. Secretly, near the beginning of June, Robinson met PowerGen CEO Wallis.

On July 27, Margaret Beckett was removed from the Trade Ministry. On September 22, her replacement, Peter Mandelson, signed off on PowerGen's takeover of East Midlands. The next day, PowerGen signed contracts for 25 million tons of British coal. The government granted Enron its waiver, then removed the moratorium on gas plants altogether.

What may appear to the ethically rigid as a creepy little fix, a deal at the edge of the law, are to the New Men of New Labour sword thrusts at the knots of government gone sclerotic with legalisms. That is why the real work of governance requires movers and shakers of business, the Geoffrey Robinsons, to move and shake the system to get the damn thing *done*.

But do not reserve all the kudos for Mr Robinson. According to the US Commerce Secretary's notes, it was Tony Blair himself who stepped over his minister Beckett to "intervene to water down the gas moratorium".

What on earth would move the prime minister of Britain to hop like a bunny to Bill Clinton's bidding, to let America swallow his own nation's power industry, then lighten the US investors' tax load, to grant special waivers to Texas Enron which ultimately, contracts or not, will seal Britain's coal mines?

US power companies were first on his gift list, but other adventuring Americans wiped their feet on the golden doormat at Downing Street. The international chief of Wal-Mart, the retail dragon of Arkansas, swallowed Asda stores following a private, unprecedented meeting with the PM himself. Britain waved in Wackenhut prison company, Columbia (private) Health Care, GTech the lottery men, televangelist Pat Robertson and his Internet bank, and Monsanto with its strange harvest in English fields – not one, but a stable of Trojan horses that Blair sees as a stud pool to breed with the mangy local stock.

Back to the power deal. The US Embassy's timing was flawless, knowing, says an internal embassy memo, that "the Cabinet may take up the issue at its June 4 meeting". How did they know *that?* There are Members of Parliament who can't get their hands on the Cabinet's agenda. But Enron's operatives had a pipe in to the Select Committee on the energy review. "Many friends in government like to run things past us to some days in advance." Enron, their lobbyist explained (unwittingly, and on tape), is "using us to influence that energy policy and we're having reasonable effects especially on the moratorium".

Buying Brazil

One humid night in July 1998, Peter Mandelson boogied until dawn in Rio with a young man named Fabrizio. Or so reported our moral watchdogs, the *Express*, Mohamed Fayed's *Punch* and William Hague. "Lord Mandelson of Rio." What the minister did without his portfolio is none of our damn business. But there were other names on his dance card – President Fernando Henrique Cardoso, tycoon Olavo Monteiro and the British Chamber of Commerce of São Paolo. And there was something on the Tropic of Capricorn more attractive than an expendable toy-boy: the Gas Company of São Paolo and other state assets, boodle worth *one hundred billion dollars* which British and American companies believed was rightly theirs, despite Brazilian resistance.

To Brazilians, an Englishman shaking his booty may be a little off-putting, but no scandal. What caused a ruckus was Mandelson, a foreigner, endorsing Cardoso's re-election on national television, supposedly a slip of the tongue, but brilliantly crafted.

While Old Labour cannot help but think of the Project as a *coup d'état* by the faction of their party who sneer at singing "The Red Flag" at party conferences, this view is small and provincial. Blairismo is the UK subsidiary of an international community, which encompassed Clinton, Mexico's Fox, India's Manmohan Singh, Jerry Rawlings of Ghana and a wide group of modernizers. Their golden child was Cardoso, whose new Brazil will provide the transforming Miracle for the Third Way religion, much as Chile provided the genesis fable for Thatcher's free market cosmology.

However, in July 1998, Cardoso's re-election to the presidency hung by a thread: his ability to maintain the stunningly high value of Brazil's currency, the real.

The World Bank and International Monetary Fund dangled a loan (ultimately $41 billion) to prevent the real's collapse, but they would hand over nothing until after the elections. Mandelson's crafty endorsement was a clear signal to Brazilians that only Cardoso had the safe hands into which Euro-American leaders would place the bail-out check.

Cardoso squeaked back into office in October. Thirteen days later, with Cardoso's re-election secured, the US Treasury gave the nod, a trap door opened and Brazil's currency plunged through, dropping 40 per cent.

Crisis has its uses. To pay its new multi-billion dollar debts, Brazil held a fire sale. British Gas picked up the São Paolo Gas Company for a song. As Brazil sank, our Texans Enron and Houston Industries picked up Rio and São Paolo electricity companies and a pipeline.

On November 23, just days before Mandelson, now trade minister, was scheduled to return to Brasilia for his victory samba with Cardoso, World Bank brass flew in to London to lay out what it modestly titled a "Master Plan for Brazil". At its center was a check-list of the bank's five measures for a "flexible public sector workforce":

Reduce Salary/Benefits;
Reduce Pensions;
Increase Work Hours;
Reduce Job Stability;
Reduce Employment.

The World Bank and its Latin stepchild, the Inter-American Development Bank (IDB), described for Britons the game plan for implementation, including the bankers' rewrite of Brazil's constitution. Five days later, Mandelson's well-briefed contingent arrived in South America ... but without the Secretary. That week, the UK press broke the story of Mandelson's Saturday Night Fever in Rio from his earlier visit, and it seemed impolitic for him to return at that moment. (And a month later, he resigned in disgrace over a secret loan from Mr Robinson. Both resignation and disgrace were temporary.)

The Transatlantic Business Dialogue

On November 13, 1998, the *New York Times* printed a truly curious letter, "IT'S TIME TO REPAY AMERICA", by Tony Blair. Britain's chief of state gushed and bubbled and, editorially speaking, lifted his skirt over his head, to thank Bill Clinton and the whole of the United States (often conflating the two) for introducing him to the simple pleasures of bombing selected dictators and to leadership the American Way. "Governments should not hinder the logic of the market ... results not theology ... free from preconceptions and bureaucratic wrangling." It was a wee bit embarrassing, like getting a Valentine dipped in perfume from an office mate. For Tony it was love; Clinton thought it was just a *business* relationship.

Yet there was more to this twosome than I had credited. In May 1998, Blair and Clinton together acknowledged the birth of their love-child, the Transatlantic Economic Partnership. This was not a press release, but an extraordinary commitment to the program of the Transatlantic Business Dialogue (TABD).

For all you conspiracy cranks and paranoid anti-globalizers who imagine that the planet's corporate elite and government functionaries actually meet to conspire on their blueprint for rewriting the laws of sovereign nations, you may in fact get the schedule of the TABD's twice yearly confabs on the web. However, you aren't invited.

Who *are* these guys? The Transatlantic Business Dialogue is the working group of the West's 100 most powerful CEOs. Before presidents, prime ministers and other transitory heads of state meet at the World Trade Organization, this more permanent grouping provides them the details of their agenda.

According to an internal US Commerce Department memo, in their September 1997 meeting, the US Secretary was to tutor his British counterpart, Mrs Beckett, on TABD. "TABD is the most influential business group advising governments on US–EU commercial relations. Your encouragement," he was to instruct Beckett, "would be helpful."

The TABD's system is masterfully efficient. One US corporate Big is paired with one European CEO for each of three dozen "sectoral" or "horizontal issue" groupings. For example, Monsanto's Robert Harness and Unilever's F.A.H. Vigeveno are in charge of Agri-Biotech. Here's where the corporations get their power: both the US government and the EC assign one official each to report to an industry pair. The TABD pairs' privileged access is not to small fry either, but top bananas such as Pascal Lamy, European Commissioner for Trade, and Erkki Liikanen, Commissioner for Enterprise and the Information Society (what you and I call Telecommunications).

In May 2000 government assignees had to report to their corporate duo on the headway they had made on each of the items on a "TABD Implementation Table". The table listed 33 environment, consumer and worker protection laws in selected nations, which TABD would then defeat or defang. The corporate chiefs then judged each minister on their progress and rendered their verdict on what TABD call "the scorecard", which was turned over, along with a new Implementation Table, including agenda items for the next WTO summit meeting.

The 1998 Implementation Table, one of the first documents obtained (grudgingly) from the EC under its Access to Information disclosure rules, makes good reading for those wanting to know what's planned for our brave new world. For example, several of the "tetra-partite groups" (the two-on-two government-business trysting sessions) seek expansion of MRA. MRA stands for "Mutual Recognition Agreement", what the TABD describes as "Approved once, accepted everywhere." It is the globalizers' cruise missile. "MRA," US Secretary Daley tutored Minister Beckett, "shows how influential the TABD can be in moving governments to act on business priorities."

Here's an example of how MRA works. Years ago Pfizer company defectively fabricated heart valves which cracked and killed more than 169 patients in whom it had been surgically implanted. Understandably, this made Europe wary of accepting contraptions merely because they were blessed by the US Food and Drug Administration. MRA brushes aside individual nations' health and safety regulatory reviews – including individual regulation of medical device manufacturing plants.

Given the ill feeling of Europe to genetic modification, the MRA rules for GM products are devilishly complex and savvy, effectively applying only to the developing nations. Does Brazil have a problem with Monsanto's bovine growth hormone? Sorry, approval by the WTO's Codex Alimentarius committee means Brazil must accept the product or face WTO trade sanctions.

The US too is a target of TABD's contempt for consumer protection. TABD's Products Liability Group, under the guise of eliminating "non-tariff" trade barriers, takes aim at American citizens' unique right to sue corporate bad guys. One TABD proposal would reverse the $5 billion judgment against Exxon in the *Exxon Valdez* oil spill case.

Businessmen lobbying their way into government offices is an old story, but the supercharged TABD version of infiltration by invitation began only in 1995 as the brainchild of Ron Brown, Clinton's first commerce secretary. Brown, who died in 1996 when his plane crashed during a sales promotion tour of Bosnia, was Clinton's Mandelson, architect of the scheme to turn Democrats into New Democrats, party of business. When Brown died, Clinton's passion for pairing with business passed also, not uninfluenced by the demolition of the New Democrats in the 1994 Congressional elections. Clinton lopped off the "New" label – take note, Tony – when his good buddies in industry, sensing his weakness, rushed back to their natural home in the Republican Party.

"But Blair really *believes!*" says economist Jagdish Bhagwati of the prime minister's globalization fervour, who attended a gripe session with business bigs in Budapest in 2000 where they rejected "dialogue" with NGOs such as Amnesty International. "I don't believe that those who were in Seattle represented somebody with a legitimate stake," fumed Peter Sutherland, head of investment banking giant Goldman Sachs UK. Sutherland, who jumped to Goldman from his post as the WTO's director, prefers the company of his own kind. "We have to be very careful on engaging in this debate as those NGOs should not have a say with government!" Interestingly, the Goldman bank chaired the TABD when Sutherland directed WTO.

Bill Clinton could blow a mean "Heartbreak Hotel" on his sax. Clinton can feel your pain. (And several women attest he felt theirs.) But Blair has none of Clinton's cynical cool, nor Bush's. Blair *believes*. He can't help it. Those handsome arched swastika brows over eyes that never blink give him away.

Dr Faust had the great advantage of knowing he sold his soul to the Devil; he could always redeem the pawn ticket. But the prime minister, giving over Britain's high streets to Wal-Mart, jails to Wackenhut, power plants to Entergy, is convinced he's sold his nation's soul to Santa Claus. The Americans will sprinkle the fairy dust of commerce know-how over his laggardly island and – presto! – Enterprise will take flight.

It's sad, really. Unlike Clinton who wised-up quickly, Blair confuses the TABD crowd's self-serving wish-list with a program of economic salvation. He trusts his industry darlings will never leave his side. But eventually, as flies to faeces, industry will return to their Tory pile. And when that happens, Blair will find that, as they say in Arkansas, he's been kissed but he ain't been loved.

8

Kissing the Whip

Napoleon said that England is a nation of shopkeepers, but then, the Little Corporal never tried to purchase simple dietary staples (organic milk, Red Bull) from Tesco's Express in Islington. I queried the manager as to why they were out of stock *again*.

"It's Friday," was the answer, as if that were an unforeseen occurrence, like a rogue tidal wave engulfing Upper Street and preventing deliveries. I began to explain that "Friday" is what accountants call a "recurring event" and *HAVEN'T YOU BRITONS EVER HEARD OF COMPUTERS – YOU KNOW THOSE THINGS THAT LOOK LIKE TELEVISIONS WITH TYPEWRITERS ATTACHED ...* and by then, everyone was looking around at that despised figure, the Complaining American.

I like that. In 1999, I left America in disgust, then discovered, to my surprise, I was some kind of freaking *patriot*.

Americans bitch, moan, complain and *demand* their *rights*. Sometimes. When our TV infotainment hypnosis wears off, when "Have a nice day" is an insufficient answer to getting screwed by the powers that be, Americans can surprise themselves, rise up and say, No thanks, we won't eat shit.

You can read my chapters up to here and get darned depressed: the big boys, the bullies, the brutal always seem to win. When your daddy was a president and your brother, the governor of Florida, counts the ballots, you don't have to win an election to become president. They don't call it the "privileged" class for nothing. Corporate cash beats democracy every time. So it seems.

But not always. It may seem like a battle of bears versus bunnies, but sometimes we little critters stand on our hind legs, fight it out and win. There's a long history in the US of biting back, from Andrew Jackson's challenge to the creation of these creatures called "corporations" to the Populist Movement's demand for public utilities commissions to limit monopolists' price gouging. In the USA, trade unions may fall, but credit unions rise.

The point of this chapter is that America has something to offer the planet besides McBurgers, cruise missiles and Madonna. Admittedly, it is a small chapter.

Blood on the Volvo

On April 4, 2000, I called America and, to my surprise, it was still there. Mom and dad in California and big sister in Washington, coming up out of their deep shelters, squinted into their first glimpses of sunlight since the night before, when Judge Thomas Penfield Jackson dropped The Bomb – his ruling to break up Microsoft.

Microsoft's CEO Steve Ballmer had warned that a judgment in the US Justice Department's anti-trust case against the company would mean the end of "the freedom that is driving our economy". The American way of life was at risk! Who knew what civil upheaval would ensue and the prudent barricaded themselves in preparation for the worst.

Yet, America survived intact. Its lovers still cry, its poets still dream and McDonald's employees still lack health insurance.

The value of Jackson's ruling to the British public – beyond the giddy satis-faction of watching a centi-billionaire nerd pantsed and paddled by the court – eluded me until, dozing through the drizzle that passes for journalism on the topic of Monopoly Bill, I was jerked awake by my newspaper's advice to the judge. Our editorial admonished the US court to impose heavy fines to punish Microsoft for ripping off Joe and Josephine Bloggs with unconscionably high charges for Windows.

Strange advice from a newssheet in London. The suggestion is better directed down the street to Her Majesty's Office of Fair Trading (OFT) which, only a month earlier, gained the legal authority to fine monopolists. For OFT, this should be a no-brainer. Judge Jackson ruled the Microsoft's evil-doings were "worldwide" in scope. And to make OFT's work easier, unlike secretive European monopoly investigations, the US Justice Department posts all its evidence on the web. UK authorities and curious insomniacs can download hundreds of hysterical, petulant and self-incriminating e-mails by Bill Gates and his buddies at www.usdoj.gov.

For the record, OFT informs me they have "no investigation and no plan for investigating" of Microsoft.

The *Guardian* (besides aiming its advice at the wrong nation), in emphasiz-ing state-imposed fines, evidenced a common misunderstanding of what makes American competition law work – at least by comparison to the sorry codes in Europe. The simple brilliance of US anti-trust law is not in punishing the price-fixers (though it does that, with fines or jail time) but in *compensating victims*. If Gates's bully-boy tactics added $20 to the price of Windows, then every PC jockey in America gets a check for $60, triple the overcharge.

Americophilic columnist Jonathan Freedland postulates that tougher, citizen-friendly anti-trust laws in the US are rooted in the progressive theories of enlightened turn-of-the-century capitalists seeking to keep the marketplace free and fair. Washington anti-trust lawyer Kenneth Adams has a closer view. "Americans have 200 million hand guns. We've always had guns. If we didn't have a way for the average guy to get his money back, there'd be war." The 1890 Sherman Anti-Trust Act was the desperate defense of America's monied class aimed at defusing the Populist Movement, a million armed farmers on the verge of insurrection against the railroad barons.

Moreover, in the US, no victim has to wait for the government to nail the bad guys. Any overcharged customer can file a Sherman Act suit, even if the government concludes no monopoly exists. That's what drives the system. While Joel Klein, head of the US Justice Department's trust-busting unit, deserves credit for bringing Gates to heel, the government's case only followed on the path cleared by private suits brought by Microsoft's injured competitors, Netscape and Sun MicroSystems.

Klein's unit has slammed monopolists for nearly $3 billion in fines over the past decade; but that is peanuts compared to the collections by millions of victims in class action suits totalling many times the government's take. In Britain, ripped-off consumers have to wait upon timid, befuddled, underfunded and politically vulnerable agencies like OFT to take up their defense. Their targets are few, action is rare and compensation is out of the question.

A month before the Microsoft ruling, Britain's OFT uncovered a ring of 14 Volvo dealers in a secret price-boosting pact. But the limp trust-buster did not order them to give the £4,000 in overcharges back to their customers. (It's against the law to fix prices in Britain, but in the past 100 years, the number of price-fixing victims who have won compensation is exactly zero.)

No question that if it happened in the US, there would be bullet holes in the salesrooms and blood on the bumpers.

Hot water again. That column got Volvo's knickers in a twist. Apparently, I was guilty of "attempted mockery". Well, there was nothing I could do but apologize to the company and my readers ...

Is my face red! In an ungracious screed about Volvo and its dealers illegally fixing car prices, I noted that the auto company had not, despite news reports, publicly confessed to whacking their customers for £4,000 each.

The day after my story went to print, the postman brought a sharp note from Volvo UK challenging the figure of £4,000. Oh, really? In other words, Volvo now *admits* it fixed prices?

Well, not exactly, the official company spokesman tells us. "I think that all our customers felt comfortable that they were getting a deal that was right for them."

Despite the jacked-up price, customers were happy?

"Yeah, or they wouldn't have bought the car would they?"

You cannot assail such logic. Accept my apologies.

But the real steam in the letter – from Company Secretary Nick Conner no less – was over this column's "attempting to mock" Volvo's program for compensating their customer-victims. That was not my intent. In truth, *I had no idea* the company had any compensation program at all, a misimpression shared by Volvo's Customer Relations office which told a Volvo "owner" (actually, an *Observer* volunteer) that they were "not aware of any program" for repayment.

It seems some Volvo customers are also in the dark about the restitution program. Volvo sold over 100,000 autos in the three-year period over which the company was accused of punishing dealers who discounted, yet fewer than 50 customers have sought money back. This is another sign of customer satisfaction, says the flak, not the result of the company's failing to notify overcharged customers.

Rather than send a cold letter to ripped-off shoppers, Volvo has concocted a more exciting system for paying its victims, kind of like a game show. First, the consumer must get past denials of its customer service gatekeepers. Then, the buyer must correctly guess the three-month period for which the company will acknowledge "isolated" dealers conspired on prices. The purchaser must then correctly name a shady dealer. Volvo's spokesman assured us all the information, names and dates, are clearly laid out in the stipulation the company signed with the government – a copy of which they would happily give us if it weren't confidential.

Might Volvo at least give customers a sporting chance by listing the bent dealers?

"That's unfair to go back retrospectively to pick out individual cases."

Have you taken any action against those dealers? Confiscated the bonuses they received from Volvo for participating in the conspiracy?

"Retrospective action is not how this company works."

One lucky woman who did match both time period and dealer came within inches of compensation. But then Volvo decided she received a high trade-in allowance on her old car. No pay-out prize for you, miss!

I accept the £4,000 figure is wrong. What, then, is the average restitution paid out?

"We haven't yet compensated anyone."

Oh. Despite such minor glitches in the program, I am quite proud this American corporation (Volvo is a unit of Ford Motor) would voluntarily compensate customers. This proves the wider policy point: there is no need for governments to impose the kind of "retrospective" price-fixing punishments found in US law, criminal fines, triple compensation for victims, jail time for conspirators.

Interestingly, the Consumers' Association notes that Volvo's cooperation with competition authorities began in earnest after the Americans took over. I am certain Ford/Volvo's rush to a deal with the OFT was not motivated by a desire to pre-empt the "Long Arm" provisions of the Sherman Anti-Trust Act. The Long Arm empowers US courts to impose draconian Sherman Act penalties on American firms conspiring to fix prices anywhere in the world – unless another government acts, as did OFT, more or less.

Phil Evans, Consumers' Association auto expert, dissents from my praise of the Ford/Volvo compensation package. "They will pay you if you suffered a loss, but they've already decided you can't have suffered a loss, so they will compensate you but it will probably be nothing. It's something out of Alice in Wonderland."

I had to warn Mr Evans he was getting dangerously close to mocking Volvo's commitment to compensation and that I could not allow him to use this column for that purpose.

Wanting to give Ford/Volvo the benefit of the doubt, I took Mr Clair to his local Volvo dealer in Cobham, Surrey. The man had been cheated, the dealer and company admitted, so I simply asked if they'd give him back the overcharge. They didn't want to talk to me. It was either my hat that put them off or my BBC camera crew. Anyway, Mr Claire got nada, nothing, bupkis. So we went to Volvo headquarters in Swindon, then to Washington DC, Brussels, New York ... and finally, Mr Claire got a check for £173. Who says there's no justice?

Ni Tuya, Ni Mia, De Todos

New York, New York, it's a helluva town. Just 15 years ago, you could walk down Third Street on the Lower East Side and count 23 boarded-up, abandoned buildings and only seven buildings inhabited. On the corner at Avenue B, the awnings of the local bank provided shelter for the open-air market where you could buy smack, crack, angel dust, you name it. In 1984, one of those dealers (no longer in the business) took over the bank – and heralded a revolution in US finance.

Mary Spink, out of prison for running a drugs network, heard news that the bank, a branch of Manufacturers Hanover Trust, was about to shut its doors and re-open in a tony Midtown location. "Manny Hanny" was the Lower East Side's last bank – if you don't count the loan sharks – and without it, the neighborhood would finally die. Spink teamed up with the parish priest and local housing activists (including a former Weather Underground wannabe terrorist) and picketed Manufacturers' Hanover Manhattan headquarters. They won a face-to-face meeting with the bank's executives hosted by the Federal Reserve Board.

In the Fed's elegantly appointed Wall Street conference room, the Lower East Side crew demanded that the $80 billion bank corporation hand over their branch building to the group to house a community credit union. They also demanded the bank kick in several hundred thousand dollars to get the credit union off the ground. The executives balked, but the Federal Reserve reminded them of the power of the Invisible Hand of the Marketplace (i.e. the iron fist of Alan Greenspan) – and the Community Reinvestment Act, CRA, a then new law obliging banks to serve the credit needs of communities in their areas of operation. Manufacturers' Hanover caved in. The launch of the Lower East Side Peoples Federal Credit Union, a novel use of the CRA, quietly marked an extraordinary shift in political power from boardrooms to the public. Their slogan: *Ni Tuya, Ni Mia, De Todos* – "Not Mine, Not Yours, But Ours".

Today's monster-sized mergers of financial behemoths, such as the Citicorp/Travelers Group combination, are akin to elephants mating. It is such a fascinating spectacle, we forget about the effect on the ants below – the poor and working-class customers for whom bank consolidation usually means bank abandonment.

But now in the US, the ants are fighting back and their weapon of choice is the Community Reinvestment Act. Armed with CRA, America's anti-poverty campaigners are holding mega-mergers hostage until banks cough up millions, and sometimes billions, of dollars for loan funds pledged to low-income borrowers. In March 1998, 130 angry citizens testified at Federal Reserve Board hearings against the takeover of Philadelphia's CoreStates by First Union Corporation. To avoid further challenge under the CRA, the banks settled with community groups by pledging to make $5 billion in low- and moderate-income loans over five years, a huge jump over current lending rates. Then Bank of America made the mother of all pledges, $350 billion over ten years, in return for the right to gobble up NationsBank. In all, merger-bound banks have signed 360 agreements to provide $1.04 *trillion* in targeted financing to underserved communities.

But Matthew Lee isn't satisfied. Lee, now head of New York's Community on the Move, rejected a plea by Citibank and Travelers to end his challenge to their merger in return for the new bank's establishing a $115 billion ten-year loan program for low-income customers and small businesses in poor neigh-bourhoods. An alumnus of the Lower East Side Peoples credit union, Lee is the Che Guevara of poor folks' banking rights. Like Che, he sports a beard. Unlike Che, he puts fear into the hearts of American capitalists. His convincing, detailed analysis of banks' lending patterns have exposed the dark, racist side of "red-lining", the practice of cutting off credit to deteriorating neighbour-hoods, thereby accelerating the deterioration. Lee wrested a commitment of $1 billion for loans to low-income customers from Charter Bank of Ohio after he exposed data showing the bank was three times as likely to reject loan appli-cations from Blacks and Hispanics as from Whites, despite little discernible difference in creditworthiness.

Lee, in rejecting the $115 billion offer from Citigroup, emphasized that CRA compliance is not a game of piling up gargantuan loan funds, but a matter of justice for the poor in the provision of credit. He cites a case of unscrupulous treatment of an African American family, the Harrises, by Citigroup's Commercial Credit Unit. While homeowners in white neighborhoods receive mortgages at a 7 per cent interest, the Harrises paid 12 per cent despite their solid credit rating. The Harrises had signed blank loan forms, counting on the integrity of the world's largest financial institution. That was a mistake, one that Lee himself did not make by signing off on the Citigroup merger deal. Lee insists that the Harrises' predicament is not isolated, that Citigroup operations systematically overcharge and underfund poor and minority communities.

It would be easy to list CRA's weaknesses – biased access to capital remains a fact of American life – nevertheless, CRA has helped boost the total number of home mortgages for Black Americans by 72 per cent in its first four years on the books. The Republicans' chief banking spokesman charges that the loan funds are simply extortion payments to activists. Yet he could not find a single banker to testify against CRA's continuation. No mystery there: banks turn a profit on these mandatory low-income loans.

CRA's producing a heap of cash for depressed areas has not gone unnoticed by Britain's New Labour "social exclusion" policy mavens. Over the last three years, HM Treasury has sent teams to the US to meet with "Che" Lee, community credit union experts and activists – and brought some of these finance industry savages back to London for display before government task forces. Introducing the Americans to her task force the then economics minister, Patricia Hewitt, proclaimed, "This government believes strongly that wider access to financial services – through positive action by the banking community – is vital." Undoubtedly, imposing a community reinvestment obligation on British banks could revolutionize the credit system.

But don't hold your breath waiting. Hewitt immediately reassured the assembled bankers – the task force was headed by the Deputy CEO of the Royal Bank of Scotland – that New Labour had not the slightest intention of mandating any new lending requirements. "I should emphasize that we are *not* planning to copy the US legislation." Rather, she merely hoped that tales of money-making low-income loans in the US would encourage British financiers to seek "profitable banking in our poorer communities".

Back on the no-longer-mean streets of the Lower East Side, Mary Spink, dealer-turned-banker (today she's treasurer of the National Federation of Community Development Credit Unions) warns the Blair government not to assume they can cajole banks into doing the right thing, into voluntarily putting money back into Liverpool instead of into international hedge funds. The Blairites believe they can win over the hearts and minds of the banking community with sweet talk of profits from lending to the working poor. But Spink suggests that CRA succeeds in the US because it obeys the dictum of General Westmoreland, "When you've got 'em by the balls, their hearts and minds will follow."

In March 2000, about a year after I wrote this, the Royal Bank of Scotland, which headed this task force on excluding small and low-income citizens from finance, finally did something about it – the bank closed scores of branches all over the United Kingdom. Barclays Bank CEO, Matthew Barrett, would not be outdone: he closed 172 branches, a tenth of his system, mostly in rural areas; and Barrett picked up a bonus of £30.5 million ($46 million).

On the Lower East Side of New York, Father Jack Kenington aided Mary Spink's activist crew by organizing immigrant members of his parish for non-violent, but in-your-face direct action, which led to the takeover of the Manufacturer's Hanover bank by the community.

When the banks closed in Britain, another cleric wheeled into battle, Rowan Williams, Archbishop of Wales. He called for turning Britain's abandoned banks into community credit unions. But rather than surround the local Barclays with pickets or sitting-in at the offices of shoulder-shrugging officials, the Archbishop seemed resigned to administer last rites to the closing branches. "It's a bit utopian to imagine that government can intervene to make the banks behave."

The meek may inherit the earth, Your Grace, but seizing the bank buildings will restore your communities' financial services. So there it is: when a good soul like the Archbishop disparages his own demand for reform as "utopian", the call to action decays into another lesson in public acquiescence.

Kissing the Whip

After he was charged with treason, Daniel Ellsberg, who made the Pentagon Papers public, was beaten nearly to death by a group of thugs on the courthouse steps. "God Bless America," he told me. In Britain, Ellsberg noted, he would have been thrown in the slammer and never heard of again. The United Kingdom has an Official Secrets Act, libel laws that effectively privatize censorship of journalism, privacy laws protecting politicians, no legal freedom of the press – and there's not much dissent over it. An unholy number of British journalists seem to have fallen in love with their shackles. (Don't get smug, America. We may have no Official Secrets Act, but we are on the cutting edge of creating a corporate secrets act – see "Silence of the Lambs" in Chapter 1). I put this notice in Index on Censorship:

On March 17, 1999, on an order from the London Metropolitan Police, my fellow reporter from the *Observer*, Martin Bright, our editors at the *Observer* and lawyers for the *Guardian* were called before a judge at the Old Bailey. On pain of imprisonment and unlimited fines, the British court ordered them to turn over all internal notes relating to stories about a former MI5 agent. Bright and the editors, Roger Alton and Alan Rusbridger, refused.

One week later at a black-tie soirée at the Hilton Hotel, I found myself in a meandering, champagne-lubricated debate with a disturbingly articulate gent defending the government's right to censor and restrict news reports. My interlocutor (and my boss), *Guardian* editor and *Observer* CEO Alan Rusbridger, the very man facing time in the Queen's dungeon for refusing the court order.

I was not surprised.

It is the subtle brilliance of British censorship and news suppression that its prime victims, the nation's editors and reporters, have developed a nodding acceptance of the principles justifying limits on their freedom, a curious custom of English journalists to kiss the whip that lashes them.

Rusbridger challenged me, "You wouldn't want a [news] photographer taking pictures of your family over your garden fence, would you?" Well, no. The death of Princess Diana – in the public's mind, a victim of invasive press hounds – has turned a concern for protecting privacy into a treacherous obsession. Privacy has become the first, attractive step down that slippery slope to journalists' accepting state censorship.

Under this banner of respecting privacy, Prime Minister Tony Blair's government obtained a court order blocking publication of his children's nanny's diaries. The convenient tool of privacy also was the cloak to conceal public ministers' salaries. Even the records of a phone call from Downing Street in which a Blair adviser privately offered to sell me access to government office – that was private too.

The news community's response to the writs against editor Rusbridger, reporter Bright and their papers was slow to form. In a land of cautious protest and measured defense, the *Observer* itself delayed for a week covering its own punishment, unsure whether readers found their paper's repression newsworthy.

Weeks passed. Finally, Stuart Weir, the first Briton since Tom Paine to understand the word "freedom", got up a petition signed by media notables. However, with their plea to the government to drop the prosecutions, the petitioners conceded, "We recognise the need to protect national security," a mannered diffidence to the state's ultimate authority over the printed word grating to my American ears. The journalists also demanded: "The Official Secrets Act should be reformed to allow a public interest defense." *Reform*? The Official Secrets Act prohibits the publication of almost any document or fact that the government chooses to conceal, from crimes by MI6 to educational statistics. The polite protesters would grant the right of the Crown to arrest journalists, but they requested wide exceptions. Petition organizer Weir knew a demand to abolish the repressive Act outright would have chased away key signatories.

The *Guardian* editorialized in its own defense, but again, its complaint was carefully circumscribed. The paper targeted the plain silliness of the government's writ. The *Guardian* had done nothing more than print a letter to the editor from a former MI5 agent, David Shayler. The government demanded the newspaper hand over the physical copy of the agent's letter (as it turned out, the computer tape holding an e-mail message) – despite the fact that David Shayler himself *sent a copy of the letter directly to the authorities*.

Similarly, the *Observer* report contained little more than a note that a US Internet site had posted information corroborating agent Shayler's accusations. Apparently, Shayler had tipped the *Observer* to this public information. While *any* communication by an ex-agent violates the Official Secrets Act, the police did not need the reporter's letter files, as they claimed, as unique evidence of Shayler's alleged violation of the law – Shayler himself had sent the government copies of his messages to the paper.

Yet, the sheer foolishness of the government's demanding documents already in its possession is evidence of a more sinister aim. By showing it will punish minor infractions of its secrecy laws, government succeeds in freezing any journalist's attempt to dig out deeper and more dangerous truths concealed within secretive agencies. Worse, journalists, defending their minor infractions, trap themselves into justifying the greater censorship. "As a newspaper," wrote the *Observer*, "we have no difficulty with secrets or with the principle that secrecy, where necessary, should be protected by the law."

By acceding to limit itself to "legitimate" inquiries, to use the timid terminology of the journalists" petition, the papers open the door to state policing to root out the "illegitimate".

Most American readers, who still think of Britain as mother of our democracy, will be surprised to learn that the United Kingdom remains one of the hemisphere's only nations without a written constitutional guarantee of free speech and press. That changed in October as Article 10 of the European Convention on Human Rights becomes UK law. The Convention will allow Britons, for the first time, "to receive and impart information and ideas without interference by public authority".

The court and government were quick to agree that the new Human Rights law applied to the current prosecution of reporter Bright and the newspapers. This was *not* good news. Whereas the US constitution states, "Congress shall not restrict the freedom of the press nor of speech" – no *ifs, ands or buts* – the European Convention adds a nasty little codicil, "Part 2". In the March 17 hearing, the judge ruled that the right to "receive and impart information" – freedom of the press – was subject to Part 2's "restrictions and penalties in the interests of national security". How fitting that in the land of George Orwell, the law bars the government's controlling the press – unless the government decides to do so. Prime Minister Blair's minions clearly intended the Guardian Group case to establish from the inception of the Act that a right is no right at all.

D-Notice Blues

On April 15, the censorship/self-censorship vaudeville opened a new act. That day, reporter Bright saw a copy of a four-year-old MI5 document detailing the security agency's bungled attempt to recruit a Libyan spy, a cock-up which appears to have led to the murder of a Libyan dissident living in London. The "TOP SECRET DELICATE SOURCE UK EYES" document can be read by anyone with a mouse and time on their hands at www.cryptome.org. Observer reporter Bright drafted a story (with Antony Barnett) about the information on the website.

Despite its open publication on the site, repeating this information invited criminal and civil penalties. (In fact, *reading* the web-site's content is a crime in the United Kingdom.) And if you think that's a joke, Blair's thought Gestapo arrested college student Julie-Ann Davies for reading letters from Agent Shayler published on his French web-site. To avoid another writ, the *Observer* contacted the Defence Advisory Committee, the "D-Notice" committee, a kind of government confessional where journalists may whisper their unpublished thoughts and information and ask, in confidence, "If we publish, will we have sinned against the state?" The agency suggested that if our paper could prove our news report contained no new news – an interesting restriction for a newspaper – then prosecution *might* not follow.

However, there was another censor yet to contact, the Treasury Solicitor, who held a two-year-old injunction against any British newspaper publishing any information whatsoever from former agents. Just five minutes before the printing deadline, the Treasury telephoned. Four hours passed (and four editions with front-page filler where the article could have run) as the government bargained with the editors and the paper's lawyers who, in the face of ruinous fines, found themselves with little choice but to fax to MI5 the unpublished draft of the story.

The paper asked two simple questions: Would publication violate the law? And, can we publish? The government said it would not stop publication, but neither would it promise not to prosecute the reporters and editor if publication went ahead. MI5's position had a serpentine brilliance: blocking the article would get them an "*OBSERVER* GAGGED AGAIN!" headline. By keeping open the *hint* – but not the *threat* – of prosecution, the official spooks meant to lure the paper into withdrawing the story, while the government could claim it censored nothing.

Laudably, the paper went ahead with publication for its last edition, though it "voluntarily" left off the web-site's address. Reporter Bright finds the procedure deadly to the ethics of news coverage. "It's crazy, but the law says we can't do what journalists should always do: check with the sources, review the key documents. We have to break the law to break the news."

Self-censorship is in the breeding

The D-Notice Committee, the reluctance to ban publication outright, the seemingly sympathetic bargaining, all serve to foster the habit of self-censorship. Rarely does government have to brandish the implements of coercion because British news people are bred to a strong sense of the boundaries of public discourse. In this class-poisoned society, elite reporters and editors are lured by the thrill of joining the inner circle of *cognoscenti* with ministers and titled military intelligence men. The cost of admission is gentlemanly circumspection.

Britons, as they constantly remind me, are *subjects* not citizens. British-born journalist Christopher Hitchens, scourge of authorities on two continents, stunned Americans by submitting to deposition by US government prosecutors during the impeachment trial of President Bill Clinton. Clearly, habits of subjugation die hard.

The state extends its power to punish unruly reporters through libel laws, which, in effect, privatize enforcement of state censorship. I have yet to publish a single column in a British newspaper as written, uncarved by lawyers fearful of ruinous court action by well-funded litigious bullies running the gamut from McDonald's Corporation to the prime minister himself.

Astonishingly, some British journalists are not shy about borrowing this brutal weaponry of the state to censor others. The government's writs to the *Guardian* followed just after closure of the magazine *LM*. The lefty periodical had disclosed that a powerful piece of British anti-Serb war propaganda, a photo of starving Bosnian prisoners behind barbed wire, was "manipulated". The pro-government photo-journalists, backed with corporate funding, made good use of the British court's revulsion with *LM*'s admittedly vile and preposterous denial of Serbian fanatics' war crimes. The legal fees, more than the judgment, bankrupted the dissident publication.

These libel laws, while crippling the work of investigative reporters (the *Guardian*'s computer won't accept any copy prior to a reporter's answering the machine's query, "LAWYERED?") hardly protect the public. England's tabloids like the *Daily Mirror* are notorious cesspools of character assassination, rumor and vicious fabrications.

When other arguments against unfettering the press fail, the ultimate defense by officials eager to censor and journalists ready to comply is that a government open to scrutiny is "not British". Certain freedoms offend what some Britons call their "culture" which, on examination, is nothing more than a debilitating combination of long-established habits of subjugation mixing too comfortably with the preferences of the powerful.

Talk about hot water, we'd done it now. Frank Fisher, managing editor of Index on Censorship *and the type of troublemaker journalism desperately needs, was left in charge of publication while his superiors were out of London. Frank slipped into the piece the actual web-site address where anyone can read MI5 and MI6 documents. In case readers missed the point, he illustrated the story with a secret service document marked confidential.*

When the chief editors returned to find the thousands of copies already printed, they called a meeting. Should Frank be boiled in oil or merely turned over to the authorities with a note pinned on him, "Do as you will"? How can we preserve the computer disks, keep the magazine running, out of bankruptcy, when the Metropolitan Police come to take the computers as they had done to the student arrested earlier? How do I prevent seizure of my passport?

No matter the consequences, the issue would go out.

But we were not prepared for the stunning attack about to come by electronic post:

Greg Palast's hastily-written article entitled, Kissing the Whip ... What on earth is Index *doing when it allows its space to be wasted, and its reputation for seriousness lowered, by ignorance and pettiness of this sort?*

Christopher Hitchens, a British transplant in America, whose posh accent and carefully hedged nastiness made him New York's favorite cocktail party revolutionary, was in high dudgeon. The mild reproving mention of his collaboration with Republican officials would not be countenanced.

Everything in this passage is either false or irrelevant. The House Judiciary Committee, which prepared the case against Clinton, is not an arm of the US government ... I did not "submit" to any process, but freely agreed to a request for my testimony ... If Mr Palast does not understand the impeachment provisions of the US Constitution, he has no business patronising the hapless Brits for their lack of a Bill of Rights.

Chastened by this dressing-down, I replied with humility.

Mr Christopher Hitchens
Washington DC

Dear Sir,

I write to you to offer a sincere apology for my words in print which appear to have deeply wounded your pride and your justly earned sense of your own worth. I did not mean to offend a person as important and accomplished as yourself in the arts of essay and condescension.

I often say that social critics such as ourselves, whose profession it is to censure others, should withstand with grace and humor that which so easily we dish out. But, given your stature and deserved celebrity, I agree we should make you an exception, and grant you an immunity from any and all criticism. For though your work seldom discomfits the powerful, it does flatter the Left at a time when we so need an appreciation of our prejudices.

I must admit that had I edited, as well as authored, the piece, I would not have concluded with any mention of your story ... your antics in Washington were not as noteworthy in my estimation as you believe.

Forgive us, for we had other things on our mind as we approached publication. *Index* exposed the vicious system of British censorship – and came close to crossing the line of the Official Secrets Act as interpreted by MI5 and MI6. We had long discussion about what to do in case *Index* were charged under the Act, our computers seized or the editors and I arrested. I admit, while focusing on the difficulties of facing down state repression, I did not give more careful attention to your personal feelings.

I am horrified that in what you rightly term my "ignorance and pettiness", I stated you "submitted" to a request to provide testimony in Kenneth Starr's prosecution of President Clinton. Had you done so, it would have been a violation of American journalistic ethics: reporters must never provide source information to aid a state prosecution. I now gladly correct the record. You did not "submit" to testify but, as you say, "freely agreed" to take part in Kenneth Starr's official witch-hunt.

Therefore, I would ask *Index* to run the following retraction:

Mr Greg Palast wishes to apologize unreservedly to Mr Christopher Hitchens whose actions are at all times honourable, commendable and always, without exception, beyond the criticism of so-called investigative reporters such as Mr Palast. Mr Palast is terribly ashamed.

Sincerely, ...

In the end, Her Majesty's intelligence services and Christopher Hitchens backed off. An English court of appeals ruled that the new European Human Rights

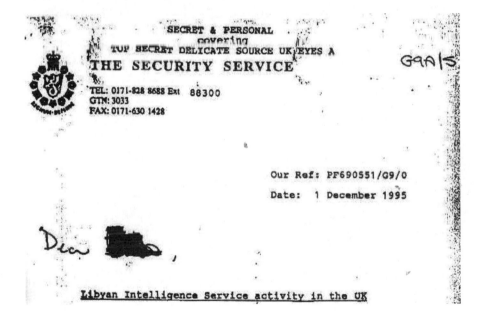

Figure 17. An MI5 document regarding an attempt to recruit a Libyan spy, Khalifa Ahmad Bazelya, allowing him to stay in Britain. The scheme failed disastrously. Bazelya was deported after the mysterious murder of a Libyan dissident living in London.

Reporter Martin Bright and the editors of the *Guardian* and *Observer* were hauled into court for mentioning the existence of the document, a violation of the Official Secrets Act and refusing to turn over information on sources. Frank Fisher, production editor at *Index on Censorship*, decided to push it a step beyond, printing the web-site location of the document and illustrating my story with a copy of the secret document. Fortunately, the court ruled that Britain's recent signing of the European Human Rights Charter barred prosecution for the crime of journalism, at least in this case. By the way, the MI5 documents can be seen at www.cryptome.org.

law trumped British official secrets hysteria in this silly matter of publishing already public information, though the pernicious Act remains to punish those who cross a line, drawn at a place unknown, in revealing official evils.

9

Victory in the Pacific – A Conclusion

I'm told readers want to know what it all means. What's there to say? Well, here's something I wrote for the International Herald Tribune. *I got some hate mail, so it must mean something.*

In 1995, veterans of Silver Post No. 282 celebrated the fiftieth anniversary of their victory over Japan, marching around the catering hall wearing their old service caps, pins, ribbons and medals. My father sat at his table, silent. He did not wear his medals.

He had given them to me 30 years earlier. I can figure it exactly: March 8, 1965. That day, like every other, my dad and I walked to the newsstand near the dime store. He was an *LA Times* man. Never read the *Examiner*. He looked at the headline: US Marines had landed on the beach at Danang, Vietnam.

As a kid, I really loved my dad's medals. One, embossed with an eagle and soldiers under a palm tree, said "Asiatic Pacific Campaign", hung from a ribbon. It had three bronze stars and an arrowhead.

My father always found flag-wavers a bit suspect. But he was a patriot, nurturing this deep and intelligent patriotism. To him, America stood for Franklin D. Roosevelt and the Four Freedoms. My father's army had liberated Hitler's concentration camps and later protected Martin Luther King's marchers on the road to Birmingham. His America put its strong arm around the world's shoulder as protector. On the back of the medal, it read "Freedom from Want and Fear".

His victory over Japan was a victory of principles over imperial power, of freedom over tyranny, of right over Japan's raw military might. A song he taught me from the early days of the war, when Japan had the guns and we had only ideals went, *We have no bombers to attack with ... but Eagles, American Eagles, fight for the rights we adore!*

"That's it," he said that day in 1965, and folded the newspaper. The politicians had ordered his army, with its fierce post-war industrial killing machines, to set upon Asia's poor. Too well read in history and too experienced in battle, he knew what was coming. He could see right then what it would take other Americans ten years of that war in Vietnam to see: American bombers dropping napalm on straw huts, burning the same villages Hirohito's invaders had burned 20 years earlier.

Lyndon Johnson and the politicians had taken away his victory over Japan. They stole his victory over tyranny.

Figure 18. When war was heroic. In 1943, Dad was in the 716th Tank Battalion in the Philippines. Mom was in the Waves, the US Coast Guard women's unit.

When we returned home, he dropped his medals into my twelve-year-old hands to play with and to lose among my toys.

A few years ago, my wife Linda and I went to Vietnam to help out rural credit unions lending a few dollars to farmers so they could buy pigs and chickens.

On March 8, 1995, while in Danang, I walked up a long stone stairway from the beach to a shrine where Vietnamese honor their parents and ancestors.

Halfway up, a man about my age had stopped to rest, exhausted from his difficult, hot climb on one leg and crutches. I sat next to him, but he turned his head away, ashamed of his ragged clothes, parts of an old, dirty uniform.

The two of us watched the fishermen at work on the boats below. I put one of my father's medals down next to him. I don't know what he thought I was doing. I don't know myself.

In '45, on the battleship *Missouri*, Douglas MacArthur accepted the surrender of Imperial Japan. I never thought much of General MacArthur, but he said something that stuck with me. "It is for us, both victors and vanquished, to rise to that higher dignity which alone benefits the sacred purposes we are about to serve."

Our deepest fear is not that we are inadequate. Our deepest fear is that we are powerful beyond measure.

Nelson Mandela

Index